Workers in Stalin's Russia

By the same author:
Managerial Power in the Soviet Union (Saxon House, Westmead, 1976).

Workers in Stalin's Russia

Industrialization and Social Change in a Planned Economy

Vladimir Andrle
Lecturer in Sociology, University of York

HARVESTER · WHEATSHEAF · ENGLAND

ST. MARTIN'S PRESS · NEW YORK

First published 1988 by
Harvester · Wheatsheaf
66 Wood Lane End, Hemel Hempstead,
Hertfordshire HP2 4RG
A division of
Simon & Schuster International Group

and in the USA by
St. Martin's Press, Inc.
175 Fifth Avenue, New York, NY 10010

Printed in Great Britain by
Billing and Sons Limited, Worcester

British Library Cataloguing in Publication Data

Andrle, Vladimir
Workers in Stalin's Russia : industrialization
and social change in a planned economy.
1. Soviet Union—Industries—History
2. Soviet Union—Economic conditions—
1918–1945
I. Title
338.0947   HC335.3

ISBN 0-7450-0315-X

Library of Congress Cataloging-in-Publication Data

Andrle, Vladimir.
    Workers in Stalin's Russia / by Vladimir Andrle,
        p.   cm.
    Bibliography: p.
    Includes index.
    ISBN 0-312-02390-1
    1. Labor and laboring classes—Soviet Union—
History—20th century.   2. Soviet Union—Economic
conditions—1918–1945.   3. Collectivism—Soviet
Union—History—20th century.   4. Soviet Union—
Industries—History.   I. Title.
    HD8526.A77   1988
– 331'.047'0947—dc19   88-17441
                                                CIP

1 2 3 4 5   92 91 90 89 88

To Tania and Noah

Contents

Preface

This is a book about Soviet factory workers and the social organization of their labour during the 1930s. It examines the circumstances in which a new working class was formed in the course of that eventful decade, and in which there was established a pattern of interaction between politically instigated campaigns for industrial efficiency on the one hand, and a structure of labour–management relations on the other. The aim is to offer an insight into, first, some of the 'from below' or 'on the ground' aspects of the 'revolution from above'; and secondly, some of the characteristics of the industrial order that became its legacy.

The arguments of the book are structured by themes rather than chronology, for they are concerned more with trends and the 'normal' phenomena of everyday collective life than with individual events and their unique chains of antecedents. *Workers in Stalin's Russia* is above all a study in sociological interpretation, but I have taken care to remain close to the historical sources – mainly press reports, memoirs and archival documents – to convey to the reader the nature of the data on the basis of which I am offering my interpretations. I hope that this will encourage at least some readers to exercise their own interpretative powers and experiment with alternative reconstructions of social life in the Soviet 1930s that can be inferred from the historical data at hand. If this book helps to engender a sense that a whole range of possibilities and nuances apply to what people at various levels of Soviet society during the period meant by their actions, how they understood their situations and what they felt about them, a worthwhile purpose has been served.

The first chapter is a brief outline of the 1930s to introduce the non-specialist reader to the period. It discusses the collectivization and industrialization campaigns, and some of the developments that took place in the party state. Chapter 2 considers the situation of workers in the highly mobile society 'outside the factory gates', their living standards and life-styles, and also their relations with the repressive agencies of the state. Chapter 3 analyses the structure of the 'industrial nexus'; the relationship between management problems and political controls, the philosophy of the industrialization campaign with its conflicting strands of strategic thought, the images of the 'backwardness' problem and the institutionalization of its 'overcoming'. Chapter 4 explores the shop-floor level; it analyses the nature of industrial work and its informal organization, and then examines the interactive strategies of government efficiency campaigns and shopfloor response. It shows the political methods of labour mobilization to have had their pragmatic element in exploiting workplace divisions and conflicts of interest.

The final chapter examines the Stakhanovite movement; the contests over its interpretation, its workplace routinization and the attempts to revitalize it. It is a hi_.ory that serves also as a summary of previously explored themes, a test case for the industrial order that had been established. And, since it coincided with the Great Purges, the discussion inevitably leads on to consider them as well. The purges of 1936–38 were a cataclysmic phenomenon of which there is only partial knowledge and no satisfactory explanation. A study of the labour–management aspect of the industrialization campaign cannot fill this gap; but it can perhaps offer a different vantage-point from which to view the purges and their context.

I am indebted to a number of organizations and a great many individuals for their support of this study. The Economic and Social Research Council provided a grant which enabled me to devote a whole year of full-time research to the project and spend valuable time exploring the sources available in the US Library of Congress and the Hoover Institution on War,

Revolution and Peace at Stanford University. My studies in the Library of Congress were also supported by a supplementary grant and general assistance from the Kennan Institute for Advanced Russian Studies, Wilson Center for Scholars, Washington, DC. At a much earlier stage, I had also enjoyed a modest but helpful backing from the Institute for Research in the Social Sciences, University of York.

The 'home base' of this study has been the Soviet Industrialisation Project Seminar held regularly, and over many years, at the Centre for Russian and East European Studies, University of Birmingham. Most of what I know about the Soviet 1930s I have my colleagues at the Seminar to thank for. I mention by name only those who acted as discussants of my papers, commented on parts of the manuscript or gave me specialist advice on sources: Professor R.W. Davies, CREES, University of Birmingham, who has made his expertise and critical care available with great generosity; Dr J.D. Barber, King's College, Cambridge; Dr D.A. Filtzer, CREES; Dr M. McAuley, St Hilda's College, Oxford; Professor N. Shiokawa, University of Tokyo; Dr S.G. Wheatcroft, now at University of Melbourne; Dr N. Lampert, CREES; and Dr J.J. Brine, the Librarian of A. Baykov Library at the University of Birmingham.

Outside the SIPS realm, I owe much to Professor M. Lewin of the University of Pennsylvania, who had inspired my interest in Soviet social history and over the years has offered many incisive comments in discussions of research problems. I am also very grateful to Dr M. Burawoy of the University of California at Berkeley, and to Dr E. Garnsey of Cambridge University, for their comments on my papers. My colleagues at the Department of Sociology, University of York, have provided a challenging intellectual environment. Of their number, special thanks are due to Dr C.B. Campbell also for taking over my administrative duties during the final stage of writing this manuscript. My students should be acknowledged, too, for their essays and seminar papers have been an important source of inspiration.

Some of the material presented in Chapter 4 had been published as an article in *Social History* (vol. 10, No. 2, May 1985) and I am grateful to Methuen & Co. Ltd, the publishers of the journal, for their permission to use that material again.

Finally, I am much indebted to Jayne Wilde for her insights into managerial problems and her general support throughout the project.

The responsibility for remaining errors and inadequacies is mine.

1 A Revolution from Above

In 1928–29, conflicts within the party leadership over the best policies for social and economic development ended not in a compromise solution such as might have been expected of political leaders in another time and place, but in the 'great breakthrough'. This was a radical departure on three main fronts: in agriculture, the collectivization of peasant farming; in industry, an ambitious programme of rapid development with a strong emphasis on heavy industry; and in the party state, an extensive reliance on political mobilization for the goals of social and economic development.

COLLECTIVIZATION

In the mid-1920s, the USSR was primarily an agrarian country with some 85 per cent of its population being largely dependent on peasant farming for their livelihood. In 1921–27, this population was linked to the urban–industrial sector of the economy by the NEP system of trading, in which the government on the whole did not interfere with the internal organization of the rural sector, but used price controls to stimulate agricultural productivity and secure the necessary levels of supplies to the towns without starving industry of much needed funds for investment. This policy had its successes and its problems. Farmers grew industrial crops and bred livestock in increasing quantities, but failed to satisfy urban demand for the main form of food – grain.[1] In 1927, a programme of industrial development was launched with a sense of urgency born of deteriorating international relations, which meant an expansion of the industrial workforce and a need to export grain to finance the import of machinery; but in the autumn, the supplies of grain actually dropped substantially from previous years' levels.

This grain crisis was an occasion for a decisive shift in the balance of power within the party as the 'left' (anti-kulak, anti-NEP and pro rapid industrialization) went into action under Stalin's leadership, to solve the grain problem by a campaign of forced procurement in certain regions where the 'kulak strike' seemed especially strong. Detachments of militant activists, party plenipotentiaries and armed forces were dispatched to the villages to find hoarded stocks, force compulsory purchases, or confiscate them by evoking laws against black marketeering. These 'extraordinary measures' were successful in bringing large quantities of grain to the cities. They were repeated on an increasing scale after the next two harvests, thus forcing the collapse of the NEP framework which had been based on the principle that agricultural supplies should be voluntary and motivated by economic self-interest.[2]

By this time, the 'right' in the party leadership were defeated. The victorious 'left' viewpoint was that a very rapid development of the economy was possible only if it was accepted that, as a process of substantial social change, it would have to be conducted as something akin to a class war. It was an important aspect of the procurement campaigns that they seemed to offer young men from the towns a share in the revolutionary glory that had been hitherto monopolized by their elders, the Red Guard and Red Army heroes from the civil war years of 1917–21. When they finished collecting grain after the harvest in 1929, the tens of thousands of class warriors with their supports of armed police were ordered to stay in the countryside, see to it that peasants formed collective farms, and at the same time 'liquidate the kulak as a class'. The latter was a wonderfully ambiguous phrase, in that it might have simply meant a process of economic reorganization whereby private property lost its powers of exploitation, but it also had a ruthless ring about it which suggested that the collectivization campaign should not stop short of physical violence to overcome the resistance of the kulak enemy. In practice it meant setting up processes of selection in the rural districts whereby roughly 5 per cent of peasant households were singled out as belonging to the kulak class. Dispossessed of their property, the kulaks were deported with their families to colonize hitherto uncultivated land in remote regions, or, as was increasingly common, they were deported without their families to serve three, five or ten years in labour camps.[3] Some were originally allocated plots of inferior land to eke out a living in their own villages, but deported later, when they failed to deliver the imposed quotas of grain in tax.[4] Many kulaks who offered some resistance or who were regarded as particularly dangerous were simply shot.[5] The non-kulak majority of peasants were coerced into forming collective farms.

The collectivization campaign developed directly out of the grain procurement campaigns, and this was what it was primarily about. Organizing regular collections of delivery quotas from some 200,000 large farms seemed administratively more feasible than cat-and-mouse games with more than 20 million households. Beyond this, there was not much clarity in the initial stages as to what sort of arrangements for agricultural production the collective farms were to institutionalize. In fact, there was so much chaos and confusion during the winter of 1929–30 that the campaign was called off in the spring, with the result that many peasants left the collective farms by the next autumn.[6] After the collection of grain from the next harvest, however, collectivization was resumed in earnest and proceeded without a halt until there were virtually no individual farms left by the end of the decade.

The collective farms settled into a relatively durable framework, after a number of policy zig-zags, by 1933. Grain and industrial crops were grown in large consolidated fields, the ploughing of which was increasingly coming under management by Tractor Stations which supplied mechanized labour, collected much of the grain for the state, and also assumed general supervisory responsibilities over the farms. The members of collective farms received a share of the total income from grain deliveries, and of the grain that was left to the farms for consumption; the size of the share accruing to a household was determined by the number of days worked by its members in the collective fields. The households were also given individual plots of land and allowed to keep small amounts of livestock for their own needs, or for sale at relatively free markets (bazaars). Some of the collectively produced foodstuffs could be also sold in the bazaars for the benefit of collective farmers, after the obligations to the state sector were fulfilled.[7]

The collectivization campaign thus ended in a degree of covert compromise where an element of individual household farming was restored within the collective farms. This element in fact provided far from negligible proportions of dairy and vegetable produce for the urban population throughout the 1930s; about a half of all the milk and one-fifth of all the eggs acquired by the urban population were bought at the bazaars according to one Soviet estimate,[8] while another Soviet source estimated that one-fifth of the total marketed food supplies came from the individual plots.[9] This compromise between collectivization and family farming never received more than a grudging acceptance from the party state which, while legislating the right of collective farmers to small plots of family land in 1935, instigated a number of campaigns against alleged capitalist abuses of this right, most notably in 1939 when the private plots were subjected to a whole gamut of extra taxes and controls.[10]

The private plot concessions notwithstanding, the new regime in the countryside provided a strong incentive for peasants to migrate into the fast-expanding urban sector of the economy, and as we shall see in the next chapter, many did. This was made more difficult by a discriminatory system of internal passports which was introduced in 1933; only urban residents were issued passports, and passports were needed to obtain urban residence permits. Collective farmers were thus in effect accorded an inferior citizen status which, in combination with the obligations to work in the collective fields while providing their own livelihood from small family allotments, was somewhat reminiscent of the situation of peasant serfs in Tsarist Russia. On the other hand, the members of 'dekulakized' families who had managed to make their escape into the urban sector along with the mass peasant exodus to some extent benefited from the decrees and party leaders' pronouncements that were issued during the run-up to the inauguration of Socialist Constitution in 1936, rendering illegitimate any acts of discrimination against urban workers on the grounds of class origins alone.[11]

The kulaks and their agents were officially considered a liquidated social class by 1936, but the effects of the collectivization campaign on agriculture were less triumphant. The only area of production which did not suffer a setback were industrial crops (cotton, flax, etc.), which continued in their healthy upward trend throughout the decade. As regards grain harvests, there were some good years and some bad years, the good ones only matching the levels that used to be average in the Tsarist empire of pre-war years, in 1909–13, when there had been 10 million fewer people to feed than in 1939. Livestock was reduced by a half between 1928 and 1932, and never recovered to its pre-collectivization level before the end of the decade.[12] Since 1931 and 1932 were also particularly bad years for grain and potatoes, this was a crisis in the provision of food which was alleviated only after the much improved harvest of 1933. We shall see below that 1932–33 were crisis years in the industrial sector of the economy as well.

Some of the western engineers, specialists and workers who arrived in Russia at the time to help out with industrialization recorded their shock at the mass poverty they encountered in their memoirs. This is what happened when a Danish traveller gave a biscuit to a beggar boy at a country railway station late in 1932:

> The news seemed to have spread around all through Telovaya that some foreigner was distributing food. A weird collection of human beings turned up and formed a circle round us. The stench was so dreadful that I felt ill and hardening my heart against them I asked a GPU soldier to deliver me from the crowd.[13]

Since Soviet social policy had by this time abandoned its earlier commitment to egalitarianism, the food situation among the Moscow party elite might be expected to be as different from the Telovaya station as cheese from chalk. It was, but not to the extent of keeping the larders in elite homes stocked. This put an interesting new dimension on gatherings in the Kremlin, as recalled by Nikita Khruschev who was then the second highest official in the Moscow branch of the party:

When the Leningraders finished presenting their report, a recess was called and people filed out of the hall to go into a near-by lounge where refreshments were served. There was hunger in the land, and even people in high positions like myself lived modestly, to put it mildly, and we often did not have enough to eat at home. Therefore we used to gorge ourselves on sandwiches, sausages, sour cream and sweet tea between working sessions in the Kremlin.[14]

City food rations were meagre, but it was in some of the rural districts that the people suffered periods of true famine, testifying to the fact that historically the collectivization campaign had evolved out of procurement offensives and it was in regard to this original purpose that collectivization proved unquestionably effective; it made it possible for the state to take grain in increasing amounts for the cities and for export, regardless of whether the harvests were good or bad and whether the farmers were left anything to eat themselves.[15] This was a degree of exploitation that could have hardly taken its course in peace. The collectivization campaign was not couched in a rhetoric of class war and 'bolshevik iron fist' for nothing; it encountered some armed resistance and plenty of 'kulak sabotage', judging by Soviet press reports. Stalin was later to surprise Churchill by stating that the early years of the collectivization campaign had been a worse crisis than the war with Germany in 1941, when the Wehrmacht overran a large part of the country and reached the outskirts of Moscow.[16]

After the disaster of 1931–33, the situation in agriculture could only improve. Food rationing was abolished at the end of 1934, and although few Soviet dinner tables ever had an occasion to groan under the weight of good meals, the collective farms with their family allotments on the whole just managed to feed the Soviet population throughout the rest of the decade. They did it with 30 per cent fewer hands in 1939 than there had been in the agricultural sector in 1926. The exodus to the industrial sector left mainly older people and women behind to work the farms, and they worked substantially longer hours than they had done in pre-collectivization days.[17]

INDUSTRIALIZATION

Unlike the campaign to collectivize peasant farming, the industrialization campaign was preceded by a few years of deliberation by government economists.[18] There were many issues to resolve as a more comprehensive programme of economic development had never been attempted before. They can perhaps be summarized as follows. First, there was the problem of estimating how much productive potential there already was in the economy which was still under-utilized. The apparent ease of industrial recovery from 1922 to 1926 suggested that there still was some slack left which could be taken up by rationalization measures. One of the first short-term effects of the policy commitment to industrialization in the mid-1920s was a series of labour productivity campaigns in industry which, in combination with growing unemployment, caused a degree of unrest among industrial workers.[19]

The second problem was closely related to the first: where should funds for new investment come from, and by what methods should they be obtained? This was an especially divisive question, as the answers to it in effect proposed that some social groups would have to sacrifice their living standards to provide funds for industrial investment. In 1927–29, the development plans that were being drafted still assumed that, if more wealth had to be obtained from the peasantry to make possible the acquisition of new industrial plant, this would have to be within the limits dictated by the NEP principles of peaceful coexistence and voluntary trade between the rural and the industrial sectors. The productivity campaigns in industry during the second half of the 1920s must have seemed to some industrial workers to indicate that it was they who were asked to pay for investment.

The third group of questions revolved around the issue of whether the initial impact of the investment programme should be directed at industries which produced consumer goods ('group B industries') such as textiles, shoes and bicycles, or at industries which produced industrial equipment such as machine tools, tractors and trucks ('group A industries'). While the former strategy held the hope that an increase in the availability of consumer goods would motivate greater productivity throughout the economy which would in turn generate more funds for investment, a concentration of investment in 'group A' industries promised a rapid accumulation of productive capacity at the risk of blocking improvements in living standards for some time. The 'group A' strategy involved a rapid expansion of the steel and engineering industries in particular, which made it an attractive answer to the task of a rapid build-up of an independent defence capability.

The fourth issue related to the question of what sort of technology should be acquired: the most up-to-date and expensive, or was a lesser degree of mechanization appropriate while labour was abundant and inexpensive? The 'most up-to-date' strategy promised to maximize the rate of accumulation of productive capacity, but also the costs; this not only because sophisticated technology was expensive, but also because its efficient utilization tended to presuppose a large degree of specialization of plant, which in turn required either a great degree of integration into the world economy by foreign trade, or a rapid expansion of the planners' ability to coordinate developments under conditions of increasing differentiation and complexity in the organization of the economy. Related to this was the final set issues: the methods of planning the targets and supplying the requirements of the various sectors and units of the economy, the role of financial credits and budgets in the coordinative process, the procedures for setting the prices of industrial goods, and all the other problems of organization which face a government the moment it assumes a major responsibility for economic development.

In the event, the construction of the industrialization programme was influenced more by a political process than economic deliberation. The military requirements on economic development gained a sense of urgency in 1927, when

Britain broke off diplomatic relations and exposed Soviet weakness in the international situation. Since the best the Red Army could offer in the way of national defence was still on horseback, its rapid modernization became a strong priority. This meant the heavy industry path, and a preoccupation with securing the rapid achievement of development goals rather than with counting the costs of doing so. In 1928–29, the still infant crafts of large-scale economic planning were swept away by the 'great breakthrough' optimism about what could be achieved if there was the political will to mobilize human effort as well as all material reserves on a mass scale. Rival groups of planners outdid each other in the bold scale and tight schedules of their proposed construction projects.[20]

The first five year plan that was eventually adopted was the most ambitious version, the coherence of which was based on highly optimistic and tenuous assumptions. From here it was only a short step to abandoning altogether any notion of maintaining inter-sectoral balances so that, from the middle of 1929, industrial leaders appeared to be less concerned with coordinated planning than with exorcising all 'fear of speed' that might be manifested by economists and managers down the line of command. Everyone was under pressure to make promises which it was impossible to honour. As in the collectivization of agriculture, the industrial construction drive now gained the characteristics of a hectic 'do or die' campaign, a socialist offensive against political reaction and economic backwardness. This yielded some spectacular results, but also many problems of coordination which called for an endless chain of *ad hoc* interventions by the political leaders to prioritize certain projects at the expense of others. These interventions served to increase further the already strong bias in favour of the heavy industry projects.

It would be hard to find a more evocative phrase for the period of 1929–31 than 'primitive socialist accumulation', although the economists who had originally coined this phrase meant a very different scenario by it.[21] It was a period of *primitive* accumulation, because it was facilitated by a substantial reduction in the standard of living of most workers in all the branches of the economy, and also, because the greatest expansion in the initial period was in labouring jobs.

Thousands of giant building sites were set up for new power stations, blast furnaces and factories, while extractive industries like lumbering and mining had to be quickly expanded to provide income from exports and with it the capability to purchase the best in foreign technology. For the time being, however, there were not even enough wheelbarrows, which left workers on some of the building projects to move earth literally in their tunics.[22]

The 'great breakthrough' of 1929–31 was also a period in which economic policy-making was under the influence of visionary leftism. Money was expected to be phased out in the longer term, while in the short term it was very much reduced in significance by a regime which combined low fixed prices with administrative rationing, and gave precedence to political and administrative commands over considerations of budgetary discipline. It was also envisaged in some of the vocal quarters of the mobilized economy (mainly the communist youth organization, *komsomol*) that workers' lives in and out of factory hours would become increasingly rooted in strongly collectivist 'labour communes' with egalitarian principles of income distribution.[23]

The visionary leftism was never unopposed in press debates, and it was shown to be out of favour in the party leadership by summer 1931, when Stalin made a speech on 'new conditions and new tasks in economic construction'. This much publicized speech made it an official policy that industrial incomes should be differentiated to provide strong individual incentives for the acquisition of technical skills. In addition, it urged organizational changes in the factories to combat the prevalence of 'lack of personal responsibility' and the general chaos which prevented workers from working efficiently, and demanded that technically competent people should be promoted to responsible positions regardless of whether they were party members, while the campaign of 'class vigilance' against the 'bourgeois specialists' should be called off in favour of treating the educated classes with 'attention and solicitude'. Finally, Stalin's speech denounced the tendency on the part of industrial managers to take decisions without a due regard for costs, and called for a system of cost accounting (*khozrashchet*) which would encourage managers to look for ways of increasing efficiency without making further claims on the supplies of labour and equipment.[24]

By this time, the industrial sector showed distinct signs of heading for a crisis. Contrary to the assumptions of the five year plan, the industrialization drive mopped up the reserves of urban unemployed labour within two years of starting, and henceforth continued under the sign of a chronic excess of demand for labour over its supply. The rate of migration from agriculture to industry also exceeded expectations, so that the underprovision of accommodation and other necessities for workers that had been assumed in the five year plan in the interest of concentrating construction resources on industrial plant in the event became much more severe than envisaged. The result was escalating rates of labour turnover which added another disruptive factor to the chronic bottlenecks in supplies of raw material and equipment. Few of the thousands of industrial construction projects that had been started were getting completed to begin their useful lives as efficient production units. Virtually all of the increase in industrial production that was achieved in 1930–31 was due to additions of workers to already existing factories, while the number of people receiving bread rations in towns rose by more than 10 million (about 40 per cent).[25]

Another problem was that the terms of international trade moved against primary products with the onset of depression in the West, which made imports of machines from the West unexpectedly more expensive for the Soviet economy. A severe balance-of-payments crisis forced the importation of technology to be curtailed at the end of 1931, causing many of the new production lines to come on stream with gaps in equipment.[26] Another consequence of the discontinuation of imports was that Soviet production lines which had been planned on the assumption of extensive specialization would in practice be required to be very flexible and versatile in their product ranges. And finally, the discontinuation of imports included tractors, which added to the problems in agriculture where substantial numbers of tractors were being transferred east to help with defence preparations in the face of a new threat from Japan.[27]

Prices of food and consumer goods rose by hefty margins both in the state sector and in the bazaars in 1931–32, while the rations of food and other necessities were reduced and even then not always honoured as supplies to the shops fell below the minimum levels.[28] While average industrial wages were substantially reduced in real terms between 1928 and 1932, the period of the first five year plan, most of this reduction must have occurred in the last two years. To cap it all, the level of industrial investment actually dropped in 1933, which was the cause of another eerie experience for the western traveller whose troubles with biscuits in Telovaya station have been mentioned above; between stations, his train passed by a number of large construction sites and new factory shells which, their windows smashed, looked totally abandoned and desolate.[29]

While the mass media never stopped urging vigilance against 'rightist-opportunists' who claimed that 'taut plans' were unrealistic, the industrial newspaper began publishing discussion articles which developed Stalin's directive about production cost accounting into proposals that amounted to a U-turn in economic strategy. They in effect argued that, to make production cost accounting really effective as a stimulus to industrial efficiency, production units should have a degree of freedom from administrative commands, with product prices to some extent decontrolled and managerial decisions made in the context of contractual agreements, profit incentives and monetary controls.[30] These arguments were similar in essence and tone to the economic strategies that had been favoured by many government economists before the 'great breakthrough' and that were destined to resurface in the 1960s as a tradition of reformist thought oriented to 'market socialism'.[31]

That such 'rightist-opportunist' views were allowed expression in 1932–33 suggested that the party leadership was divided in its opinions about the wisdom of continuing with the 'taut plans' strategy of industrial development in the face of the fact that the first five year plan was ending in an economic crisis. The issues were complex, but they could be summarized in one question: did direct political and administrative pressures for 'bolshevik speeds' in construction, production and accumulation constitute the best possible method of economic development? The second five year plan, for 1933–37, had to give an answer. It did, but only after a delay of one year, at the beginning of 1934.

In the meantime, the tone that was set in a keynote speech by Stalin at a plenary session of the party central committee held in January 1933 sounded like a compromise which was rather favourable to the case for abandoning the 'taut plans' strategy. While he reaffirmed an uncompromising attitude to the situation in agriculture, he argued in regard to industry and the 'thunderous speeds' of the first five year plan had been necessary to overcome backwardness and raise the defence capability of the country to a sufficient level, but this was now achieved. Now it was 'obviously' not necessary to continue 'to whip the country and drive it on' (*podkhlestyvat' i podgonyat' stranu*). If the slogan for the first five year plan had been the 'acquisition of an industrial base', the slogan for the next period should be the 'mastery of technology'; Soviet workers and engineers had to learn how to use the new equipment for cost-effective and good-quality production, which required that the plan should allow for the annual rate of growth of industrial output to drop from 22 per cent to 13 or 14 per cent, 'as a minimum'. This was indeed a modest target, given the fact that it was envisaged for the years during which the heavy investment in new technology should start bringing results in substantial productivity increases. The 'as a minimum' proviso, however, testified to the existence of less moderate ambitions among party leaders. Stalin concluded the speech by proclaiming that only Trotskyists and Zinovievites might want to perpetuate scurrilous rumours that the proposed relaxation of pace represented a turn away from the policy of rapid accumulation.[32]

By the time the 17th Party Congress eventually approved the second five year plan in February 1934, the balance of opinion in the party leadership appeared to have moved some way back towards the 'taut plans' strategy, albeit in a more moderate form than had been the case in 1929–32. After an ostentatious show of disagreement between two members of the party politburo, Molotov and Ordzhonikidze, over the rate of growth targets, the congress adopted the latter protagonist's proposal for 16½ per cent p.a., in preference to his inter-locutor's 19 per cent p.a.[33] It was envisaged that this rate of growth would be achieved by substantial improvements in labour productivity rather than by further transfers of labour from agriculture to industry, but in practice this was not to be. While overall industrial output in the rest of the 1930s did rise at an average annual rate which was not far off the target of 16 per cent, output per industrial worker increased at an annual rate of about 11 per cent, which was well below the plan.[34] This pattern of results, where gross output targets are achieved while targets pertaining to labour productivity and production costs are not, is a testimony to the fact that the 'taut plans' strategy of industrial leadership became the domi-nant policy again. The 'market economy' type of proposals had disappeared from the pages of the press in the course of 1933. 'Mastery of technology' remained the slogan for the second five year plan, but a much publicized speech by Molotov at the party congress made it clear that industrial efficiency had to be pursued at the same time as, not at the expense of, the pursuit of planned output targets.[35] The changes in the structure of government and economic admi-nistration that were made at this time reflected concerns for management rationality, but without taking anything away from the prerogatives of the political leadership of the party state to enforce priorities and generally intervene in the running of the economy as it saw fit, by direct political and administrative methods.

However, the industrial economy was growing much too complex for the structure and principles of its management to remain a settled issue for long. The number of industrial enterprises grew from 9000 in 1929 to more than 45,000 in 1934, and then to more than 64,000 in 1938.[36] The market economy proposals of 1932–33 may have been rejected, but the escalating number of production units that had to be coordinated was calling for some sort of self-adjusting system in industrial decision-making in preference to direct interven-tions by commands from the centralized party state. Inevit-ably, the call seemed to be, again, for factory production plans to be at least in part determined by contracts between industrial suppliers and customers rather than by detailed production targets imposed from above, and for a system of monetary accounting. One of the large firms in the iron and steel industry was put on an experimental system where financial subsidy from centralized government funds was withdrawn while a large part of the profits that were made remained at the disposal of the enterprise management for reinvestment and distribution in incentive schemes for staff.[37] There was also some flexibility allowed in the setting of product prices so that they could reflect the actual costs of production. In keeping with the political culture of the decade, the beneficial results that were claimed for this experiment in terms of labour productivity and general cost-effectiveness were spectacular and probably exaggerated. However, their validity was disputed by the director of another large firm within the same industry, who alleged that the impressive results were due to eccentric accounting methods, product price increases and the fact that the experimental firm enjoyed a privileged treatment by the Commissar for Heavy Industry. The dispute continued on the pages of the specialist press with increasing bitterness in 1935–36 and was 'resolved' only in early 1937 when Ordzhonikidze's sudden death was followed by an escalation of the Great Purge among the managerial stratum, in the course of which the director of the experimental firm was arrested and his opponent promoted.[38]

The years 1935–37 were also ones of altogether a different experiment in industry, the Stakhanovite movement. Since the scene of this phenomenon was on the shopfloors as well as in managers' offices, it will be discussed in more detail in Chapter 5. In the meantime, it is worth noting that the nature of this experiment was itself subject to conflicting interpretations which to some extent reflected tensions between the commitment to 'taut plan' strategy on the one hand, and the promotion of industrial cost-efficiency on the other hand.

Despite the economic crisis, there were many new production lines coming on stream in 1932–33; and the three years that followed, 1934–36, were probably the best ones of the decade for the industrial economy, as workers became more skilled in operating the new production lines and managers began to find viable ways of discharging their responsibilities.

In 1937, however, economic performance was adversely affected by the escalation of purges and arrests among managers, while in the last years of the decade the economy was severely disrupted by preparations for war.

The estimation of changes in the total value of industrial output is generally a complicated art and it is not always easy to explain exactly what the statistical series that are made available by economic historians represent. At the same time, it seems hardly appropriate to conclude a discussion of the industrialization campaign without giving some indication of overall results. Let it be said therefore that the total amount of what was produced by Soviet industry in 1940 was five or six times greater than what was produced in 1928. This stands out as a very large increase for the amount of what was produced by industry in 1929 was less than one and a half times greater than the amount produced in 1913. Within the overall growth of industrial production in the 1930s, there were considerable differences between the various branches of industry. Engineering was the biggest growth industry, with almost a twenty-fold increase in its annual output between 1928 and 1940. In the course of these years, a peasant country became a large producer of airplanes, vehicles, tractors, machine-tools, turbines, pumps, tanks and all manner of gadgetry for industrial and military use. In the food and light consumer goods industries, the growth was so small that there is some doubt as to whether it made up for the loss of small artisan workshops that had to close down during the 'great breakthrough'.[39]

There are other shadows of doubt that might be cast on the triumph in heavy industry. Product quality is a difficult factor to quantify; it would seem that substantial improvement in this respect was widespread in 1934–35, but some of it was subsequently sacrificed to 'speed up' campaigns. It is probably fair to say that, throughout the decade, product quality approached international standards only when and where this became a high-powered priority such as could not be accorded to every production line. In respect of production efficiency, I have already noted that labour productivity probably did not grow as fast as could have been expected on the basis of the high rate of investment in new technology.

Furthermore, it is an open and difficult question whether the great growth of heavy industry vindicated the methods of the industrialization campaign, especially when it is remembered that the original goals of 'industrial culture' were wider than those reflected in gross output statistics. This is a problem to which there will be occasion to return in later chapters.

DEVELOPMENTS IN THE PARTY STATE

The class struggle aspect of the 'great breakthrough' in party policy on agriculture had its counterpart in the industrial sector. In spring 1928, a group of engineers were arrested and later, at a show trial, convicted of organized sabotage. This marked the beginning of a campaign of 'class vigilance' against the people who, having had the benefit of university or specialist education during the days of the Tsarist empire, still worked in responsible economic and governmental posts.[40] Known as 'bourgeois specialists', their position in the 'proletarian state' always had been a bone of contention. Few of the educated strata were Bolshevik supporters, especially as some of the managers and engineers associated the concept of the 'dictatorship of the proletariat' with disagreeable memories of being put in carts and ceremoniously wheeled out of their factories by insurgent workers during the heady days of 1917.[41] It did not take long, however, before Lenin went out of his way to persuade the educated strata not to emigrate and take their full part in the reconstruction of the devastated economy. He backed the specialists in their demand for the restoration of managerial authority and enticed them by high salaries.

While this never was a universally popular policy within the party or the Russian working class, the Revolution having left a strong legacy of egalitarian expectations, popular resentments against the 'bourgeois specialists' must have only increased when the latter found themselves in the position of chief implementors of government campaigns to raise labour productivity in the factories. 'Rationalization measures' became a byword in the second half of the 1920s, which, from the workers' point of view, all too often meant just more strictness and strain in their work regimes, to reduce alleged overmanning although urban unemployment was on the rise. At the same time, some of the educated professions appeared to have a better access to give advice on their needs to the government and party leaders than most party members.[42]

The campaign against the kulaks struck a responsive chord among some sections of the party and the working class, and this was only more true about the show trial allegations that some of the privileged intelligentsia were active 'class enemy' after all. There was probably enough pent-up resentment of the 'bourgeois specialists' among the workers and the urban poor to overcome the awkward likelihood that the engineers who were prosecuted at the show trial were quite innocent of any gross negligence or intentional sabotage. In any case, by all accounts there was no shortage of denunciations and innuendos made by the rank-and-file against educated people and other 'class aliens' in positions of administrative or managerial authority. 'Specialist-baiting' was a common phenomenon in the next three years as party activists, *ad hoc* workers' commissions, the militia, the procuracy and the secret police busied themselves with 'class vigilance'. 'Bourgeois specialists' were investigated in their thousands and many were sacked or sentenced to terms of corrective labour.[43] It is also true that many were released and reinstated in responsible jobs on appeal, but, according to the engineers' professional association, 17 per cent of its members lost their jobs by April 1929;[44] it is not known how many were victims of 'specialist-baiting' by the time this was declared to be clearly against the party policy more than two years later.

It would probably be wrong to jump to the conclusion that many 'bourgeois specialists' were made to pay for this assigned status with their lives. Only a minority of those who were investigated were sentenced to terms of servitude in labour camps, and of those who did, chances were that they served on industrial projects in their professional capacity, and that they would be eventually able to return home. In so far as the scattered scraps of evidence that are available in relation to this topic allow any hunches, it would seem that the ranks of the 'bourgeois specialists' would eventually emerge from the 1930s less depleted by coercive repression than either the kulaks or the broad ranks of communist administrators and military officers who fell victim to the Great Purge in 1936–38.

Nevertheless, the period of 'specialist-baiting' that was started by the Shakhty trial in 1928 was certainly repressive enough to discourage most 'bourgeois specialists' from putting their weight behind any opposition to the 'taut plans' industrialization strategy. Another aspect of 'specialist-baiting' which contributed to the 'great breakthrough' momentum was the fact that, since the 'bourgeois specialists' could be assumed to disagree with the idea of industrialization by 'bolshevik speeds', the party leaders who also disagreed with this idea now found themselves in a compromising position on the wrong side of the suddenly revitalized class division.[45] It is an intriguing possibility that, had Bukharin, Tomskii and other party leaders who opposed the abandonment of gradualist policies had the foresight to make a strong stand against the unjust prosecution of the Shakhty engineers in spring 1928, they would have not suffered so comprehensive a political defeat as they did in the year to come.

But the significance of the movement of 'class vigilance' against 'bourgeois specialists' was not limited to shifting the balance of power in favour of crash collectivization and industrialization. It quickly escalated into a movement of radical enmity against many values of the old urban culture that the 'bourgeois specialists' represented; in other words, the renewed 'class vigilance' carried some of the hallmarks of a 'cultural revolution'. This is how the period 1928–31 has been recently characterizied by a western historian:

Cultural revolution had many facets. It was a worker promotion movement linked to a political campaign to discredit the 'Right Opposition' within the Party. It was an iconoclastic youth movement directed against 'bureaucratic' authority. It was a process whereby militant Communist groups in the professions established local dictatorships and attempted to revolutionise their disciplines. It was, finally, a heyday for revolutionary 'theorists' and 'hare-brained schemes', whose blueprints for the new society not only attracted disciplines among the Communist cultural militants but also in many cases gained solid institutional support.[46]

In the arts, aesthetic values were put under pressure from a radical, social commitment stance strongly reminiscent of the 'proletarian culture' (*proletkult*) movement which had been active during the first years of Soviet power.[47] In education, theoretical approaches to knowledge and anything else that smacked of academic elitism had to give way to the requirement of mass promotion of workers to positions that used to be monopolized by the old educated strata. The proportion of workers among students in higher education rose from 30 per cent in 1928–29 to 58 per cent in 1932–33. For workers, academic entry requirements were reduced to primary schooling and the completion of apprenticeship training.[48]

In jurisprudence, the noble communist vision of the withering away of the state was thought by some leaders of the profession to have a worthy and practical vehicle in a doctrine that counselled the 'withering away of the law'. According to this doctrine, legalistic conceptions of justice had developed to serve the principles of private commodity exchange which lay at the basis of bourgeois society; as the notion of 'equality before the law' served to reinforce the much more fundamental inequality of class in bourgeois society, the struggle for socialist transformation would be only hampered by it. The main criterion in judging criminal acts and civil disputes should be therefore not the letter of the law but social expediency.[49]

Radical reforms of the criminal law were proposed which would make it possible for an action (or non-action) to be judged as a crime even if it did not appear to fall within any of the categories of crime described in the law books. Judges would no longer be obliged to determine whether a criminal act was intended, its social consequences being more important to the case than an individual's motives. In the same vein, judges would no longer be obliged to keep to any set penalty scales in their sentencing decisions; they would be guided in this respect by who the accused was as a social person rather than the nature of the alleged act that had brought him before the court. It was envisaged that the bulk of cases against individuals would be tried before lay 'comradely courts' in workplaces and neighbourhoods while professional judges would be primarily concerned with the arbitration of disputes between corporate bodies. Although these reforms of the law were only proposed and never in fact accepted by the government, there was a time during the 'great breakthrough' period when some of the judges were sufficiently confused to think that the proposals already were law, which, incidentally, increased further the already high propensity of judicial decisions to be overturned on appeal.[50]

The 'purge' (*chistka*) was another phenomenon which, while not entirely new, gained unprecedented prominence in the wake of the Shakhty trial. Here I have in mind neither the party purges which will receive their due attention below, nor the police hunts for 'wreckers' and enemy agents, but the numerous occasions on which people in positions of petty authority – housing clerks, local government officials, teachers, retail shop managers, etc. – were called to account for themselves in public meetings. This is how the phenomenon was described by a worried young woman on the eve of her appearance before one of these gatherings in summer 1931, as recollected by a western memoir writer who was then a worker in a Leningrad factory:

. . . every two years workmen's commissions are sent to public offices to scrutinise the work of the officials, whose antecedents and loyalty they endeavour to ascertain. If they suspect any particular person, they cite him or her to a public *chistka*, where anyone can bring forward accusations. After the evidence has been heard the commission then makes its decision, according to which either the 'purged' one may be declared innocent, let off with a warning or dismissed.[51]

Every tenth official of the government who came before the purge commissions was dismissed from his post in 1929–30.[52]

The disdain for apolitical aesthetics and academic elitism in art and knowledge, the rejection of procedural legalism in the administration of justice, the penchant for bearing white-collar souls in front of workers' gatherings, the insistence that there was no valid reality other than that defined by the class-struggle version of history; all these themes in the manifestations of the 'great breakthrough' were recognizably leftist, as were the dreams of communality without the coercive blessings of the state that made a fleeting appearance in the public media before getting swept away by the dialectic which held that the party state only had to grow in strength and importance as victory in the class struggle drew near. Few of the leftist calls could be still heard after 1930, except of course the one that identified 'socialist construction' with 'taut plans' industrialization.

After 1933, the dominant trends in cultural and social policies were moderate rather than radical. Artists were asked to be popular and entertaining as well as ideologically committed. Higher education and science were reformed again, marking a return to the principles of academic merit and selection if not to academic autonomy.[53] In the legal sphere, judges were asked to abide by the letter of the law and to insist that accusations were supported by evidence linking the accused to the alleged criminal act; neither the class origins of the accused nor his confessions were to be regarded as sufficient evidence.[54] Notions of citizen equality and legal rights, regardless of class origins, were enshrined in the new Constitution that was adopted in 1936. At the same time, however, the organs of the secret police remained beyond the jurisdiction of the judges, while their own powers of sentencing of suspected subversives in closed summary courts were reaffirmed and enlarged. The secret police (at various times known as the *Cheka*, *GPU*, *NKVD* and *OGPU)* also took over from the judicial sphere the management of penal institutions, where it became possible to re-sentence inmates to further terms, again in closed courts consisting of state security officers. Unlike in the judicial sphere, criteria of 'social expediency' retained precedence over legalistic criteria of proof in the operations of the secret police. The 'legal nihilism' of left-socialist jurisprudence was thus disallowed in normal open courts, but retained behind the closed doors of secret policemen's offices.[55]

The purges, too, remained a feature of the 1930s after other 'cultural revolution' movements were over. Simple 'specialist-baiting' was denounced in 1931, but activities of 'criticism from below' continued to be promoted as a check against abuses of authority by petty officials. The Workers' and Peasants' Inspectorate *(Rabkrin)*, which had been originally established by Lenin for the purpose of organizing rank-and-file vigilance against 'bureaucratism' on the part of administrators, was abolished at the beginning of 1934, but its functions were taken over by the trade unions and it would appear that there remained plenty of scope for workers who wanted to take part in various inspections of the low levels of administration. At the same time, however, the findings of such inspections tended to be passed on for decision to the Procuracy (state law enforcement agency) rather than to workers' meetings. Semi-public spectacles of soul-bearing became a rare occurrence until the tradition was revived in 1935, in the context of the party purges; however, since the conclusions of these proceedings became an object of interest for the secret police in 1936, it is unlikely that workers' participation at the meetings was very spontaneous in character. The main medium of rank-and-file participation in the purges became the anonymous letter of denunciation, which could be a deadly weapon of revenge but hardly what the earlier left-socialist fighters for popular controls over administrators had in mind.

Within the party, purges were centrally instigated and monitored in four grand campaigns: the purges (*chistki*) of 1929 and 1933, the 'verification of party documents' in 1935, and the 'exchange of party documents' in 1936. The campaign that started in 1929 must have been connected with the 'great breakthrough' and the desire to minimize the influence of the 'rightist-opportunities' within the party ranks who disagreed with it. The membership that was lost to the party as a result of the purge was compensated for by a busy recruitment campaign, primarily among workers and peasants, which more than doubled the total size of the party between 1929 and 1933.[56]

We shall see in the next chapter that the period 1929–32 was one of large-scale social and geographical mobility, which affected party members at all levels as much as the rest of the population. Neither the system of membership files nor the networks of face-to-face contacts coped with the fluidity of members' movement between branches, with the result that a large proportion of members found themselves beyond the reach of calls to party duty. As this was not a good state of affairs for countering the general slump in morale that accompanied the famine and industrial failures in 1932, the party leaders got worried about disorder in their own house, imposed a freeze on further recruitment and ordered another comprehensive screening of existing members. Political resistance, too, must have been a worry to the party leaders as this was the time of the famine, open disagreements about the merits of 'taut plans' industrialization, and oppositional expressions such as the 'Ryutin platform' in the party central committee. By the time this campaign was completed in 1934, 18 per cent of the total membership were expelled, mainly recent entrants. Of these expulsions, 21 per cent were officially due to violations of party discipline and 17 per cent were of members who were found to have given false information about their social origins. It transpired in the course of this screening that 200,000 party members had lost their membership cards or had them stolen. It was also found that 1000 blank cards had been stolen from party offices and another 47,000 had been issued, but it was not known to whom.[57]

The 'verification of party documents' was therefore ordered in 1935 to spot people who came by their cards in unauthorized ways but, after a few months, the central committee also requested that the rank and file become more widely involved in the 'verification commissions', and that the process should put some emphasis on 'self-criticism', especially by party members in official positions. This the local leaders countered by meticulous checking of all denunciations, with the result that the central committee accused them of 'family-mindedness'. About 9 per cent of party members were expelled by the end of the 'verification' process, but few of them were, it would seem, people in positions of authority. As the inspection of party documents found many cards in bad condition, new cards were printed and issued to all members in exchange for the old documents in 1936. This again was to be an occasion for further screening, causing another 2 per cent of the membership to be expelled.[58]

In the meantime, the general atmosphere of public life became distinctly denunciatory as party leaders urged vigilance against 'bureaucratism', while secret policemen betrayed the signs of being under pressure to discover hidden conspiracies against the party, in the wake of the murder of the Leningrad party secretary Kirov in December 1934, by a former member of the communist youth organization, the *komsomol*. This trend reached a new stage after the trial of Zinoviev, Kamenev and others in summer 1936, and the subsequent replacement of police chief Yagoda by Ezhov.

The next two years were dominated by the bizarre spectacle of a huge wave of arrests sweeping over the party–state establishment. This campaign depleted the highest and middle levels of industrial management, the party *apparat*, various branches of the government and the army officer corps. There were grotesque show trials with famous Bolshevik leaders some of whom had once been Stalin's rivals or their supporters, but many of the people who were arrested and sent to concentration camps of forced labour as political criminals had none other than impeccable credentials as loyal servants of the regime. The public media and meeting halls were filled with frenzied denunciation contests between sets of officials, reports of self-confessions, reprieves and reinstatements on appeal, and exhortations to further vigilance against the 'hidden enemies' who had supposedly infiltrated Soviet organizations. Police interrogation cells were filled with officials who were still in their posts during the day but under questioning during the night, as well as by officials who had been already arrested.[59] Ezhov's campaign (known as the *ezhovshchina*) was halted only after the chief himself and a number of his *NKVD* officers had been arrested and shot. In March 1939, the delegates to the party congress were told that mass purges were no longer necessary.

The phenomenon of a regime turning its instruments of terror against its own supporters makes the events of 1936–38 go down in history as one of the great historical puzzles. There is no complete explanation. While the gaps in documented knowledge are many, uncontested facts are also plentiful, but here the problem is that they tend to present themselves in contradictions. The *ezhovshchina* started while the state was adopting a constitution which heralded the end of class warfare and gave legal rights to all its citizens. The main spokesman for due process of the law and its guarantees for the rights of the individual took a starring role as the prosecutor in the most infamous and perverse show trials.[60] The height of the terror within the party coincided with official campaigns for party democracy and elections of party officials by secret ballot.[61] While there was a high sense of urgency about the tasks of preparing the country for a fast-approaching war, the party became consumed by its own affairs and the army as well as the strategic industries became subject to severe disruption from far-fetched fictions of over-zealous policemen.

Another prominent feature of Soviet public life became the cult of the leader. The Bolshevik revolution always had been something of a charismatic movement, with Lenin and his band of associates gaining mythical dimensions to their personalities in their lifetime. The charismatic aspect became only more pronounced on Lenin's death when the corpse was embalmed and placed on permanent display as a national shrine. Since Stalin became the undisputed leader of the party in 1929, his revolutionary past was built up to exaggerate the closeness of his association with Lenin, and his contemporary pronouncements were quoted as a source of infallible authority in commentaries on government policies. There was still some functionality about the way his name was used; ritual displays of sheer adulation were still rare, the emphasis was more on praising the policies of the party under his leadership than on praising the superb qualities of his person. There was also some sharing of the limelight as the other members of the Politburo were quoted as source of authority for policy interpretation, too, although less frequently. Some of them ('Sergo' Ordzhonikidze, L. Kaganovich) were even built up by the media as charismatic and strong personalities in their own right, although their own devotion to Stalin was never allowed to be in doubt. Things got onto a different plane in 1935–36. There was little in public life that was allowed to remain unsanctified by Stalin's image and quotations, and by songs of praise in his honour. The effect of the greatly increased frequency of reference to him in the printed media was enhanced by the new custom of printing his name all in capital letters or in italicized characters, or, just to make sure that there was no doubt left of the distinction between the sacred and the profane, in italicized capital letters. Any act that could be possibly construed as making light of the leader's authority was liable to denunciation.

Two other features were characteristic of public life during the 1930s, pertaining to the rhetoric that was common in the printed media. One of the functions of the media was to further the cause of socialist construction by exposing and criticizing various shortcomings that could be found in the practice of implementing party policy in the workplaces and offices throughout the land. Since the conception of the policies was one which placed them in the 'dialectical' context of pursuing social development by uncompromising 'class struggle', the rhetoric was rather strident. Good-humoured criticism was less common than heavy irony in the reports from the 'fronts' ('textile production front', 'technical education front', 'securing the supplies of timber to building sites front', etc.), which often bristled with pejorative neologisms and ascribed bad intentions to the ways in which people dealt with the problems they encountered in their work. This tendency, again, became extreme in 1936–38. It was not, however, the case that the persons who were criticized in the press were thereby irrevocably doomed to a downfall, not even in the virulent days of 1937, when published retractions of previous denunciations were almost as common as fresh allegations.

The other feature of public rhetoric throughout the 1930s was exaggeration, as if what was not blatantly grandiose could not have any significance.[62] The gigantomania was evident in the plans of construction themselves, which favoured huge projects and plants, spectacular and the biggest in the world. There may have been some economic or technical reasons for the 'big is beautiful' philosophy, but there clearly was a symbolic factor as well; since the industrialization campaign relied on the political mobilization of work effort in a backward country, the projects had to be spectacular if the 'pathos of socialist construction' was to catch popular imagination. Similarly, an achievement apparently was not worth talking about if it was only gradual and measurable in mere single figures. The statistics of productive successes had to be in double or triple figures, anything less was obviously considered too subtle to impress. This went for the custom of undertaking voluntary obligations as well. Promises had to be big to count for something when they were made; whether they were also realistic did not seem to matter so much. Like most negative phenomena, this one, too, came under criticism, even from Stalin himself, but to no avail.

It is impossible to evaluate with any quantitative accuracy the costs or the benefits of the 'revolution from above'. The hardships and the casualties suffered by the Soviet population in the 1930s were clearly immense, but unlike wartime casualty statistics, similar measurements pertaining to the 'socialist construction' decade remain a closely guarded state secret. Untimely deaths, their causes, and the numbers of arrests and imprisonments in forced labour camps are therefore a matter for more or less ingenious estimates based on scattered and diverse bits of information. The mystery is compounded and worst suspicions fuelled by the fact that the results of a general population census carried out in 1937 were suppressed, with the census office staff added to the victims of the Great Purge.

Another census, however, was carried out in 1939, allowing comparisons to be made with the census of 1926, and on that basis extrapolations about the number of 'unexpected' or 'excess' deaths occurring over the 13 years. There is also some information on birth rates and mortality rates based on partial surveys carried out in certain years of the decade. The data of the 1939 census, various economic and employment statistics, together with statistics pertaining to people deprived of electoral rights, provide clues to the size of the labour camp population.[63] Another important statistic is provided by the population census carried out in 1959, which gives a breakdown of the population by sex and age cohorts. This reveals an excessive deficit of males compared to females especially in the cohort born in 1900–1904;[64] this cohort was probably too old by the time of the war with Germany for the excessive deficit of males to be explained by active war service, but just the 'right' age in the late 1930s to fit in with the profile of the typical victim of the *ezhovshchina*. Other than that, there are various reports from emigrés who were able to provide information about the particular penal establishments they themselves had had the misfortune of knowing from the inside.

A 'low estimates' methodology leads to the hypothesis that

there were between 4 and 5 million people incarcerated in forced labour camps in 1939, and that about 5½ million people died prematurely during the 1930s as a result of the hardships inflicted by the famine and the deportations, and as a result of police executions.[65] Most of the victims were peasants who had found themselves on the wrong side of the collectivization and grain collection campaigns in 1929–33. The second major category of victims, much smaller in size than the first, were the victims of the *ezhovshchina* in 1936–38, mainly urban men in positions of authority. The residual were a heterogeneous collection of individuals who found themselves entangled in the peculiar deductions of class-vigilant minds for a wide variety of 'reasons'.

Although only half as high as the estimates offered by the most frequently quoted western authority on the subject of the Great Terror,[66] these are terrible statistics. They tell us that every twenty-fifth person of working age was in a forced labour camp. This was in addition to the people who, while not imprisoned in the camps, had their freedom severely restricted by terms of exile or deportation. The ranks of those who retained their basic freedoms, but only after bruising experiences of being denounced, harassed and interrogated, should also have their place in the casualty count. As regards the untimely deaths, there clearly were pockets of concentrated disaster where epidemics of typhoid and malaria preyed on people weakened by inadequate diet. The labour camps and places of deportation must have been particularly susceptible, as were some ordinary rural districts. And cutting across geographical distinctions is the especially depleted generation of men born between 1900 and 1904, every twentieth of whom was killed by the peacetime violence of the 'socialist construction' policies.[67]

On the other hand, however, these statistics allow for the possibility that some strata of the population, such as ordinary workers in the urban sector, did not have to fear arbitrary arrest quite so much if they kept outspoken political opinions away from secret police ears. In other words, mundane matters of industrial workers' discipline were not within the scope of the secret police hunts for 'enemy agents', in which case blanket references to police repression do not explain everything about the developing customs and social relations surrounding industrial work. But that is a topic for the chapters to follow.

2 Workers in a Changing Society

NEW WORKERS

Ivan Gudov would become a famous Stakhanovite hero, shake hands with Stalin and Ordzhonikidze in Kremlin gatherings, remain an honoured personality of the Soviet establishment and eventually write an excellent book of memoirs to which we shall have recourse more than once.[1] But he knew none of this when he arrived in Moscow in search of a better life in 1934. Travelling with his wife, two children and bundles of possessions, his first impression of the capital city was that the railway station and nearby streets were crowded with immigrant countrymen like himself. Railway station scenes crowded with peasants who 'looked as if they had been waiting for days on end or as if they had decided to camp provisionally in the hall and on the platforms', and who 'dragged the most incredible things about with them just as Indians, Chinamen and Japanese did in America',[2] feature strongly in the memoirs of western visitors, too.

Railway stations were places where people joined three-day queues to depart for new opportunities, or simply to escape 'class vigilance'; they were also places where 'class-liquidated' kulaks reported for deportation, or where their relatives waited for a chance to give parcels of practical gifts;[3] railway stations were temporary shelters for arriving immigrants with no accommodation, unofficial labour exchanges where truant workers met labour-poaching managers from other firms,[4] and the haunts of thiefs, racketeers and all manner of petty opportunists such as tend to be created in

31

their thousands by poverty and migration. Queue-jumping officials setting out for month-long business trips and organized groups of youth going off to build great power stations and blast furnaces must be also mentioned to complete the picture, and, from 1938 on, also the large groups of young men going off to join the army.[5] There was much of Soviet life in the 1930s that could be seen in a single railway station, for the period was one of much geographical as well as social mobility.

The population census that was carried out in December 1926 found 26 million (18 per cent of the total) living in towns and 121 million (82 per cent) living in the countryside. According to the census of January 1939, the total population amounted to 171 million;[6] 56 million (33 per cent of the total) living in towns and 115 million (67 per cent) in the countryside. Almost one-half of the town-dwellers in 1939 were recent (post-1926) arrivals from the peasant countryside. Eighteen million peasants had moved to the cities within the six years 1929–35; the peak year for migration was 1931, when more than 4 million countrymen arrived in the towns as fresh immigrants, while another 7 million peasants moved around the country on temporary labouring contracts. During the first five year plan alone, the cities grew by 44 per cent, that is as much as they had done over the preceding 30 years.[7]

Impressive though they might seem by any standards of rapid urbanization, these statistics still understate the amount of movement that in fact occurred. While in 1926 almost all rural residents had been found by the census to live mainly off agriculture, in 1939 there were 30 million people who were registered as rural residents while depending for their livelihood mainly on incomes from state employment outside of the agricultural sector.[8] Of the 86 million urban and rural residents who now belonged to the non-agrarian sector of the economy, only one-third had non-agrarian backgrounds going further back than 1926. But this shows only the extent of population transfer from the rural to the urban sector of the economy, not the mobility of the life that followed after the peasant homestead had been left behind.

In any one year of the first five year plan period, the wage clerks of the average industrial enterprise had to make more deletions from the pay-roll than the average number of people on it, and even a greater number of new entries. In other words, the annual turnover of labour in most enterprises exceeded 100 per cent. The only exception in this respect were the older and rural-situated cotton mills.[9] Annual turnover rates generally tended to drop below 100 per cent after 1932, but still remained very high throughout the rest of the decade. Bewildered newcomers trying to find their way round was an extremely common sight in most places of work in the 1930s. There were many people who were well practised in being bewildered newcomers, having changed jobs more than once between one birthday and the next.

Identifying the causes and proposing measures to reduce labour turnover was almost another industry in itself, but it might be said that in general the underlying cause lay in the contrast between the conditions in which most employees were finding themselves on the one hand, and the job opportunities elsewhere that were beckoning on the other hand. There were new jobs for political administrators, industrial managers and technicians, retail managers and assistants, planners, book-keepers, inspectors of many kinds, security guards, policemen, educators, bathing attendants and medical personnel, to name but some of the fast-growing types of non-manual employment, as well as for manual workers in extractive industries, construction, transportation and manufacturing.[10] The expansion mopped up existing urban unemployment before the second year of the first five year plan was out,[11] and henceforth it was a question of most employing organizations looking for new staff without being able to provide the sort of conditions which would encourage newcomers to settle down and resist rumours of greener pastures. Carpet-bagging movement from one employment to the next almost seemed a type of adaptation to the hardships of 'primitive accumulation' under the first five year plan; there were groups of workers who would make their disappearance on receiving boots or work-clothes or their ration cards for food from a new employer,[12] these things being highly priced commodities on the black market, and there were many newly hired workers who moved on when they found out that there would be administrative delays in the provision of these necessities which they desperately lacked.[13] During the second five year plan, a promise of better accommodation or better conditions of work and pay were the frequently occurring factors in the decisions to pack up bags yet again.

It was in this generally migrant environment that the social class which interests us most, i.e. manual workers in manufacturing industries, grew from some 3 million jobs in 1928 to 6 million in 1932 and over 8 million in 1940. This was not, incidentally, an entirely unremitting growth as there were two years in which the ranks of industrial workers decreased. There was a freeze on staffing imposed in connection with the economic crisis in 1933, which resulted in a negligible decrease (0.02 per cent) in the overall number of industrial workers in that year, and, in 1939, a large-scale draft of men to the army reduced the industrial workforce by more than 3 per cent.[14] The years of the greatest growth, in both relative and absolute terms, were 1930–31, during which the industrial workforce increased by 75 per cent.[15]

There could not have been more than one-half of the 3 million workers who had been in manual factory jobs at the beginning of the first five year plan still in similar jobs at the end of 1932. It was difficult for a worker to avoid a promotion into positions of authority in those years, for it was the working class that was relied upon to provide the political armies of collectivization activists, fill the mushrooming posts in the various branches of the state, and provide the expanding industry with its managerial and engineering corps. Many older workers were appointed directly to administrative posts from the shopfloor while many of the younger ones were recruited to be higher education students. The fast disappearance of skilled and experienced workers from the factory shopfloor alarmed the party leaders to the extent of decreeing a stop to the mass promotions (*vydvizhenetstvo*) at the end of 1930 and then again a few months later, but these decrees shared the fate of many other ones in that their impact on what was happening in practice was limited.[16] In addition, of the experienced workers that remained on the shopfloors, many were inevitably appointed to the fast-growing number of posts for foremen. If we call workers who joined manufacturing industry after 1928 'new' and all the rest 'old', there were at least three new workers for every old one by 1933, and seven or eight new ones for every old one by 1937.[17]

Some 60 per cent of the new workers came from peasant backgrounds, but not directly.[18] Ivan Gudov, whom we have already witnessed stepping off the train in Moscow in 1934, was typical in this respect, in that his route from the family farm to a Moscow engineering plant (manufacturing machine-tools) had taken him via a good number of labouring jobs in lumbering. Many workers joined manufacturing industry after a period on construction sites; it was in fact a widespread practice to recruit workers for new plants from the construction workers who built them. A rising proportion of the new workers were women, so that their share of the total industrial workforce increased from 29 per cent in 1928 to 42 per cent in 1937.[19] Furthermore, whereas women workers used to be concentrated mainly in the textile industries in the 1920s, they formed substantial minorities in the new industries by the end of the first five year plan. For example, 24 per cent of the manual workers in the brand-new Gorkii Automobile Works *(GAZ)* were women in 1932, and this proportion was expected to rise to 40 per cent within the next three years.[20] New women workers tended to be more urban and working-class by background than new men workers a good majority of whom had come from the peasantry.[21]

Above all, however, the accent was on youth. In this respect Ivan Gudov was untypical, because he was about 30 years old when he joined the engineering industry, and that was old. From 1930 on, some 70 per cent of newcomers to industry were below the age of 23, quickly creating a very young age profile of the industrial workforce. By 1933, 41 per cent of all industrial workers were under 23 years.[22] The workforce of the newly-built plants was particularly youthful; to give an example from the Gorkii Automobile Works again, 'up to 60 per cent' of its workers were younger than 23 years when the plant started production in 1932, and only 20 per cent were older than 30.[23] The industrial workforce began to age slightly after the main influx of new recruits was over in 1933, so that in the second half of the decade the typical shopfloor worker was in his or her late twenties rather than early twenties. Few of the new workers were illiterate, most having had four or five years of general schooling, and the situation improved further from this point of view after 1933, when the proportion of apprenticeship graduates (mainly graduates of *FZU*) among new recruits began to approach 70 per cent.[24]

The new working class that was formed in the 1930s was very youthful and highly mobile. Its single largest component consisted of young men with migrant peasant backgrounds, while men from urban backgrounds tended to be quick to leave shopfloor work for higher things. The majority joined the ranks of factory workers in the early years of the decade. Young women of urban as well as rural backgrounds formed the second largest subgroup. It would appear from incidental data that workers of all backgrounds were prone to leave one factory for another to a similarly high extent, the exception of this rule being perhaps constituted by the women workers in the longer established and rural textile mills, where the rates of labour turnover were substantially lower than in the rest of manufacturing industry. We shall see below that the youthfulness and mobility of this industrial workforce was to some extent reflected in its lifestyles, and also in its relations with the repressive agencies of the state. But first, it is appropriate to give some consideration to its living standards.

LIVING STANDARDS

Available comparative statistics of food consumption during the crisis years 1931–33 suggest that industrial workers were better off than some other strata of the population. Moscow workers are recorded as having consumed, per capita, 20 per cent more grain products than average for non-agricultural population, and slightly more meat. Comparison with agricultural population was even more favourable, as workers were able to consume 60 per cent more of meat products per capita than rural workers who had to compensate by eating relatively more potatoes and dairy products.[25]. The relative advantage enjoyed by the average worker over the average person outside the industrial sector was maintained in the provinces too, as workers in the heavy industries such as mining and steelmaking had rations which were the envy of engineering workers in the capital cities, and because many of the large firms in the favoured industries owned their own farms for the benefit of their workers.[26]

Nevertheless, the relatively privileged position of the favoured industries did not shelter workers from the harsh realities of the crisis. Although outright starvation was rarely in evidence according to the American engineers who helped to manage industrial projects at the time, both in European Russia and in the remote regions,[27] evidence of serious poverty among all groups of workers was overwhelming in its consistency. Hunger featured strongly in the memories of the crisis years recollected by the Ukrainian workers who emigrated to USA at the end of the war fifteen years later,[28] and the meagre diet of the Soviet workers received a frequent comment in the reports of western engineers and visitors.[29] The Soviet press also provided much evidence of the unsatisfactory situation. It made the proper management of factory farms, bread shops and canteens one of its major campaigns, and the seriousness of the food situation came out in the course of campaigns for shopfloor discipline and efficiency as well; press reports showed, for example, that a worker's pursuit of a flat-mate suspected of the theft of a 5 kg bag of potatoes from the communal kitchen was acceptable to management as a good enough reason for missing two days' work, and that arranging workplace meals for workers was among the more effective things that foremen could try to reduce absenteeism.[30] Workers' inspections were given national publicity when they caught shop assistants selling slightly underweight portions of bread.[31]

The factory-owned farms were believed to vary in quality, thus contributing another reason for workers to want to move from one firm to another.[32] Since a worker spent three-quarters of her wages in the shops and canteens managed by her factory,[33] it is understandable that rumours of better provisions in another factory could prove irresistible. The press often criticized the fact that, in the general context of shortage of competent managers, the factory farms and retail establishments (*ORS*) tended to be managed by people who had already showed their incompetence in other appointments.[34] How true this could be in extreme cases was shown by one of the Ukrainian emigré interviewees who reported to have worked in a factory where the *ORS* manager was a retired Red Army officer who, having distinguished himself in action during the Civil War, now enjoyed high political patronage which kept him in managerial posts. Already preceded by something of a reputation, he did not disappoint expectations when, on his arrival to take up office, he demonstrated a broad-chested commitment to workers' welfare by deciding that the factory farm should immediately switch its meat production from chickens and rabbits to cows, because the proletariat deserved beef. Forty thousand chickens and rabbits were therefore slaughtered by the innovative method of mass electrocution, resulting in a glut of meat singed beyond edibility. The future was meatless because the beef programme predictably faltered on a shortage of things that cattle would eat. The cavalry hero's reign over the supplies of provisions continued after this setback and became distinguished by characteristics stemming from the fact that he loved workers to have a good time at generously lubricated celebrations, hated accountants, and signed chits of paper without being able to read.[35] Such cases of colourful incompetence apart, not even the best-managed factory farms could altogether escape the general difficulties of agriculture in the famine years.

The general recovery of agricultural supplies that started after 1933 was not fast enough to reassure workers that food was no longer a problem. The press reported 'Trotskyist agitation' at workers' meetings that greeted the abolition of rationing in 1935 by expressions of misgivings about prices and availability.[36] The sense of uncertainty about the food situation was also shown by the popularity of a government policy which, in contrast to earlier suspicions about hypothetical corrupting influences of peasant pursuits on proletarian consciousness, charged the trade unions with the task of making allotments of land available for workers who wanted them. It was originally planned that the number of plots of land allocated to employees of the non-agrarian sector of the economy would reach 1½ million in the course of 1934, but this number was in fact exceeded by another million before the end of that year.[37] Campaigns for supplying allotment-holding workers with seeds and implements, and for protecting their produce from the attentions of requisition agencies, were a major preoccupation of the trade unions in 1933–35.[38] In the latter year, sales of farm livestock on favourable terms to shock workers and to workers with large families became one of the well-publicized ways in which factory trade unions displayed a caring approach to their members.[39]

That the abolition of food rationing was justified by improving supplies was shown by the fact that prices of bread on the free peasant markets dropped to one half in 1935 of what they had been in the previous year.[40] There was much truth in Stalin's proclamation, to the congress of Stakhanovites in autumn 1935, that 'life has become easier, comrades, life has become gayer'.[41] But we know from the examination of agricultural performance in Chapter 1 that, welcome though it was, the post-1933 improvement was not substantial enough to restore the food aspect of workers' living standards to the levels of the late 1920s. Neither did the shift of responsibility for distribution from the factory *ORS* shops to general retail networks occur without some local difficulties. Newspaper reports of workers forming pre-dawn queues for staple provisions became rare in the second half of the decade, but they still made the occasional appearance, in addition to renewed criticisms of factory managements for slackening their care for workers' provisions.[42] These criticisms were often made in the context of the finding that there was a sharp drop in the number of meals sold to workers in factory canteens. The abolition of rationing had been accompanied by an increase in the prices of the food retailed through the state distribution network, which also caused an increase in the prices of the food retailed in the factories. The drop in canteen custom might have been interpreted simply as a confirmation that workers could now enjoy home-made sandwiches in preference to standing in canteen queues, but there was in fact much concern that workers could no longer afford to pay for hot meals under the new system.[43]

Clothing was another aspect of workers' living standards which testified to their poverty. This shortage was caused by

the mass exit of the population from the peasant economy
wherein much of the weaving, spinning, dress-making and
boot-making had previously been done, together with the fact
that light industry was the recipient of a very inferior share of
overall industrialization investment. As with food, the worst
years were the ones under the first five year plan, which were
followed by a modest rate of improvement during the second
five year plan. Inevitably, the improvement was halted in the
last years of the 1930s when a large transfer of industrial
resources had to take place in favour of the military sector.
The ragged appearance of Soviet workers in the 1930s received as much dismayed comment from western visitors as
the prevalent dietary standards, but the most eloquent testi-
monies to the seriousness of the situation were borne by
Soviet press reports which, in the context of criticizing factory
managements' failures in respect of their legal obligation to
provide workers with safety clothing, publicized cases of
barefoot workers on the shopfloors of heavy industry, and of
steel-workers who could be singled out from the others in the
street by singed clothes, because they had no change of
clothing for work.[44] Gudov recalls in his memoirs that he had
owned only second-hand clothes before he became a rich and
famous Stakhanovite in autumn 1935, thus implicitly posing
the question of when the less high-flying members of the
Moscow working class would be able to buy their first sets of
new clothes.[45] The lack of good-quality clothing and footwear
must have been experienced by workers as a major hardship
during the winter seasons.

The third basic ingredient of material living standards –
shelter – was also in short supply. The housing construction
programmes of both the first and second five year plans were
underfulfilled, while the number of new workers coming in to
claim housing in urban areas was far above the plan. In the
capital cities (Moscow, Leningrad, Kiev) most workers lived
in shared apartments, a substantial minority in factory-owned
barracks, and some, including Ivan Gudov and his family
before he became a Stakhanovite and got a self-contained
apartment, lodged in peasant huts in nearby villages. In the
rural-situated textile mills, many workers lived in their own
peasant huts, or lodged in them. In the new industrial com-

plexes that were built under the auspices of the five year plans in the provinces and remote regions, factory-owned barracks were the most typical abode for workers.[46] This is the break-down of the population of the new iron and steel city of Magnitogorsk by categories of dwelling, as compiled by an American worker who spent most of the 1930s working there: 50 per cent lived in barracks, 25 per cent in makeshift dwellings dug in to the hillsides (*zemlyanki*), 15 per cent in apartment blocks, 8 per cent in peasant cottages and 2 per cent in large elite residences and the hotel.[47] Whether living in factory-owned barracks, city-owned apartment blocks or peasant-owned cottages, the vast majority of workers' homes were badly overcrowded. It was a good fortune for a couple to have a small room of their own even if it had only shared facilities, while a single worker in a room of his own seemed a suspicious anomaly.[48] Small self-contained apartments were a coveted luxury to which only the families of managers, engineers, some old workers and leading Stakhanovites might aspire with any degree of realism. Living with strangers at close quarters was normal for the great majority of indust-rial workers.

The sharing of facilities was very intensive. An American worker in Leningrad found his Soviet friends living in an apartment block where fifteen families shared one kitchen and one bathroom; this may have been a little worse than average, but a lot better than the apartment blocks with forty rooms per one toilet, which were mentioned by a trade union leader in the course of his criticisms of bad housing.[49] The average floorspace available to a worker was about large enough for a single bed and one or two small pieces of furniture. Many people lived in apartment corridors, in kitchens and in cellars. Some of the wooden barracks built by factories to provide temporary accommodation for single workers consisted of large shared rooms. In one such room in Leningrad, the living space of 5 by 6 metres was shared by a family with two pre-school children, another young married couple, plus a single person. At more than four square metres per person, this amount of floor-space was about average for Soviet workers.[50] The lack of privacy was perhaps rather worse than the Soviet average; 200 families lived in this particular building, 'all craving for a small but separate room'.[51] There were, however, many factory barracks which provided nothing better than long dormitories with endless rows of beds separated only by narrow aisles.[52] The Soviet press did not shrink from publicizing the deplorable extremes of the housing shortage suffered by many workers at least temporarily, for example shift-workers who had to take turns in barrack beds, or workers who had to sleep on bare boards.[53] Inadequate heating, frozen waterpipes and inordinate amounts of bed bugs were also acknowledged as common facts of life in factory housing.[54] The bed bugs even earned their place in a speech by Ordzhonikidze, the high-powered Commissar of Heavy Industry.[55]

The general rise in living standards that occurred during the second five year plan did not extend to the housing situation.[56] On the other hand, it should be noted that, whereas the years of the first five year plan were ones of a substantial decline in material living standards relative to the late 1920s or indeed the late Tsarist period, housing standards had always been bad as far as both the peasantry and the industrial working class were concerned. Workers' overcrowding had been even worse in 1913 than in the 1930s, but the improvement that took place in the 1920s was largely limited to the extent made possible by dispossessing the rich of the Tsarist order of their excess housing space.[57] As regards the mass of the peasantry, their best living standards were achieved in the late 1920s, when their housing standards were described by a visiting American builder in the following terms.

The best homes were, of course, those belonging to the kulaks. They were 'substantially built and fairly comfortable', but living quarters and stables for livestock were under the same roof. Water for general use was brought by women from the river flowing through the village, while drinking water was drawn from wells and boiled before use. A bathhouse would be in a separate building, some distance from the living quarters. 'The weekly trek across the barn yard and the manure pile to the bath house, especially in wet weather, was hardly conducive to the full enjoyment of one's weekly bath.' These were the kulak residences. Poor peasants lived in squalid and congested huts with dirt floors and no bath-houses. Needless to say, kulaks as well as poor peasants tended to share their living space with large extended families.[58]

If a lack of private living space was nothing new to most workers, regardless of whether their backgrounds were peasant or urban, electricity, sewerage, running water and central heating were new to the ex-peasant majority. Some of the barracks that housed industrial workers had all of these amenities. It is unlikely that the new workers experienced their housing immediately as a bad drop in their living standards. It was different rather than worse. The report of the Leningrad barrack inhabitants who craved small rooms of their own, however, suggests that accommodation which provides a modicum of privacy is a need that becomes urgent with time, *after* the migrant has settled into urban life. It is interesting to note at this point that an experienced American engineer, who worked in new copper mines in the remoter regions of Russia where the accommodation for workers presumably was not any better than average, found the conditions there to be generally similar to those 'in the mining camps' in America only 30 years earlier.[59] Whereas sufficient food and clothing was a major preoccupation for most Soviet workers in the early 1930s, sufficient private housing probably became the major preoccupation in the later 1930s. If that was so, the actual economic development was not far off the mark in its general trends; there was an improvement in regard to food and consumer goods during the second five year plan, and there were signs that average housing standards began to improve with the beginning of the third five year plan in 1938, although this upward trend was soon to be reversed by the devastations of the war.

It is sometimes said about the Soviet economy that, because of the consumer scarcities and the proliferation of different distribution networks, money wages are less important than the wage-earner's standing with the authorities. This is a partial truth which is easily exaggerated. In regard to the 1930s, it is truer to say that the size of the wage-packet and its insufficiencies were a constant issue in a workers' life. The main instance where a stroke of an administrative pen could

make a greater difference to a worker's living standards than
large changes in earnings was when the pen assigned a room
in a municipally-controlled apartment, thus providing a home
which was better and cheaper than renting a room-share by
private   arrangement,   and   in   some   cases   even
cheaper than a bed in a factory barrack.[60] Otherwise, everything cost money and few people earned enough to be able to
regard their fortnightly salary slips with indifference. In the
early 1930s, the prices of rationed goods were not exactly
paltry by the standards of an average worker's wage, and,
given the low level of the rations, the ability to supplement
them by costly purchases at peasant market-stalls was rather
important to one's well-being.[61] I have already noted in
Chapter 1 the price increases in the early 1930s, to the
awareness of which should be also added the price increases
that took place in the middle years of the decade following the
abolition of rationing. After 1932, increases in wages were
large enough to outstrip price inflation, but this is talking
about averages; in practice there were many workers who had
to worry at one time or another about being able to make
their money go far enough to provide basic subsistence.

That there were surviving islands of serious poverty among
industrial workers on average wages was brought out by press
reports of welfare activities in the factories, especially in the
summer months of 1935, when industrial authorities were
under a special pressure to display their care for workers'
welfare. According to one such report from welfare activists
in a Leningrad heavy engineering plant, thirty families of
semi-skilled workers were found living in the sort of poverty
that was made evident by children suffering from rickets and
workers collecting leftover scraps of bread from canteen
tables, although they kept no chickens at home as many of
their fellow Leningraders apparently did. Some of the
workers were reduced to this sort of poverty because they
spent too much of their wages on drink, some because their
wives were not working, there being no nursery places for
their children, and in some cases the problem was heavy
indebtedness.[62]

That falling into heavy debt must have been all too easy was
evident from the press reports which publicized details of

shopping sprees by newly affluent Stakhanovites in the winter of 1935–36. One customer in a special shop set up for high-flying workers in the Kharkov Tractor Works, for example, paid 850 roubles for one pair of leather boots, one pair of slippers, one pair of shoes, one winter coat and material for one suit; another customer paid 1460 roubles for one pair of boots, one pair of shoes, one pair of women's shoes, material for a men's suit and material for a woman's coat.[63] The average wage in state employment overall was 190 roubles per month in 1935;[64] the average worker in a shoe factory earned 196 roubles in June 1935 and 249 roubles in June 1936;[65] the average wage for workers in heavy engineering was 260 roubles per month in 1935;[66] the workers who were found in urgent need of welfare support in the Leningrad heavy engineering plant mentioned above were milling-machine operators earning 200 to 250 roubles per month.[67] Not surprisingly, many workers found it necessary to supplement their incomes by taking additional part-time employment. Ivan Gudov, for example, worked not only as a milling-machine operator in a machine-tools plant, but also three shifts a week as a wagon-loader in a railway depot.[68] Incomes from second jobs amounted to 16 per cent of the total money earned in state employment in 1936; this amount of state-registered 'moonlighting' was considered to represent a welcome drop from the levels of previous years.[69]

A discussion of workers' living standards would not be complete if it did not include some consideration of the fact that some workers were better off than others. In the first half of the 1930s, the 10 per cent highest-paid industrial workers were earning more than three times as much as the 10 per cent lowest-paid ones.[70] Wages were differentiated by industrial branch, skill grades and output performance. The highest-paid workers were in the metallurgical plants and in deep mines, while the lowest-paid workers were concentrated in municipally-controlled 'small-scale' industries and in light industry. Each industry had its own wage tariff which prescribed basic hourly rates of pay for each of seven or eight grades of skill, where grades 1 and 2 were for unskilled workers, grades 3 and 4 required some training and grades 5 and above were for skilled workers. Grade 3 was the most widespread grade in the early years of the decade, and grade 4 in the later years.[71] Workers on piece-rates had higher tariffs than hourly-paid workers, and shift-workers were paid more than workers who worked only during the day. And finally, with the removal of the safety-net of minimum hourly rates for workers on piece-rates, by a government decree in 1934, piece-rates became another source of differentiation in earnings.[72] Overall data of earnings distribution of industrial workers in the latter half of the 1930s are not available, but, since the fight against 'petty-bourgeois egalitarianism' was one of the central planks of government pay policies after 1931, and since it was found that the 10 per cent best-paid workers earned more than five times as much as the lowest-paid 10 per cent in 1946,[73] differentials must have been increasing in the latter part of the 1930s. The most dynamic period in this respect was clearly the Stakhanovite movement in its early stages, in the winter 1935–36, when there were widely publicized cases of workers achieving monthly earnings in excess of 1000 roubles,[74] which was four times higher than the industrial workers' average. But these were exceptions. Few rate-busters managed to pull off such spectacular feats more than once. A survey of engineering workers carried out a year later found that Stakhanovites in skill grade 4 were on average earning only 25 per cent more than rank-and-file workers in the same skill grade.[75]

Apart from wage differentials, an obvious factor that distinguished a small minority of privileged workers from the rest was accommodation in self-contained apartments, usually in blocks otherwise reserved for higher ranking managers and engineers. (It should be noted that many of the younger engineers lived in barrack dormitories, in overcrowded conditions which were no better than those suffered by the majority of manual workers, although their periods of waiting for more permanent housing perhaps were shorter than manual workers.[76]) This leaves us to consider the extent to which other welfare benefits constituted another source of differentiation within the working class.

The 'social wage' in the form of free or subsidized education, sick pay, paid maternity leave, retirement pensions, subsidized use of sanatoria and rest homes, summer camps for children, nurseries and kindergartens, and financial welfare funds for loans and grants, has been estimated to constitute an addition to real wages amounting to between 20 and 25 per cent of the total in the 1930s.[77] The disposal of these welfare benefits was in the hands of factory trade union committees, who were under conflicting pressures in regard to the principles of distribution; they were supposed to use benefits as an additional incentive to good behaviour and production efficiency on the part of the workers, but without being really freed of the principle that welfare benefits should be made available mainly to workers in special need.

That welfare benefits should constitute a material incentive for better work behaviour was decreed by the party central committee in October 1930, and by the government legislation that followed in 1931. In this instance, the main objective was to reduce labour turnover. Workers who had served the 'basic industries' for more than two years were rewarded by three extra days of annual leave. Sickness benefit was also gradated by years of service, and the whole range of welfare benefits was to be administered in favour of longer-serving workers and 'shock workers'.[78] There were calls for years in service to be defined for these purposes in terms of work in a single enterprise rather than in industry in general, but they never became actual policy.[79] The 'anti-levelling' trend in the disposal of benefits, however, continued to the extent that, by 1936, factory trade union officials boasted in the press that full sick pay was being made available to 'shock workers' only.[80] We must note, however, that about one-third of all industrial workers were registered as 'shock workers' by this time, and that the boast was quite likely to mean that only workers who were registered in 'socialist competition' for the title of 'shock worker' qualified, which was a category comprising about two-thirds of all workers.[81]

Since the 'provision for need' criterion for the distribution of benefits was never renounced, the relevance of the particular living conditions and adverse circumstances faced by individual claimants tended to be reiterated even in those policy statements which were otherwise meant to encourage the differentiation of highly productive and disciplined workers from others. While a trade union could be criticized, for example, for granting a pension increment to a worker 'simply because he had a wife',[82] the trade union could also be criticized if it showed a 'bureaucratic disregard' for individuals' needs. Undue stinginess in granting the full rate of sick pay was publicly denounced even in 1936, during a campaign for reducing 'overspending' of sick pay budgets.[83] Despite all the resolutions and decrees according to which exemplary workers should be allowed to jump queues for sanatoria and health resorts, medical personnel were not denied favourable publicity when they complained that these establishments were full of 'patients' who had no need of the particular medical facilities available there. Medical representatives were called upon to play a more active role in the sittings of the commissions that distributed the passes to sanatoria.[84]

Welfare benefits must have come nearest to serving as an instrument of the 'anti-levelling' policies of stimulating high work performance during the winter 1935–36, when the excesses of the Stakhanovite movement reached their heights and factory trade unions boasted in the press of the special care they lavished on their best-performing workers. They sent them to rest homes, set up special shops for them, visited them in their homes to find out what their needs were, chauffeur-drove them to nurseries if they happened to be breast-feeding mothers, and lent them money (sometimes on a 'non-returnable basis') to buy furniture, radio sets, bicycles and in a few cases even private cars.[85] But these privileges were much more widely publicized than widespread. According to a report of the distribution of the 'self-help' fund published by the Kharkov Tractor Works in January 1936, for example, 13,850 roubles were lent to 35 Stakhanovites to help them acquire private cars, but this was not a great sum compared to the 300,000 roubles paid out in loans and grants to 4500 workers, mainly to help them through periods of sickness (presumably because they did not qualify for the full rate of sick pay), or to compensate them for loss of pay caused by looking after sick members of the family, or to help them buy clothes.[86] A lot more of the welfare money was spent on alleviating hardship than on augmenting the living standards of the highest-paid workers.

The dispensation of passes to vacation resorts owned by the trade unions was probably a more consistent instrument of the 'anti-levelling' policies, but this observation must be tempered by the fact that there were fewer passes to be distributed than there were accredited Stakhanovites to claim the privilege. In Gudov's machine-tools plant, for example, there were over 700 workers accredited as Stakhanovites in the summer 1936 (out of 4000 workers overall), but only 300 passes to vacation resorts could be issued in the first seven months of that year.[87] Judging by frequent press reports, some of the privileged minority with rest-home passes found that the privilege was not worth very much, as many rest homes were notorious for being underfunded, understaffed and giving rise to many complaints.[88] There is also some evidence that the dispensation of passes to the better establishments was at times influenced by bribery rather than the applicants' standing and work-performance records.[89]

The provision of welfare benefits was often criticized or appealed against by workers in the press on various grounds, ranging from hardship to status and achievement. The overall conclusion must be that, the publicity stunts involving 'non-returnable loans' for the purchase of cars, etc. notwithstanding, the administration of workers' welfare on the whole was not something that added much to the differentiation of living standards within the working class, because it remained to some extent oriented to the 'levelling' task of alleviating poverty where it was pressing the most. To recall the example of the Leningrad heavy engineering plant where the trade union organized a campaign to help the workers who collected bread crusts from canteen tables for the benefit of their families rather than their poultry, financial aid was granted to all the thirty families who were found to need it, regardless of whether their financial distress might have been thought to be caused by some of their members' drinking habits.[90] As a factor of differentiation, the administration of welfare paled into insignificance beside wage-scales and the abilities of workers to benefit from piece-rate schemes. The administration of housing, however, was a strong factor which visibly identified a small elite of manual workers as equal in status and material living standards to managers and engineers.

In the late 1920s, the highest-paid workers were found among the 45–49 year olds. It is not surprising that the fast social mobility of the industrialization period should bring the age of the shopfloor elite down; in 1937, the best-paid workers in the engineering industry were in the 30–34 age-group, with 80 per cent of toolsetters and 70 per cent of highly skilled lathe-turners (grade 6) being less than 34 years old.[91] There were substantially more women among the shopfloor elite in the second half of the 1930s than ever before, but they were still under-represented, among both the top skill-grades and the shock workers and Stakhanovites.[92] (Although Soviet women were reported to be better workers than men by the American engineers who had worked there in the early 1930s.[93])

Soviet workers were the beneficiaries of a progressive legislation in so far as conditions of employment were concerned. Shifts were normally seven to eight hours long (not counting dinner breaks), every sixth day was free (every fifth day in mines and some metallurgical plants), and there was an annual minimum of another 16 days of national holidays and paid vacations.[94] Physical conditions at work clearly varied, but managers were under a lot of pressure to make improvements a priority, which they sometimes did, judging by proud press reports of new facilities like 'hygiene corners' with gleaming wash-basins and polished mirrors opening up in the factories, and by the comments of some of the ex-Ukrainians in USA who thought that conditions in the new Soviet plants were 'really good' and improving, in contrast to the conditions they found on taking employment in their newly adopted country.[95]

On the debit side from the point of view of workers' quality of life, many of the plants in the high-priority industries worked on three-shift systems, and most of the rest on two-shift ones. The worst feature of the working schedules, however, was the so-called uninterrupted working week (*nepreryvka*), that was being introduced into a growing number of factories in the first years of the industrialization campaign. The plants that worked on this type of schedule had no closing days, which meant that, to enable each worker to have the fifth day off while keeping each workplace going without closing days, the workforce was on five different week-cycles. This created something of an organizational nightmare in the factories, as workers had to be frequently transferred from one machine or one team to another, and at home as well, since friends and families often found it difficult to get free days together. The drawbacks of this system brought the party leaders to declare a retreat from it and allow factories to stop production every sixth day without being accused of underutilizing equipment, but some factories evidently still were on uninterrupted schedules in 1934, that is, three years after the retreat was first called.[96]

Another mixed blessing was overtime. There are no data which could reliably show what the average hours of work actually were.[97] In itself, overtime working might not be always unpopular with workers, if it boosted wages by extra rates of pay, but this did not always happen, as anti-overtime legislation and wage-budget cash limits often forced managers to try to get overtime from workers without extra pay. This could be sometimes arranged fairly amicably, by allowing workers to take extra leave in compensation for overtime work, but there is a plethora of press stories which show that the terms on which overtime was worked were a frequent source of grievance, especially where workers were asked to turn up for work, at short notice, on their free days.[98]

LIFESTYLES

Since characterizing a lifestyle tends to boil down to the question of what a person does outside the factory gates, a part of the answer has already been supplied by the discussion of living standards. For many workers, there could not have been much time left after the basic business of earning a living, as some did a lot of overtime, and some had second jobs. It might also be worth noting at this point that the poor housing conditions and underdeveloped municipal services forced some workers to spend a lot of time in transit between home and work. To take another example from Ivan Gudov's pre-Stakhanovite days, he had to walk 10 km every day, and presumably more than that on the three days when he also moonlighted; although it should be noted that he did not think this too bad by the standards of the village life he had been used to.[99]

After the business of earning a living, there was the time-consuming problem of buying necessities that were in short supply. In the latter part of the 1920s, Russian working women evidently spent daily on average 5 hours 47 minutes on housework.[100] Shopping presumably formed a substantial part of this time, and also home-based activities like the making and repair of clothes. In both these respects, the demands on workers' time must have been greater in the 1930s, when the retail network was sparser, queues were longer and the lack of availability of ready-made clothes greater than had been the case at the time of the 'time-budget' surveys in the latter part of the 1920s. Futhermore, if basic shopping became a little easier after 1933, we have seen in the previous section that many workers' families acquired allotments of land for the purpose of producing some of their food, which must have been a time-consuming activity, especially where the allotments were situated some distance from workers' homes.[101]

But the society in which the working class was forming was not only poor but also very mobile and in many tangible respects young. Opportunities to join the ranks of skilled workers, the technical intelligentsia and administrators were beckoning, and there was no shortage of energy among young workers for taking advantage of the facilities that were available for self-improvement. The main means of travelling up the job ladder was education; evening and correspondence courses at all levels, from basic literacy to university degree level, were widely available, and the acquisition of a higher qualification usually led to a higher-paid job. The incentives for study became especially strong in the second half of the decade, with the widening of the wage differentials between jobs on the basis of the required qualifications. And even if the route to relative wealth that was taken by an ambitious worker lay in becoming a shock worker or a Stakhanovite rather than an engineer or an administrator, it still required that effort be expended at the school desk as well as at the machine.

The government in fact wanted a situation where every worker under the age of 35 was a further education student.[102] While this remained one of the many underfulfilled targets, and while the quality of some of the courses that workers attended was quite possibly rather below par, successive 'get educated' campaigns made sure that enrolling on new courses and passing more exams was a prominent aspect of workers' lives. During one of these campaigns in 1936, 84 per cent of industrial workers were studying at 'technological minimum' courses alone; a year later, 33 per cent did the follow-up courses for Stakhanovites and 'masters of socialist labour'.[103] This was not counting the students on other courses. A Stakhanovite worker spent on average 2 hours 47 minutes per day on study and a non-Stakhanovite worker 1 hour 38 minutes, according to a survey carried out among industrial workers in spring 1937.[104] Even John Scott enrolled on a course during his time in Magnitogorsk, obviously not being able to resist the opportunity of becoming the first American to get a 'communist academy' (*komvuz*) degree; he found in the academic year 1933–34 that, of his 24 co-habitants in the factory barrack, eight were students in some organized school, spending up to four hours in certain evenings of the week at school desks, sometimes after overtime shifts and on empty stomachs.[105]

The self-denial exercised by the studying workers was to some extent mitigated by the fact that alternative ways of spending an evening were not always particularly alluring. The overcrowded housing could not offer much by way of relaxing quiet evenings at home, and although there were new factory clubs with cafés and pleasant leisure facilities opening up during the years of the second five year plan, places to go out remained among the many things that were in short supply.[106] In this context, going out to an evening class might have been found quite attractive by many workers, and the same could be said about the gamut of voluntary activities that came under the heading of 'social work'. In 1937, the average amount of time spent daily by industrial workers on 'social work' was 36 minutes among the Stakhanovites and 24 minutes among the rest.[107] Organized by the party, the Communist Youth League (*komsomol*) and, mainly, the trade unions, these activities encompassed the whole range from taking part in the work of state inspectorates and purge commissions to visiting sick colleagues and planting trees in factory yards.[108] The majority of workers, however, probably spent most of their 'social work' time mixing passive attendance with private socializing at meetings and at occasional sessions of unpaid labour in collective farms or other institutions over which their factory exercised 'patronage' (*shefstvo*).[109]

Not all of the activities which dominated the lives of many workers were as readily admissible to the interviewers of officially sponsored surveys as taking part in further education and in 'social work'. The most important case in point was *blat*, i.e. the business of cultivating and using networks of personal contacts for the purpose of obtaining scarce resources which should have been distributed as state property in a centralized and planned economy, in accordance with official and impersonal rules. *Blat* might have in various instances involved elements of theft, fraud, bribery and black marketeering, but, rather than in outright crime, its essence lay in the ability to pull strings, i.e. to claim a personal favour from someone whose job put him or her in a position of privileged access to some scarce resource. Even an ordinary worker was in a position of privileged access to something; for example, by being entitled to sturdy work-boots, or by virtue of handling scarce tools and materials, which formed a basis for his ability to promise reciprocity when claiming favours. By all accounts, success in obtaining valued goods by 'pulling strings' (*po blatu*) could make a lot of the difference between living in serious want and living bearably well for many workers.

It is interesting to note in this context that some of the evidence of workers' devotion to the wheelings and dealings of *blat* suggests a difference of attitudes between old workers and new workers. This is how one of the ex-Ukrainian interviewees recalled the crisis years of the early 1930s:

The old workers were in the worst position. They did not use the *blat* as often as we did, I mean young workers. They were too proud, they used to say this was their factory. They really believed this during the *NEP* times, later on, they felt that they had been cheated. You know, after the revolution, the older workers could fight even the Party and the management through their trade unions. Later on, the power of the trade union was taken away from them. It was obvious that they felt deeply hurt and they still tried to strengthen the trade union. We younger workers, we saw that there was no use in it, therefore we jumped into the *blat* deals.[110]

It is also possible that, apart from not having any expectations to the effect that workers ought not to be obliged to hustle for their supplies of basic necessities, pulling off *blat* deals held an intrinsic satisfaction for immigrants from the peasant countryside, an agreeable sense of 'having arrived' after the alienation of uprooted poverty. A sense of intrinsic satisfaction was certainly apparent in some of the recollections of *blat* made by the ex-Ukrainian interviewees, one of whom made a general point of it while recollecting the pleasures of being able to steal things from his factory under a manager's conniving gaze.[111] After all, *blat* networks provided a practical context for the familiar communal virtues of personal reciprocity and loyalty, social settings in which the rules of conduct were understandable and the rewards tangible.

The *blat* that played a part in working-class life in the 1930s had two features that should be noted here. First, the networks had a vertical dimension, in that they tended to cut across the levels of status created by official hierarchies. In other words, the *blat* networks were settings within which ordinary workers could have understandings with people in more elevated positions.[112] This was perhaps natural in the context of the high social mobility, in which it was common for a worker to enter the higher realms of officialdom within a short period of time.[113] There was also the fact that the new positions of responsibility tended to be exposed to the attentions of various inspectors and scrutineers, which could make it in some circumstances quite valuable to have friends on the shopfloor as well as in high places.

The second feature of the *blat* networks was predictably related to the first. The networks cut across the agencies of state repression as well, and it was a widely shared belief that this was indeed so. And, if these agencies were within reach of *blat* networks, they could be used for *blat* purposes, too. Making denunciations, threatening to use personal contacts in the party or the secret police, making bluff claims of such contacts – all these were ruses which could be used by *blat* cliques in their struggles for scarce resources. In the society of uprooted migrants where future opportunities seemed high and present poverty pressing, and where there was no law above the common struggles and chaos of daily life, reaching for the triggers of enforcement was perhaps almost as natural as reaching for the gun may have been in the pioneering days of the American West. That this phenomenon was one of an unsettled and changing society rather than the result of a lack of democratic traditions in the cultural background of the people is suggested by the admission of some of the western experts that they, too, were quick to learn the ruse of threatening to use the agencies of state repression in their daily struggles.[114] This is how one of the ex-Ukrainian emigrés explained the phenomenon: 'We have a proverb in Russia, "when you are among the wolves, you ought to howl like them"; that's how you get your share of the spoils.'[115]

The best way to illustrate the close connections between *blat* and the organs of state repression in the ordinary lifestyles of the period is to let the veterans tell some stories. The first example, which, it should be said, came from someone who was a factory clerk rather than a shopfloor worker, is striking by the apparent assumption that people who tried to stay away from *blat* were misguided enough in their morals to deserve malevolent victimization:

The place where I worked in 1939 had an official car. The driver of this car was quite a s.o.b. We tried to talk to him so we could use the car during the day and go to the town and do perhaps some shopping or just to have a sip of vodka. But this bastard was so devoted to duty that we couldn't do anything with him, so we tried to fix him up for good. Yeah, we fixed him up. One day we saw through the window that he was standing in line in front of a shop where butter was being distributed. Immediately, we reported him to the Trade Union Committee and the Trade Union Committee brought his case to *RKK* (factory disputes commission). The *RKK* decided to fire him. Brother, what joy there was among us. The Director wanted to keep him, but he had to fire him because of the 'breach of the law concerning labor discipline'. You know, all the workers laughed because everybody was in the line waiting for butter. The next day, there was a new driver, the guy with whom we had previous contacts, and who was *blatnyi* [a person who takes part in *blat*].[116]

The next story is typical in many respects, including the way in which it ends; by a defence manoeuvre consisting of bringing another agent of state authority into play.

I was living with my wife in one room together with another family composed of my friend, his wife, and his father. Incidentally, let me tell you about that. One day we were eating supper and a group of young men just broke in with a *komsomolets* (communist youth league member) whom I knew, as their leader. He started to shout that I am an enemy of the people and my friends too, and he got a special certificate from the Party Committee to evict us. You see, it happened on Saturday, and at that time, I was working as a worker and the factory in which I worked was closed. That gave me the idea that evidently he got this certificate from one of his pals in the Party and it was arranged to come to evict us on Saturday because the factory was closed and nobody would be able to help me. So we got together and we kept them for a whole night in a corridor, pushing the doors back and forth and fighting with each other, until the morning hours of the next day. At that time, the Director came to his office and my wife ran to him, and he came and saved us from eviction. You see what it really was, this *komsomolets* got this certificate *po blatu* [by *blat* methods].[117]

The noise of banging doors that reverberated to announce another rowdy dispute in the second anecdote serves to remind us that workers' housing estates were overcrowded with migrant males in their late teens and early twenties. That the pursuance of further education, 'social work' and '*blat*' did not quite exhaust the collective leisure-time energies of the spirited youth is suggested by the alarmed stories that were printed in the Soviet press about hooliganism. There evidently were workers' housing estates where damage to property, muggings, knife-fights and general 'terrorism' by gangs were normal occurrences. On pay days everyone was well advised to get home from work before dark.[118] Even cases of rape by adolescents were reported in this context.[119] In 1931, one-seventh of all the sentences meted out in the courts, amounting to almost 200,000 in the Russian Federal Republic alone, was for hooliganism.[120] About one-third of the convicted hooligans were described as workers by occupation; in the city of Moscow, 60 per cent.[121] By all available evidence, there was no other offence in respect of which workers were better represented among the ranks of convicts than hooliganism, and the latter was perhaps the most usual category of offence that brought workers into these ranks.[122]

The offence of hooliganism, and the policies of the punitive agencies against it, therefore constituted an important nexus between industrial workers and the state.

Only the most violent episodes of hooliganism ended up before the courts, as it was much more usual for the police to conclude their interventions against rowdiness by fines and warnings. Consistently with other areas of state repression, workers were, it would seem, treated markedly more leniently than peasants; if only one-fifth of the people apprehended by the police for alleged hooliganism were referred to the courts in rural areas, the corresponding proportion in the cities was one-tenth.[123] This was not because the urban *militsia* were particularly active in trying to control rowdiness in urban areas by their powers of 'administrative repression', i.e. warnings or fines; some of the press reports from the workers' housing estates suggested that the overstretched police was reluctant to intervene at all against violent gangs unless the fights ended in actual loss of life.[124] Mere fist-fights were non-events. Ivan Gudov managed to get himself arrested for one, but that was because it was a policeman he attacked, who prevented him from boarding an overcrowded bus; he was released without any charges when he proved that he was a Stakhanovite.[125]

Of all the categories of criminal offence, the one that was most specifically applicable to industrial workers was the one called 'production hooliganism'. This usually referred to cases of violent insubordination, physical attacks on workers who cooperated with production speed-up campaigns, or wanton damage to equipment.[126] The available evidence about court rulings on cases of alleged 'production hooliganism' suggests that, like most of the violence that happened outside the factory gates, shopfloor fights had to draw some blood to count as serious 'production hooliganism'.[127] Convictions for the latter offence constituted only a minority of the total of court sentences for hooliganism.

Another category of offence which directed punitive measures against industrial workers was created only in 1939, when acts of industrial indiscipline such as absenteeism and tardiness became punishable by short terms of incarceration in labour camps. Earlier in the decade, in 1933, workers were the target of a short propaganda campaign which accompanied a show trial with two workers who, having been sacked for 'chronic absenteeism and bad quality production', forced entry into the factory and knifed the person who tried to stop them. Since both of the workers apparently came from 'class alien backgrounds' (priest and trader), and since the apparent motive for their crime was to take a revenge on the foreman who had had them sacked, the crime was treated as a serious political offence rather than mere 'production hooliganism'. One of the culprits was sentenced to death and the other to five years in labour camps, amidst a blaze of publicity and staged mass meetings of factory workers demanding tough sentences for the accused and promising to fight the counter-revolution by improving standards of discipline.[128] This show trial case, however, was not followed by other similar ones, and there is no evidence of any wave of repression against workers in the course of which acts that might have been classified as 'production hooliganism' were punished as political crimes.

Another short-lived campaign, which was not targeted primarily on industrial workers but affected some of them, also took place in the winter of 1932–33. This concerned the issue of passports and residence permits to the urban population, in the course of which the requisite documents could be denied to immigrant (i.e. post-1929) residents in the cities, if they were pronounced 'socially dangerous'. The 'socially dangerous elements' were then banned and evicted from the cities.[129] Passports and residence permits were issued or denied by special committees which had 'old workers' and 'shock workers' on them, and which were by all accounts able to employ a wide range of criteria in their decisions.[130]

Hooliganism, whether of the 'production' type or some other variety, however, remained the main category of criminal offence which brought workers into the arms of law enforcement. In the early 1930s, three-quarters of court sentences for hooliganism were terms of 'corrective [forced] labour without deprivation of freedom', in which the punishment usually boiled down to an extra tax on income (up to 25 per cent).[131] To serve this punishment, the sentenced culprits had to make arrangements with so called 'bureaux of forced labour'. If they were sacked from their normal employment as a result of their offence (only a minority were), they had to take whatever job was arranged for them by their 'bureau of forced labour'. The latter in a minority cases entailed residence in special colonies, but the regime in these establishments was not particularly punitive. The terms of these sentences were rarely longer than three months. The remaining one-quarter of the sentences for hooliganism were divided between straight fines, suspended sentences of various kinds, and sentences to terms of 'deprivation of freedom' by exile or deportation, or in labour camps (harder regime than the colonies mentioned above). Few of these terms were longer than two years, and only 30 per cent served the whole sentence.[132] The 'deprivation of freedom' penalties for hooliganism were increased to a maximum of five years in labour camps in 1935.[133]

It was symptomatic of the state and society in the early 1930s that far from all of the court sentences were in fact served. A large proportion were overturned on appeal, and as for the rest, the enforcement agencies simply could not cope. Prior to the introduction of passports, it was enough for the accused to give a wrong address, or to claim permanent residence elsewhere, to put the local 'bureau of forced labour' off his tracks. According to a survey of 6000 sentences meted out at Moscow courts, only 2273 culprits made themselves available for serving their punishments by providing the courts with correct Moscow addresses. In 1931–32, the Moscow 'bureau of forced labour' was faced with lists of evasive persons with up to more than 6600 names on them.[134] This situation must have changed in favour of the law enforcement agencies after the introduction of passports in 1932–33, but it was still reported in 1935 that about one-quarter of the people sentenced to terms of corrective labour did not in fact serve any sentence.[135] Inefficiencies on the part of the 'bureau of forced labour' were blamed for this situation, but there was also the fact that obtaining new and desirable personal documentation was not beyond the scope of the *blat* networks. We have already mentioned in the previous chapter the tens of thousands of blank party cards that could not be accounted for in the course of the party purges; the exchange of trade union cards revealed a similar problem, as did inspections of shock workers' books, etc.[136] As regards passports, we note with interest that a part of the policy of relaxing political attitudes to new workers with unproletarian pasts was to instruct trade union officials that workers should not be obliged to produce passports when exchanging their trade union cards in 1936.[137] At least two of the 26 ex-Ukrainian interviewees had equipped themselves with pristine personalities in the course of the 1930s, by using *blat* to acquire new passports.[138]

Judging by this account of law enforcement, industrial workers did not have much cause to experience the repressive powers of the state as especially harsh or efficient. This, however, still raises the question of how much they had to fear from the secret police. After all, the suppliers of inmates to the labour camps did not consist solely of the criminal courts, but included also the secret police with its special powers of repression against alleged counter-revolutionary agents. It might be hypothesized, for example, that the secret police terrorized industrial workers by sending a good number of them to labour camps on charges of industrial 'wrecking'. There is, however, more evidence against this hypothesis than for it. Some of the people who had been in secret police custody during the 1930s support this hypothesis by general statements in their memoirs according to which, for example, some 20 per cent of their cell-mates were workers, but then it transpires from their examples that the people they counted as 'workers' were in fact engineers or managers by the time of their arrest, from foremen upwards, or conversely, they were destitute people who were not in industrial employment.[139] Other first-hand accounts by victims of secret police vigilance are quite explicit in their view that ordinary factory workers were not well represented among political prisoners. According to an assessment made by someone who was in the labour camps during the *ezhovshchina* years, from 1937 to 1939, about 80 per cent of the people arrested at the time were members of the intelligentsia, and the other 20 per cent were 'Mensheviks, Petlur's men, a lot of Poles, and some other nationalities'.[140]

This is not to say that industrial workers were immune from secret police attentions. The 'Mensheviks' in the last account, for example, may well have included politically active 'old workers' in their ranks. Most of the ex-Ukrainian interviewees remembered fears of the secret police among their experiences, and some of them were able to provide witness accounts in which workers were at the receiving end of secret police activities; suspected ring-leaders of protest marches against bread shortages were arrested in these accounts, and so were workers who made loud comments about Stalin in shop queues. The secret police was also present during the campaigns to get workers volunteer parts of their wages for 'loans' to the state.[141]

However, neither of the two interviewees who were able to report any first-hand experience of being subjected to any arrest or court proceedings were workers at the time, and there is nothing in their stories to suggest that the normal work processes on the shopfloor, which were full of disputes and rule-breaking as will be seen in later chapters, exposed manual workers to charges of industrial 'wrecking'.[142] The special powers of the secret police to take repressive measures against 'counter-revolutionary wrecking' were to be applied 'with special strictness' in relation to the 'white-collar workers [*sluzhashchie*] of state institutions and enterprises' according to a government decree issued in 1933, and on the whole, that is indeed how they were applied.[143] As regards the laws that provided the criminal courts with their harshest sentencing powers, the 1932 law on protection of socialist property was applied primarily against peasants, the 1933 law on protection of production quality was applied primarily against managers, and the laws against speculation and illegal trading affected mainly the people working in wholesale and retail organizations. The ministrations of the officers of state repression were a hazard in the factory worker's day to a much lesser extent than in the workdays of the people in other occupations.

One of the former Ukrainians witness' accounts of state repression implies a surprising attitude to labour camps. It tells about an accountant who was frustrated in his wish to move to another job by the regulations surrounding the issue of labour books to all state employees in 1938, which made it difficult to leave an employing organization without its formally certified consent. The accountant, however, wanted the new job badly enough to make use of a new decree which made it a criminal offence, with mandatory labour camp penalites, to fail to turn up for work or be more than 20 minutes late without any acceptable reason. He deliberately reported to work late one day, was duly found guilty by the courts, and, as a convicted wrong-doer, fired by his employer at the same time. 'That was exactly what he wanted. He went to this labour camp for 3 months and afterwards, went to a new job which he had dreamt about.'[144]

We do not know what made this man so confident that he could return from a labour camp unmolested and on schedule. He might have believed that there was a hard-and-fast distinction between political prisoners and all the others in respect of the treatment that they could expect to receive in the labour camps, or it is possible that the labour camps at the end of the 1930s had not yet earned the reputation they would acquire in the post-war period. This raises the question of what image of the labour camp system was likely to be prevalent among workers in the 1930s.

In the first half of the decade, the labour camp population was dominated by the kulaks and other peasants who had been accused of resisting collectivization and grain deliveries. At the same time, the collectivizing and 'dekulakizing' villages were also providing migrant labourers for extractive industries and construction sites, many of whom would soon become industrial workers. The migrant labourers must have been aware of the labour camps, for after all, there must have been many in their ranks who had left their villages in a hurry, to escape the possibility that they, too, might be counted in with the kulaks and their suspected agents. They must have been therefore interested to find themselves working alongside deported kulaks and other prisoners in their new jobs in pits and on construction sites. Some of the large construction projects also brought forced labourers into contact with the young men and women from the cities, who had left their schools to take part in the great projects of the first five year plan. Experience of contact with deportees and labour camp prisoners was therefore not uncommon among the people who were soon to join industrial workers' ranks.

Some of the Americans who worked in the Soviet Union at the time also found themselves in surprisingly close contact with forced labourers. John Scott found in Magnitogorsk that the chief engineer there, i.e. the second highest-ranking manager on site, was a prisoner serving ten years for 'industrial wrecking', after being sentenced to death for the alleged offence in 1929. He was evidently discharging his duties just as any other manager in his position would, with normal managerial authority and as an equal participant in the policy-making deliberations of the top management team. Among the manual workers, Scott was able to befriend a kulak prisoner who was serving a five-year term after his brother had been killed in the course of a gun battle with the secret police officers who had come to arrest them. This prisoner had the position of a gang-leader (*brigadir*) on the construction site, with immediate authority over 18 labourers of whom only two were also prisoners. The prisoners seemed no worse off than other workers in regard to their work conditions, food and clothes; the only difference was that their lodgings were in a large supervised camp of tents – which must have been chilly in low winter temperatures.[145]

The following excerpts are from a report by another American, who worked as a consultant engineer on Soviet copper-mining sites for two years, until the end of 1933:

I found the kulak political prisoners among the best and most intelligent of workers, quick to learn . . . The kulak workers, with whom I came into contact, received wages like any other workers, but lived in a separate quarter, for the purpose of a better check-up. It would have been folly to try to get away, as it might mean being shot, if captured . . .

I heard an high official explain the status of the kulak, at our camp, to the plant officials. He said that they were going through a period of probation, having been taken from districts where they were formerly located, for not cooperating. They were to be returned to their former homes, if they so desired, after collectivisation had been accomplished in their districts, at which time they would see the errors of their old ways, and observe how much better for all, the new way was. He advised the men to marry kulak girls, as he had found them excellent housekeepers, and that many Communist girls could learn much from them.[146]

According to Scott, it was common for the forced labourers in Magnitogorsk to have 20–60 per cent of their sentences commuted for good work. This situation, however, changed after 1938 when releases on remission became rare, 'probably because *NKVD* felt reluctant to release workers when so few new ones were coming in'.[147]

There may have been labour camps where conditions were a lot worse than those which could be witnessed by foreign workers, but if there were such camps in the 1930s, they were hidden from the sight of Soviet workers as well. Most Soviet workers who worked alongside political prisoners quite probably thought them unlucky to have been caught on the wrong side of a class warfare campaign, but not much worse off than army conscripts. To workers who had decided to leave their peasant pasts behind, the repressive policies of the state did not seem beyond the scope of matter-of-fact acceptance.

The period of the 'revolution from above' was one marked by widespread migration and occupational mobility. It took the young generation of the peasantry away from the villages and moved it around the industrialization projects where the conditions of life were hard and the rules of competition for scarce resources uncertain. It also offered an abundance of opportunities for acquiring credentials and moving upwards in the new world. The lifestyle of the new workers was taking shape in the cross-pressures of having to earn a living wage, needing friends to obtain scarcities and acquiring enemies in the process, seeing opportunities for advancement, and having to cope with neighbourly aggression. One had to live by one's wits as well as hard work. In this lifestyle, the state with its repressive agencies was feared more as a possible tool in the hands of personal antagonists in the Hobbesian struggle for survival than as an efficient instrument of law and order. The other side of this coin was that the state with its authorities and agents was sought by new workers for help in their struggles, as well as feared. Workers' anxieties were on the whole more concerned with making a living than with the dangers of being sent to labour camps for political crimes. In this respect, they had the relative advantage of being at the bottom of the list of priorities for police vigilance, which meant that, unlike the people in more exposed occupations, they could expect to stay out of prison if they observed a few relatively simple rules of conduct.

Ivan Gudov's political education progressed as follows. When his mentor in the machine-tools factory, an old worker of skill and experience, was fired for excessive cleverness in taking advantage of incentive schemes, Gudov drew the correct lesson that 'not only technical education was needed, but also political'. By the time his own rate-busting efforts made him enemies on the shopfloor, Gudov was educated enough to suspect a conspiracy when the party secretary started to chat him up about the resemblance of his preference for working nights to Stalin's nocturnal habits. When his factory director got the sack and came under investigation in 1937, Gudov knew how to listen to the comment that, who knows, someone like that just might be guilty of something after all. For a fuller understanding of Gudov's and other workers' political thoughts, we shall have to investigate the shopfloor relations in the context of which they were formed. In the meantime, let it be said that, on the day of his election to the Supreme Soviet, a persistent chorus sang in Gudov's head: 'Who was nobody now will be all.'[148]

3 The Politics of Industrialization Management

MANAGEMENT ACCOUNTABILITY TO THE PARTY STATE

Soviet industrialization was a political campaign in pursuit of an ostensibly economic goal. It was also a radical campaign in that it intended to change the lives of most people within a few years, to which end it stimulated and endeavoured to channel the motive forces born of class antagonisms. Hence the 'dialectical' solutions to the problems of backwardness. If the agrarian problem was one of insufficient grain production and deliveries, the answer to it was to remove the best farmers, the kulaks, from their farms, on the premise that the radical uprooting of the problem required the liquidation of the class relation that was limiting the overall productive forces in the countryside. It was then ideologically quite sound of party officials to approve and administer the 'liquidation of the kulak as a class' policy and at the same time to admire the kulak prisoners and their families for being better workers than most Russians. In the industrial sphere, the answer to the problem of technological insufficiency included an attack on the 'bourgeois specialists' who were the only people actually qualified to manage technology, because they were expected to be too burdened by 'technological conservatism' to support great leaps forward. The attack on 'bourgeois specialists' also helped to stimulate workers' enthusiasm for the 'great breakthrough', by conveying the message that the new policy was fundamentally different from the much re-sented 'rationalization' campaigns that had taken place on the shopfloor in the previous three years.

The workers who were promoted to managerial and administrative positions would be able to enjoy only a short-lived advantage of working-class background. The dynamics of the industrialization leadership created and also used a new antagonism, in the context of which even the new Soviet cadres became vulnerable to political attack. The new antagonism was promoted under the broad heading of struggle against 'bureaucratism'. Like the campaigns of 'class vigilance' against the 'bourgeois specialists', it helped to stimulate interest in party policies among at least some of the workers who had not been promoted to executive positions.

The 'great breakthrough' policy was bound to have problems with 'bureaucracy'. At the policy-making stage, some of the voices of administration and management were liable to make themselves heard in opposition to the radical proposals. To the extent that their role was to give advice on the implementability and likely costs of ambitious industrialization plans, the involvement of professional administrators and managers in the policy-making process was likely to put into question the assumptions about reality on which the bolder plans of development were based. As with all political radicalism, the desire for a 'great breakthrough' was based on an optimism about the behaviour of 'the people when given the chance', whereas 'the people' were known to be a troublesome object of control in the experience of administrators. To radical politicians who considered the status quo to be in urgent need of change, however, the administrators' lack of enthusiasm for the 'great breakthrough' would seem a destructive attitude born of selfish disinclinations to change their own routines.

At the policy implementation stage, the new policies would come into contact with old realities, with some unintended and undesired results, presenting policy-makers with the difficult question of whether disasters were due to bad policy or incorrect implementation. There were two general possibilities that could make a policy suffer a defeat because of faulty implementation; administrators might fail to make sufficiently flexible responses to unforeseen problems, preferring to hide behind formal rules and pass the buck, or, they might be too flexible, to the extent of corrupting the principles of the policy.

These were general 'problems of bureaucracy' that any modern radical politician would have had to encounter. I have deduced them from the notion of political radicalism itself. But if there could be no radicalism without its bureaucracy problem, this maxim applied to the Soviet case especially. To start with, the political leadership had to make do with administrators and managers few of whom were particularly pleased to see the Bolsheviks in power. This problem could be controlled by a network of political commissars and party secretaries in the first post-revolutionary decade. In the 1930s, however, when the industrialization policies made the number of administrative and managerial posts grow much faster than the supply of qualified personnel, the problem was made worse by widespread incompetence. While there undoubtedly were many executives who learned fast and grew into their new posts of responsibility, there were also those whose existence bore eloquent testimony to the Peter Principle according to which people in bureaucracies, where promotion is the main form of reward for competent work, eventually end up stranded above their level of ability.

The main source of the 'bureaucratism' problems, however, could be found in the method of the industrialization drive itself, i.e. the taut plans. The targets of the first five year plan in particular reflected the radical assumption that hitherto unseen reserves of resources could be released by the mass mobilization of workers at all levels to inspired work. The philosophy behind the taut plans was that the shoulders of the industrial body would grow with the desired speed only if they were asked to carry greater loads than those recommended by precedent or conventional wisdom. Positive thinking was the order of the day. Pointing out detrimental circumstances and giving reasons why a set of targets was unlikely to be achieved amounted to a treacherous 'demobilization tendency'. Thus the difficulties in the organization of the economy, which were soon becoming all too evident, were countered by the bold slogan of 'five in four', which meant that plan schedules should be tightened further so that the five year plan could be accomplished in its main parts in four rather than five years. This is how the policy was summed up in a leading article printed in a journal for managers:

> The character of our difficulties is quite clear. They are the difficulties of growth. Only rightist-opportunist panic-mongerers and 'leftist' loud-mouths do not understand this. The difficulties contain within themselves the means for their overcoming. There must be no talk of reducing the speed of development.[1]

Managers were exhorted by the press headlines to 'storming' campaigns to 'take the plan' in the initial years of the five year plan.[2] It was soon recognized that short-lived campaigns of extraordinary exertion were not much good if they were followed by blatant slow-downs, and the custom of 'storming' to catch up on work that should have been done before (*shturmovshchina*) became known as a tell-tale sign of faulty management. But the requirement on managers that every effort should be expended on meeting plan targets, regardless of what they thought about the realism of the plan schedules, remained emphatic throughout the decade. 'Plan is law' proclaimed the headlines, and managers who defended their lack of success in meeting plan schedules by 'whimpering about hostile uncles', i.e. by referring to adverse conditions beyond their control, stood to be accused of anything from 'unmanliness' to 'wrecking'.[3]

Protests by managers against unrealistic plan targets were considered immoral and from time to time punishable behaviour, while failures to keep up with plan schedules exposed mangers to charges of incompetence or indeed 'wrecking'. There clearly was a delicate game to be played by the people in charge of implementing the taut plans. They had to be seen to be responding positively but at the same time try to negotiate more favourable targets for their enterprises which would give them a better chance of success. It was in their interest to underestimate their 'reserves', hoard resources where possible and conceal them, and also to give promises which they knew they could not honour.[4] John Scott described a typical meeting of top managers in Magnitogorsk in which the party secretary, the director and the chief engineer (who was in fact already serving a commuted death sentence for 'wrecking') were deciding what sort of unrealistic promise to give in response to an even less realistic demand, issued by a high government authority, for a new schedule.[5] The situation was complicated by the fact that such interventions from higher authorities in enterprise plans were becoming more frequent, to the extent that annual production plans were in effect dissolving into a constant stream of new targets and demands, as the higher authorities tried to troubleshoot the narrowest links in the chains of bottlenecks which were caused by imbalanced plans and erratic achievement rates throughout industry. 'Managers must be flexible,' proclaimed another leading article in the managerial journal.[6]

The upshot of this system of taut 'planning' was that while lip-service had to be paid to the 'plan is law' commandment by all members of the burgeoning officialdom, and while percentages of plan fulfilment remained the measure of managerial success that tended to override all other considerations, it quickly became apparent that managerial and administrative careers in fact could be made in part by attracting favourable *ad hoc* and *ad hominem* judgements from superiors in the course of playing bureaucratic politics. This did not preclude tangible achievements in setting up production lines and getting them going. Industry was undoubtedly growing. But it was hard to tell for its workers whether their labour was being well channelled into results they could approve of, or squandered by incompetent bosses, or in effect misappropriated by self-seeking careerists. The apparent socialist rationality of the economic plans of development was concealing something that looked like an almost anarchic competition for scarce resources within the state system of administration, the rules of which were as yet not always clear to insiders, let alone outsiders.

The path to success in plan fulfilment often required managers to resort to many practices which were not envisaged by the plan, and which were in some cases explicitly forbidden by various rules and laws. Managers bartered some of the scarce equipment and material assigned to their enterprises with other institutions, augmented the salaries of valued employees by giving them phantom second jobs, and ordered production to run in breach of safety regulations, to name just a few of the many common ways in which managers were known to cut legal corners in their pursuit of production results. They were therefore vulnerable to being found out as wrong-doers, which gave them another incentive to cultivate their places in networks of personal contacts that could facilitate protection from the enforcement of government rules. This was an aspect of official authority that was well understood by ordinary workers who were themselves often involved in *blat* networks, and also by the leaders at the centre of the party state who thus had reasons to believe that their policies were being implemented only at the dubious discretion of the unofficial cliques of officials that were forming in the localities. 'Localism', 'family-mindedness' and 'one hand washes another' arrangements were sins of which managers and administrators were generally believed to be guilty.

The policy of rapid industrialization made certain aspects of the backwardness it was designed to escape only more acute, at least temporarily, by creating too many managerial, administrative and technical jobs too quickly. While the number of industrial workers increased three-fold between the censuses of 1926 and 1939, the number of state inspectors and political officials increased five-fold, the number of middle and higher-level managers in industry seven-fold, the number of engineers and technicians ten-fold, and the number of industrial foremen sixteen-fold.[7] The policy at the same time created a system of management and administration which generated conflicts and mistrust within its ranks. It also made it difficult for industrial managers to develop their professional expertise in practice and make themselves respected for professional competence and integrity by the policy-makers at the centre of the party state as well as by the technical staff and shopfloor workers within their factories.

The political leaders were to some extent aware of these problems; industrial managers were therefore enabled to have their own newspaper and journals which to some extent gave a voice to their special interests and discussed professional problems, leading managers of the heavy industry were supported in cultivating their professional identity in the meetings and lectures organized under the auspices of their 'business club' (*delovyi klub*), and precious hard currency was not spared in sending engineers and managers abroad to learn from their colleagues in the greatest American and European firms. Some of the generals of the industrialization campaign, especially Ordzhonikidze, also gained a reputation for having a realistic grasp of managers' problems, and for being able and willing to protect deserving managers who fell on the wrong side of administrative–discipline enforcement or the drives against 'bureaucratism'. The problem of managerial incompetence in industry was also to some extent mitigated by the high priority that was accorded to the industrial sector, so that a high proportion of the total educational resources, and of the ablest personnel, were channelled into it.

On the whole, however, the dynamic of circumstances that was created by the taut plans – the shortages of supplies and the gamut of organizational crises which had to be dealt with to avert threats of damaging failures – favoured 'flexibility' above all else, i.e. the willingess of managers to keep changing their immediate goals in response to new directives from their superiors and party leaders. This requirement militated against attempts to put on a stable legislative footing the relationships between policy-making and policy implementation, i.e. between the central authorities of the state and its branches, localities and enterprise organizations. The problem was one of managerial accountability in the absence of the sort of competitive market relations that could have provided objective indicators of managerial performance in the form of profit accounts. Since the rates of plan fulfilment could not fill this gap if the plan targets were known to have uncertain bases in unreliable estimates of actual capacities, the central authorities had no means of telling when the pressures on industrial managers should be heightened to make sure of the best possible production performance, or when they should be relaxed to give managers room to develop and implement medium-term strategies for the productive organizations in their charge.

The party leaders had a major problem on their hands if they wanted to keep control of the industrial–administrative complex that was growing under the five year plans. A part of their response was to search for an optimal administrative structure by establishing, abolishing, splitting and merging the various commissariats, trusts and corporations at the middle layers of industrial administration. They also considered reintroducing some elements of the market economy that would make it possible for production units to have an officially acknowledged autonomy and a consensual assessment of performance on the basis of profit accounts (*khozraschet*). In the main, however, the central authorities relied on three methods to keep control over industry: they moved managers around from one appointment to another, which had a disruptive effect on the protective networks of personal contacts and the degree of actual autonomy that could be built up locally;[8] made them subject to numerous rules, instructions and inspections which could end up in court sentences ranging from terms of 'corrective labour at place of work' to years of 'deprivation of freedom'; and campaigned against managerial 'bureaucratism'. In other words, managerial accountability to the party state was instituted in a mixture of personal, legal and political terms.

The political leaders feared that the industrialization drive would lose its momentum if managers acquired the ability to remove their factories from the reach of centrally initiated 'mass mobilization' campaigns. The momentum was maintained in the way it had been gained in the 'great breakthrough' days, by the political methods of intervention and leadership in the productive sphere, of which the struggle against the varied symptoms of 'bureaucratism' was a key feature. The accent was on the political processes whereby the social body of the state was to deliver itself from its backwardness: multiple channels for scrutinizing the work done in the offices and factories throughout the land (the principle of *kontrol'nost'*), the involvement of workers in these processes, i.e. 'control from below' (*kontrol' snizu*), 'self-criticism' (*samokritika*), and the purges.

It is possible that the insistence on these forms of managerial accountability caused industry to perform better than it would have done otherwise, given the absence of the motivating forces of market competition, although it did not do much to help solve the organizational problems within industry. The fight against 'bureaucratism' also helped the cause of political stability in the face of upheavals and hardships inflicted on the population by the industrialization campaign, in so far as the top political leaders were seen to act against a popular enemy when they attacked local managers and bosses on the grounds of incompetence, carelessness, 'soul-less attitudes to workers', 'divorce from the masses' and personal immorality. The political leaders were thus able to take advantage of an old theme in Russian political culture – the myth of the good Tsar being deceived by wicked lords and officials into letting them exploit the people.

But the role of Russian traditions should not be overestimated in this respect. That attitudes were fashioned mainly in the context of the taut plan methods is suggested by the fact that the mixture of admiration for the top Soviet leaders and contempt for middle-level officials was found also among the American engineers who worked in the Soviet Union at the time. The following excerpt refers to a letter that had been in part printed in the *New York Times* early in 1936:

I had ventured the opinion that Stalin is a much underestimated man, by the outside world, as well as his immediate advisers, but that between them, and the workers, there was an inefficient block of Communist Party bureaucrats, who were the causes of many failures.[9]

Some of the American engineers in fact thought that periodic inspections and purges of technical, managerial and administrative staff were a good idea, at least in principle, even though reservations had to be made about the way the 'cleaning' of the executive ranks worked in practice:

The workers' and peasants' inspection was a very useful institution and did much good, but was somewhat cumbersome and was not used enough. It has been superseded by a system of Soviet Control, which is more effective and works more quickly and more intelligently and is satisfactory, but generally works only in case of some special complaint. The system of cleaning should be effective but too often is manipulated to favor the cleverest and too often develops into a white-washing operation, or by clever planning an unsuspecting victim can be swamped by accusations he has not opportunity to defend himself against.[10]

Apart from the problem of manipulation by local cliques, some of the American engineers noted that the inspections and 'cleanings' (i.e. purges) could be counterproductive if they added to the high turnover of technical staff, and if their political terms of reference were used by both inspectors and inspected to divert attention from their lack of technical competence.[11] But on the whole, the Americans were too impressed by the shortcomings of the Soviet managerial stratum to find the processes of the 'fight against bureaucratism', crude forms of managerial accountability though they were, abhorrent in principle. And among those who worked in manual jobs, sympathy with Stalin's reputed stand against 'bureaucratic avoidance of responsibility' (*obezlichka*) by the 'honourable rhetoreticians' (*chestnye boltuny*) and 'Soviet barons' (*sovetskie vel'mozhi*) in executive ranks[12] evidently in some cases survived even the blatant excesses of the terror in 1936–38. The following excerpt, referring to the campaign under the slogan that 'every industrial accident must have its name and patronymic',[13] is from John Scott's memoir:

Beginning with 1936 any fatal industrial accident became the subject of criminal investigation. Often they tried the wrong people, but in Russia this is relatively unimportant. The main thing was that the technicians and workers alike began to appreciate and correctly evaluate human life, both their own and other people's, and this was extremely important in a country where tyranny, war, famine and strife had made life very cheap.[14]

The American engineers' views of their Soviet colleagues were strikingly similar to some of the criticisms that were often made in the Soviet press in the context of the switch from 'functionalist' to 'line' principles of management in 1932–35. Soviet managers, especially the newly educated ones, were evidently given to much posturing at meetings to display their theoretical erudition and boldly progressive attitudes, but they were reluctant to take personal responsibility for practical action even when circumstances made this urgent. They also tended to frustrate other managers' attempts at practical action by insisting on wide-ranging discussions first, and by letting their personal unpunctuality and inefficiency in handling administrative matters add further to the time wasted in unproductive meetings.[15] In short, 'the lack of organising capacity was astounding and a serious handicap'.[16] The Americans also noticed that some of the Soviet engineers, both old and young, were rather preoccupied with their intellectual status and reluctant to involve themselves with the menial detail that the quest for technical progress sometimes made necessary,[17] and this theme of criticism would be soon adopted by the Soviet press as well, in the context of its support for the Stakhanovite movement.

But there were other criticisms of managers made in the Soviet press, which were certainly not echoed in the American engineers' reports. Allegations of 'fear of speed' (*tempoboyazn'*) and 'technological conservatism' on the part of Soviet managers belonged to this category of specifically Soviet observations, as did complaints about 'technological bureaucrats' (*chinovniki*) who resisted party interventions in industrial affairs. In addition to frequent attacks on the variety of managerial sins known as 'bureaucratism', the critical press also frequently alleged that Soviet managers suffered from tendencies to 'tailism' (*khvostism*), i.e. a weakness of resolve in the face of irresponsible pressures from 'backward' workers. Managers were also regularly upbraided for insufficient care about raising the 'cultural levels' (*kul'turnost'*) of the work methods and organization in their factories, and for unhelpful attitudes to 'shock workers', Stakhanovites and 'socialist competition' in general.

The rapid industrialization policy, which suddenly created a large stratum of inexperienced managers and made them vulnerable to the varied charges of 'bureaucratism', combined within itself two conflicting tenets: a radical faith in the socially transformative powers of mass mobilization and class politics on the one hand, and a rather technocratic belief in the necessary laws of a fundamentally technological universe on the other hand. The policy required the radical mood to live in active interaction with technical rationality, which was not always easy because each attitude generated its own fears. Radicalism feared that the rapid industrialization policy might fall prey to mass demoralization which was bound to follow should managers, administrators and party leaders succumb to corrupt desires for a comfortable life. Rationalism feared that the industrialization policy might fail should no systematic routine emerge to replace the wasteful chaos of *ad hoc* crisis management. Radicalism wanted managers and administrators to be subject to political vigilance and mobilization campaigning. Rationalism wanted them endowed with clearly delimited authority and steady conditions in which professional expertise could be developed and the 'cultural levels' of production raised.

Another contrast of orientations that was evident in discussions of managerial accountability could be described in terms of the conceptual difference between *effectiveness* and *efficiency*, where *effectiveness* is about getting a close match of goals and results, while *efficiency* is oriented to getting the best possible results relative to the expenditure of resources. The pursuit of effectiveness does not always coincide with the pursuit of efficiency; chasing a particular goal 'regardless of cost', for example, may well prove effective in that the goal is achieved, but it is unlikely to be efficient if the costing of alternative courses of action has not played a prominent part in the decision-making process. Conversely, series of decisions which are taken in strong regard to comparative costs are likely to amount to an efficient policy in that overall benefits outweigh overall expenditures, but it is possible that the benefits have stopped well short of the outcomes that were most wanted. The radical mood of the 'great breakthrough' rejected the prevalent state of economy and society for being unacceptably backward, and postulated the rapid achievement of an industrial civilization as a goal of supreme value which should inspire millions to heroic deeds. Industrialization by taut plans, at least in its initial stages, put a strong premium on the goals, i.e. concerns with effectiveness, to the extent of discouraging concerns with economy of action, i.e. efficiency.

Efficiency was half-removed from the nomenclature of managerial objectives as a result of the banishment of market economy from industrial life. It is, after all, market economy that makes possible the comparison of all kinds of benefits and expenditures within a single scale of measurement, the monetary balance account, in the knowledge that the gains over expenditures have a definite value in providing the option of access to certain quantities of scarce goods. When the principles of marketability are abandoned, the best that the financial balance sheets can indicate is a degree of success in pursuing government priorities; this would be so in the unlikely event of the process of economic planning being deliberate and logical to such an extent that it was possible to fix price-tags to goods and services in a consistent reflection of government priorities.

But this certainly was not the case with the Soviet planning in the 1930s, which was the result of a variety of political processes rather than of a single, detailed and painstakingly coherent masterplan. In this context, the prices of things were known to be quite arbitrary, and the value of the difference between production output and input shown in a financial balance sheet was uncertain. The state of the financial balance sheet was only one of many different indicators of success in the performance of a productive enterprise, and a relatively unimportant indicator at that, because its actual meaning was too uncertain to have as compelling a significance as the fulfilment of the production targets that were set in physical terms of output measurement, such as tonnes or pieces. Industrialization, after all, was about setting up an economy which provided an abundance of artefacts, so that it was not unnatural to set economic goals in terms of numbers of wanted artefacts. And, since the production of each additional artefact generated an additional demand for some other ones, and since the taut plans did not provide for these relationships between inputs and outputs very precisely, individual production schedules had to be frequently changed in the interests of economic coordination; this put an additional premium on the value of timely fulfilment of particular, the latest, production targets. As has already been stated, management objectives in this system of political economy tended to be defined in terms of effectiveness rather than efficiency.

But efficiency would not be banished from the realm of industrialization management concerns. One opening through which it kept coming back was the political process of assessing production reserves. Clearly, more could be asked of a production unit as it stood, without enlarging it by additional resources, if it could be argued that an improvement in its ways of working would make more with less. Fulfilling the taut plan production targets was then to some extent a question of good management in the sense of cutting down on 'waste' (*poteri*) in the usage of existing resources, wherever it became apparent. This, then, was what political mobilization on the 'production front' was partly about: 'uncovering reserves' and 'fighting against waste' to make possible the achievement of higher production targets. By the same token, that was also what much of the criticism of management for incompetence and 'bureaucratism' was about: the visible manifestations of 'waste'. Concerns for efficiency thus returned in the form of worries about 'waste'.

There are, of course, many kinds of 'waste' that may become apparent to the critical eye. Raw material is 'wasted' if the method of working it is different from the one that is known to leave the smallest percentage of it for scrap. Tools are 'wasted' if they get used up 'too quickly', or if they do not get used very often; machines are 'wasted' if their work-load is below capacity, if they are used only some of the time, or if they are overused at the cost of increased wear and tear; skills are 'wasted' if skilled workers do unskilled work some of the time, labour power is 'wasted' if the pace of work is not always as fast as it perhaps might be, labour time is 'wasted' when workers have unscheduled periods of rest; people are wasted if they live in a state of perpetual fatigue and frequent ill health. It is impossible to remove 'waste' in all its forms. Making sure of no 'waste' in raw material may require the slowing down of the production process, using all tools and fittings to the full may require a frequent stoppage of machines for resetting, keeping machines going at their full productive capacity may require the presence of spare workers who will stand idle some of the time.

In 1928, an article in the managerial journal could make the point that good management consisted not in the removal of all forms of 'waste', but in organizing the production process in such a way as to allow 'waste' to exist in its various forms, in quantities which were optimal in the context of maximizing efficiency overall.[18] But this was assuming the existence of a reliable accounting framework for the measurement of over-all efficiency, while the semblance of it that had been made available under the mixed economy of the NEP would soon be swept away by the 'great breakthrough'. From then on, it was rare for a manager to be commended for the wisdom of allowing any sort of 'waste' or spare capacity. The new political economy that was taking shape did not provide any positive measurement of managerial efficiency in industry, but it promoted an awareness of 'waste' in its varied visible forms which it made into objects of contention in the 'dialectical process' of struggling for higher levels of 'productive culture'.

This was a process in which everyone could be involved. The press played an important role in this respect, supporting as it did the industrialization drive by exposing particular instances of 'waste' in reports from all the sections of the 'production front' (and thus incidentally providing us with a source of vivid information about the conditions and practices in various workplaces). These reports became items on the agendas of party committee meetings at which the managers responsible for the criticized phenomena had to account for themselves and undertake to make improvements.[19] Managers with a good record of production plan fulfilment were not immune from this process. After all, one never knew whether the production targets had not been set too low, and in any case, there were no managers who could boast of effectiveness in regard to all the plan targets – the volume of main product, other products, staffing limits, wage-budget limits, investment-budget limits, equipment-depreciation limits, fuel and energy limits, increments in labour productivity, etc. The press also encouraged workers to write reports on the managerial inefficiencies that were apparent from their point of view. Then there were the various 'social organizations' – the Communist Youth League, the trade unions, commissions of Production Conferences, to name just some of the institutions for the 'mass mobilization' of workers charged with the tasks of 'criticism from below', that were called upon by the party to the battle against 'waste'. And some of the numerous government inspections, too, were out to catch managers causing 'waste'.

Since some 'waste' could be always found and no manager was above criticism according to the 'dialectical' principles of overcoming economic backwardness, and since there was no reliable method of proving a good standard of managerial performance in regard to efficiency as well as effectiveness, a manager's career rather depended on his ability to impress the scrutineers that he was a competent person for the job who really cared about doing it well. He had to learn how to attract positive judgements which were made on the basis of what I have already described as a mixture of personal, legal and political grounds. But the 'legal' grounds were neither consistent nor firm, while the 'personal' grounds were not devoid of meritocratic elements and the 'political' grounds were not simply about ideological commitment, party loyalty or class allegiance. The manager helped himself if he appeared responsive to the campaigns against various forms of 'waste'; if he could show that the quantitative performance indicators highlighted by current campaigns were moving in the right direction; if he succeeded in controlling the output of the scrutineers without getting accused of 'bureaucratic cover-up' or 'suppression of criticism'; and also if he looked and sounded like someone who had already internalized the qualities of industrial 'production culture', which included a good understanding of technology but went beyond it into the less tangible realms of a certain form of 'culturedness' (*kul-'turnost'*). This is not to forget what must have been the single most important factor of executive success, the ability to judge which of the many demands and cross-pressures merited a priority response next. But this ability was pertinent to what was essentially short-term decision-making. Industrial managers, however, were also expected to run their production units with a longer-term outlook in mind, in which respect they had to inspire confidence as people who knew the value of efficiency.

The managerial objective of efficiency was devoid of a positive and reliable overall performance indicator, but it was alive in the form of mobilization campaigns against particular sorts of 'waste'. It also had a positive, if somewhat diffuse, presence as a cultural value which was particularly representative of the new civilization that the industrialization drive was to bring about.

The industrialization decade, however, was not homogeneous in this respect. The first five year plan was primarily about the determination to get large projects of industrial construction done, against all odds and 'at any cost'; it put a strong emphasis on managerial effectiveness in this respect. The second five year plan, however, was inaugurated under the slogan of 'mastery' (*osvoenie*) of the technological base that had just been acquired; it was about getting the full productive use out of the expensively acquired machinery which, gleaming as it did with the mystique of a promised future, heralded prosperity to be a reward for efficiency at work. The politics of industrial leadership rejected the option of financial budget autonomy in management, but it made the search for industrial efficiency and a 'high standard of productive culture' (*proizvoditel 'naya kul'turnost'*) into its major preoccupation.

THE PURSUIT OF INDUSTRIAL CULTURE

The goals of the industrialization campaign were in part the goals of a cultural transformation. In this respect, they represented a distinctive continuity with the 'westernizing' traditions of Russia's struggles with her past. Lenin's slogan, 'to learn, learn and learn', was widely understood in the industrialization context as an injunction to learn the best from the West. 'For we Russians are very far behind and very, very stupid,' explained a party propagandist, without a trace of irony in her voice, to one of the would-be memoir writers during one of his train journeys in 1933:

When the second five-year plan has been carried through, everything in Russia will be good . . . Then we shall drive in motor-cars along splendid roads, and we shall have plenty to eat and good clothes to wear.[20]

The admiration for the western variety of 'industrial culture', which after all was the only one in existence then, would come under some attack with the advent of the Stakhanovite movement in 1935–36; but until then, it was a strong theme in the managerial literature in particular, which coexisted in quite curious ways with the other ideological themes of the 'great breakthrough' period. The managerial literature made it clear that the things to learn from the West extended beyond technology to the arts of organization and further still, to the values and attitudes that were believed to make the most efficient technology and organization work. Many of the published discussions also implied that a claim of direct contact with western industry, be this at the level of theory or practice, was at the same time a claim of professional competence. It was a proof of excellence on the part of a Soviet manager when he was said to be respected by foreign specialists,[21] a proof of miscarriage of justice by a state attorney when he decided against the expert opinion of 'two committees and a foreign specialist, an utmost authority',[22] and it was clear that 'systematic travel abroad' by shopfloor managers would be a good thing because 'it would give their decisions the authority that is now given to proposals made by foreign specialists'.[23]

Even the merits of phenomena that might have been expected to be treated as worthy by virtue of their Soviet character were discussed in the managerial press as worthy of backing from western authority. The taut version of the first five year plan which was decreed by the party at the end of 1929 was backed in the managerial press by quotes from western industrialists about the Soviet productivity slack,[24] and the coming on the scene of the 'socialist competition' movement brought in its wake lengthy reports about a 'campaign against waste' that had been conducted by General Motors on the pages of its company newspaper, *Reflector*.[25] The experience of other American firms with suggestion boxes was also disseminated in aid of 'socialist competition', as were the activities of the League of Time movement.[26]

There was a substantial traffic across the borders when it came to industrial experts. Thousands of foreigners were employed on temporary contracts in Soviet industry, and their impressions were frequently quoted in the management press in the course of its campaigns. Speeches by American visitors were reported verbatim even if they were hardly original in proclaiming the sound organizational principles of 'the right thing in the right place at the right time', or in making the point that this could hardly be so in factories where the gangways were dirty and cluttered because labourers were allowed to dump things where they pleased.[27] The ranks of American engineers even contributed a famous hero of the industrialization campaign in the person of John Calder whose exploits as the Chief Engineer of the construction of the Stalingrad Tractor Works were dramatized in a frequently performed theatre play called *Tempo*. The leading character of this play was one Mr Carter whose first action on being appointed the Chief Engineer was to move his office from a plush directorial suite to a shack in the middle of the construction site where he spent most of the time, close to the action. He was a practical man who had little patience with paperwork, but who had a healthy determination to get things done despite the morale-sapping problems in the shape of buck-passing colleagues who loved meetings too much, foremen who were never short of argument against implementing whatever had just been decided by their superiors, and truck-drivers who kept wrecking prepared sites by driving their vehicles across them. Not a man to shrink from what had to be done to impose the discipline that was necessary for effective work organization, Mr Carter outshouted the foremen and persuaded his superiors to arrange for the building sites to be protected from careless truck-drivers by armed guards with orders to shoot at trespassers.[28]

The border traffic in the opposite direction, by Soviet engineers and managers on study visits to western firms, was large enough to make it evidently worthwhile for a Berlin firm of gentlemen's outfitters to print a Russian version of their catalogue and regularly place an advertisement in the Soviet managerial journals, which showed a picture of an elegant young man carrying a briefcase and wearing a double-breasted suit with a matching flat cap. The advertisement gave the Berlin address of the 'large specialist enterprise for men's clothing both made-to-measure and off-the-peg', where 'those who travel abroad buy their good-quality clothes'.[29] The clothes shop was well advised to present itself as 'a large specialist enterprise', because that indeed was the sort of outfit from which a progressive man of industry would expect only the best. But the advertisers probably did not know that their cause had its support in the highest places. It was at that time, in the middle of the first five year plan, that the director of a large specialist enterprise for the manufacture of automobiles was told by Stalin to wear better shirts. The spruced-up director in turn made frequent comments to his subordinate managers on their standards of appearance.[30] The battle for 'industrial culture' was fought on many fronts and it was believed that managers had no hope of freeing factory gangways from obstructive clutter and protecting construction sites from molestation by casually driven trucks, if they themselves wore dowdy clothes and forgot to clean their shoes. Ivan Gudov, too, was told to get himself a new suit when he became a leading Stakhanovite.[31]

The managerial journals published many reports from study-trips to large and famous western firms, which were full of things to admire. They in fact tended to be written in a style which contrasted the descriptions of what had been seen on the visits with what was allegedly prevalent at home, as an ideal to emulate in opposition to a Russian backwardness that had to be overcome. The Soviet travellers were apparently deafened by the silence that ruled in the corridors at Siemens headquarters because its 6000 office-workers were busy at their desks, 'just like machine-operators at their machines'; delighted to find that they could set their watches by the regular movements of Metro-Vickers workers; tempted to picnic on Ford factory floors which were kept so sparkling clean.[32] They reported a 'cultured organization of production' such as they seldom encountered in Soviet industry, for which it was now their heartfelt duty to struggle. Inspired by what they witnessed in the best western firms, they adopted policies in their own factories, which ranged from making simple improvements to production equipment and organization to 'forging a new sort of person who likes cleanliness which in turn awakens in him an affinity for precise and economic work'.[33]

One does not have to be a connoisseur of books like *Working for Ford* to suspect that the reports from western firms were perhaps a little idealized.[34] In fact, while the themes of impeccable cleanliness, discipline, precision and organization in the western firms, in contrast to the sloppy spontaneity that was said to characterize Russian working traditions, remained constant, some of the other achievements of western management that were reported by the Soviet travellers appeared to change with the prevalent orthodoxies of Soviet management thought. The favoured structure of management in the factories was a case in point. When an extensive division of managerial authority between specialist personnel, and a large degree of centralization of decision-making in planning offices, i.e. the 'functionalist' principles of management, were favoured by Soviet management theory during most of the first five year plan, many of the idealized reports of impeccable organization were from German factories where 'all the "brain" aspects of production were worked out by the enterprise management beforehand'.[35] When this 'functionalism' was found to breed irresponsibility and the more traditional 'line' structures of authority came back to favour at the end of the first five year plan, the reports from abroad, as well as the dramatized exploits of Mr Calder-Carter, conveyed the message that good management was made by practical men who were not afraid to get their hands dirty and knew how to take responsibility; and the best of the West was now found in America rather than in Germany.[36]

The Soviet industrialization was undertaken in the belief that the attainment of western prosperity required western technology and also cultural attitudes which emphasized the virtues of cleanliness, methodicality and self-discipline. This belief was strongly supported by some of the western industrial experts who found that:

The lack of sanitation all over Russia is noticeable and I could see no improvement in this line. The animal habits of these people are not conductive to efficient working habits. Factories, offices and mines are lacking in order and cleanliness. A dirty man, unfed and unwashed will never do good work . . . The average Russian doesn't like intensive continued work.[37]

The Soviet industrializers shared this view of their nation's backwardness and viewed their responsibilities as being in part those of a civilizing mission. The activities of Ford's Sociological Department, which had been set up to teach immigrant workers from peasant Europe to become soap-using Americans with savings accounts, must have seemed almost as relevant to the Soviet leaders as the technology of Ford's production lines. After all, Ford's widely publicized management policies had been largely formulated in response to problems of labour behaviour which were not dissimilar to those now faced by the Soviet industrializers. (Labour turnover rates at the Detroit factory had reached 370 per cent p.a. by 1913, and absence rates 10 per cent.[38] Soviet managers were certainly expected to care about their civilizing responsibilities, and showing that they did was evidence of a longer-term perspective in their approach which was considered to augur well for their standards of production efficiency, alongside technological erudition and the knowledge of practice in advanced western firms.

There was another importation from the West that was available to Soviet managers for the cultivation of their professional identity and longer-term perspectives in the face of short-term pressures: the theoretical school of 'scientific management', 'rational organization', or, if one can use the term in its broader meaning, Taylorism. This was the only theoretical school of management thought that was developed well enough to exert influence on Soviet management thinkers at the time of embarkation on the industrialization programme.[39] Formulated at the historical meeting-point of immigrant peasant labour from Europe with the demands of machine-based industry in the New World, Taylorism reflected the virtues of 'industrial culture' as clearly as the philosophy of labour management that was proclaimed by Ford.

A summary of the principles of Taylorism must start with its most basic proposition, which holds that there is only one best way of accomplishing a work task. The best way can be determined with scientific accuracy if the work task is first analysed as a set of elementary components which are measured, with the application of scientific laboratory methods, in regard to the minimum expenditure of time and effort that is necessitated by them. On the basis of these measurements, the work task can be redesigned as that sequence of its elementary components which minimizes the sum of elementary effort-and-time expenditures. Then it is also possible to find the best possible division of labour for the work task, and to describe each job in explicit and unambiguous written instructions which make the most efficient method available to anyone who can read. These instructions are important not only because they make the best way of doing a job known to inexperienced newcomers, but also because they enable supervisors to recognize time-wasting by workers when it is taking place.

Another principle of Taylorism is that each job, or each component of a work task, has an appropriate speed or performance standard set for it, on the basis of the time-and-effort measurements that had been made on the elementary components. And, since the elementary components are, unlike whole work tasks, the same in different factories and production lines, job performance standards which are set on the basis of elementary measurements make possible wider comparisons to be made with some objective reliability. This would provide a consensual basis for resolving wage-comparability issues in industrial relations, and for setting performance incentive schemes. Taylorism is aware that the usual management practice of reducing those piece-rates which enable some workers to earn above-average wages motivates groups of workers to impose restrictions on their work performance, and holds that properly set piece-rates should remain unchanged even if some workers did rather well on them.

Taylorism also makes the claim that its analytical methods of job design make it possible for work tasks which have been previously the exclusive domain of skilled craftsmen to be carried out with equal efficiency by workers who have not had the benefit of long apprenticeship training. This reduces wage costs as most of the work incentive schemes can be based on semi-skilled rates of pay, and it undermines the power of skilled workers to control management decisions on the shopfloor by threatening to withdraw goodwill in applying their scarce skills. Taylorism is in this sense an offensive against the traditional status of skilled workers on the shop-floor, as well as against 'irrational' methods of work. However, its claim of making craft skills unimportant does not mean that Taylorism always assumes all workers to be freely interchangeable. Rather, it assumes that each job makes demands on certain aptitudes, that workers may well vary in this respect, but that the analytical method of work study makes it possible to identify the necessary aptitudes clearly and thus to lay a basis for developing aptitude tests that could be employed in the selection of workers for particular jobs. Again, it is assumed that a reduction in the occurrence of mismatches between workers and jobs would also reduce the incidence of conflict and restrictive work practice on the shopfloor.

Finally, Taylorism believes that the analytical method of job design should be applied to managerial tasks as well. This means that, in contrast to delimiting the authority of managerial posts in terms of groups of subordinates, as is the case in the hierarchical 'line' type of authority structure, management structure should be 'functionalist', i.e. delimiting the scope of authority of each post in terms of specialized aspects of management. At the shopfloor level, the introduction of management 'functionalism' would bring about the replacement of the 'universal foreman' by a number of specialized instructors and supervisors, each being accountable to a specialist branch of centralized factory planning. By making the scope of authority of a manager coincide with his area of specialist expertise, 'functionalism' would be perhaps more compatible with democratic values than the traditional military lines of command, thus reducing tension in industrial relations. In addition, Taylorism considers 'universal' foremen to be the bearers of shopfloor traditions alongside craftsmen, standing in the way of 'rationalisation' of work, so that a 'functionalist' reform would be a positive step in reducing their power.

The preference for paying wages in the form of piece-rates, with which Taylorism tends to be identified, has been in fact neither specific nor central to Taylorism, in contrast to the claims made for the analytical methods of work study and job design.

I shall argue in the next chapter that Taylorism is probably wrong in claiming that the analysis of work into elementary components can do away with the issue of wage comparability in shopfloor relations. But the existence of doubt in this respect does not necessarily doom the theory to practical failure. It is within the scope of the theory to consider the peculiarities of work conditions that are present on a shopfloor, and take them into account as a quantitatively expressed 'fatigue factor' in the calculation of the work performance standards that should be applied there. In other words, the laboratory calculation of the essential time-and-effort content of a job gets enlarged to allow for shopfloor conditions, and the standard of work performance on the shopfloor gets correspondingly lowered. The determination of the appropriate 'fatigue factor' in practice allows some sort of negotiation between the time-study man and the worker to take place. In the last analysis, the practical success of work study lies in the achievement of a reliable and relatively efficient work-flow on the shopfloor, and it does not really matter if the time-study man sees his job as grounded in science while workers view it as a bargaining game.

We must note, however, that the approach to shopfloor management that is advocated by Taylorism requires that the conditions of work on the shopfloor are stable, otherwise the fine division of labour, detailed operational procedures and precise timings will keep losing any consensual validity they may have previously achieved by the process of negotiated adjustment. Taylorism presumes that production is specialized, standardized and taking place in long uninterrupted runs; this is the production engineer's paradise where neither the order books, nor the supplies of whatever is required in unlimited quantity and homogeneous quality, pose serious enough problems to distract from the pursuit of all the productive efficiency that is allowed by the available technology.

The history of western industry provides two paradoxical lessons in relation to the production engineer's requirements. One is that, while it could be said that this century has belonged to large specialized plants with long runs of standardized product, these plants have been surrounded by networks of small, less technological but flexible businesses ready to do any service for the giants, which leads one to suspect that these small-scale satellites have played an important role as a sort of buffer-zone enabling the modern production lines to have their stability despite a not so stable wider environment.

And secondly, it appears that the objective of production efficiency (the maximization of the difference between output and costs) is denied exactly at the point where the usage of technology approaches full capacity. It has been found that 'working at full capacity is notoriously inefficient', as in this description of a bankruptcy-through-a-boom period in a Chicago engineering plant in the 1970s:

Excessive overtime, frequent changes in jobs and set-ups to meet short-term demands, problems of scheduling etc., sent production costs soaring. When a new delivery of castings came into the plant, 'hot jobs' would appear, and operators would have to drop everything and rush the job through, breaking set-ups where necessary. The monomania for output was further stimulated by the drive and dominance of the manufacturing manager, whose departmental interests were directly linked to producing as many engines as possible, irrespective of costs.[40]

This period was also long remembered on the Chicago shop-floor as one which put management–worker relations under considerable strain. Paradoxical though it may seem, the pursuit of organizational efficiency may well require that production lines are allowed to operate at below-capacity levels, contrary to the precepts of Taylorism, where the full usage of technological capacity is both a starting point and an objective of 'rationalization' of shopfloor work practice.

However, these reflections on the validity of Taylorism are only speculative, because there are very few examples of its full-fledged implementation. The painstakingly analytical approach to work study and job design, and its practical application to shopfloor organization, have been generally considered by western industrialists to be too expensive in overheads. Besides, many managers thought twice about the wisdom of initiating a head-on collision with the traditional authority of craftsmen and foremen. Various elements of Taylorism have been widely adopted in western industry, but only in piecemeal and diluted forms.[41] The fact remains, however, that Taylorism, and its version of 'scientific management' and 'rationalization', had a virtual monopoly in the first decades of the century as the only definition of labour management expertise that could be counterposed against the supposed flair, charisma and practical wisdom of capitalist owner-managers.

Taylorism had Lenin's blessing as one of the fruits of capitalist civilization that was worthy of serious study,[42] but this was not the only reason that made it attractive to the Soviet industrializers. Taylorism was quite easy to fit into a Marxist frame of mind. Marxism sees the production of wealth primarily as a process of organized work activity, the 'labour process', and it can be held to follow from this premise that socialist production ought to be organized on the basis of scientific knowledge of this process. Taylorism also takes the process of organized work activity to be the key to economic prosperity, and its analytical methodology of work-study and measurement clearly bears the hallmarks of science. Marxism considers advanced industrial capitalism a fertile ground for the growth of socialist phenomena among which efficient production engineering might well be counted. Taylorism represents a production engineer's view of rationality in the organization of production, which is compromised in capitalist conditions by the twin obstacles of profit-maximization and labour resistance. Taylorism could be then viewed as one of the 'forces of production' that would provide a better service under socialism than under capitalism. Production engineering, Taylorism and Marxism are at one in viewing the questions of economy in industrial production in the physical terms of inputs, outputs, labour-times and technological capacity, rather than in financial terms. And finally, Taylorism also had some pragmatic attractions for the Soviet industrializers; it seemed to value scientific methodology in management higher than practical experience, which must have been excellent news in a country where experienced industrial managers were clearly in short supply, and the same methodology also promised to reduce the need for experienced and skilled workers at shopfloor level.

To say that Taylorism was indeed influential in Soviet management thought would be an understatement. F.W. Taylor himself was equal to Marx as a routinely quoted authority in the theoretical articles in management journals. This was a clear point of differentiation between the management journals and the rest of the media, and it was self-conscious in that some of the managerial writers made explicit their belief that Taylorism was a practical application of Marxism. While others thought that this perhaps went too far, they at the same time reaffirmed Taylor's importance and subjected to criticism 'popular' propagandists for dwelling too much on Taylor's capitalist background, and Soviet publishing houses for neglecting to republish Taylor's classics.[43] Interestingly, when the Soviet 'science of organization of production' eventually became subject to controversy on the pages of its journals in connection with the Stakhanovite movement, only an oblique reference was made to an excessive obeisance to 'foreign principles and methods', while Taylor himself was quoted with approval again, this time for his pragmatism in deviating from his own theoretical orthodoxies in practice.[44]

However, Stakhanovism did not see the light of day until the middle of the decade, prior to which Taylorism ruled with unchallenged supremacy in the theoretical sections of the managerial journals. The latter devoted much space to the task of scientific job design and the determination of performance standards. Painstaking time-and-motion studies of various elementary manual operations were reported in lengthy articles, as was research on the 'fatigue factor' in various jobs and conditions.[45] The task of standardizing work-study methodology also commanded a lot of attention in the management press, and this was not confined to the journal that was devoted to the arcane arts of 'technical norm-setting' especially.[46] Also in correspondence with the spirit and letter of Taylorism were lengthy articles devoted to complex administrative systems of continuous data collection from the shopfloors, which were thought necessary to facilitate the good work of 'technical norm-setting bureaux', 'rationalization bureaux' and 'intra-plant planning departments', and at the same time to put the shopfloor tendencies to 'artisan spontaneity' under the high degree of control that was required by the incessant pursuit of 'rationalization'.[47] The management journals also kept their readers in constant touch with developments in the western 'rationalization movement', even when the European branch of the latter became somewhat embarrassingly associated with Italian fascism.[48]

Taylorism played its part in the politics of the 'great breakthrough' optimism in the late 1920s. It was claimed, for example, that its implementation in USA brought about the doubling of labour productivity there, and that this benefit should be even greater in the Soviet case.[49] This claim was made for the introduction of 'scientific management' alone, before the benefits of imported technological hardware were taken into account. The Taylorist principles of factory organization, complete with their heavy emphasis on 'technical norm-setting' and 'functionalist' structure of authority, duly became government policy, alleged inertia in respect to its implementation getting a frequent mention amidst examples of 'bourgeois specialist' conservatism.[50]

There was, however, one important aspect in which the 'great breakthrough' policy was in conflict with the Soviet school of Taylorism. Some of the leading protagonists of the school put a strong emphasis on the desirability of even pace of work on the shopfloor, and in fact made it clear that the achievement of getting all workers to work with a continuous and smoothly coordinated regularity was a management aim of key significance for the attainment of 'industrial culture'; and industrialization would not bring the desired prosperity if it failed at the level of 'work culture'. Regularity was more important than speed in their books, and speed-up campaigns therefore were not a good idea. This is how the point was put in one of the industrial dailies in autumn 1932, when the industrialization drive was reaching its crisis point. (The occasion was the 50th birthday of the foremost protagonist of Taylorism in Bolshevik ranks, 'the master of work culture', Alexander Gastev.)

A skill in working means above all else the ability to sustain a continuous and regular work-pace. This idea of Gastev's is now generally accepted in the Soviet Union . . . Once upon a time the theses of *How to Work* seemed very extreme and unrealistic. Now there is nothing in them that is not agreed by anyone who writes or speaks on the subject. Although the theses have not as yet been generally adopted in practice, in principle they are disputed by nobody. The basic idea of the theses is persistence, the ability to work at a sustained pace . . . This work culture is at the heart of the *TsIT* purpose.

Without this purpose, intensification of labour would make inevitable an exhaustion of the worker's organism, frustration and the undermining of the basic productive force, as Marx called the working class.[51]

Gastev had been also quoted in another journal nine months

earlier for this view pertaining to the political campaigns for 'norm-revision', i.e. speed-ups:

The operational regime of a machine-tool should be on the whole neither minimal, nor maximal, nor indeed optimal, but one which in the end harmonises best with a number of other places.[52]

The opposition to speed-up campaigns, however, was best developed in two books by Professor Ermanskii,[53] the second of which was much criticized, but at the same time paraphrased and quoted. Ermanskii made a point of distinguishing the pursuit of 'labour productivity' from the pursuit of 'labour intensity'.[54] 'Labour productivity' was made of factors like product quality, thorough preparation of the work process and its efficient coordination, that is, the 'qualitative' characteristics of management, the unceasing improvement of which was the proper criterion of managerial success. 'Labour intensity', on the other hand, was a 'quantitative' concept of effort expenditure by workers, and in this respect the hallmark of good management was not an upward-sloping curve, but on the contrary, a care to keep it within the bounds of acceptability for workers' health. Managers should avoid making excessive demands on the workers' effort; instead, they should take advantage of the reduction in fatigue and improvement in efficiency that could be found in routinizing the workers' movements, not forgetting, however, the 'dulling influence' of monotonous work. Ermanskii thus confronted the awkward fact that industrial efficiency demanded a high degree of monotony on the shopfloor, and in effect proposed that this problem was best resolved by allowing workers to work at a relatively easy pace, because this would allow them to develop successful ways of adapting to the rigours of time-bound discipline without danger to the 'psycho-physical optimum in energy expenditure'. Management policy which pursued higher labour productivity by putting pressure on workers to increase labour intensity was in essence capitalist, and it ought not to be adopted by Soviet managers.[55] Ermanskii had apparently put his weight behind some of the workers' protests that had taken place in response to intensification campaigns in the 1920s, for which he was denounced as a Menshevik wrecker in one organ of the managerial press early in 1932.[56] His books, however, remained available to trainee engineers and managers at least until 1936, at the beginning of which year he still occupied a chair at the prestigious Bauman Institute in Moscow.[57]

The ways in which the views of Gastev and Ermanskii on labour-intensification campaigns percolated through the pages of the managerial press during the years of the first five year plan were interesting exceptions to the rule that nothing should contradict the political mobilization methods of industrialization, on which the party leadership had been relying since the 'great breakthrough', alongside Taylorism and technology. There clearly was a contradiction between the search for clockwork regularity on the shopfloor that was dictated by the Taylorist version of 'rational organization of work' on the one hand, and the campaigns of 'socialist competition' for 'Bolshevik speeds' on the other hand. The managerial journals handled the contradiction by aloofness to 'socialist competition' initiatives, leaving the rousing fanfares to 'shock-work' heroics to be played elsewhere.

However, they could not ignore the fact that the political leadership of the industrialization drive insisted on annual campaigns of increasing work performance standards by wholesale revision of the output norms for individual shopfloor operations. This problem was handled by the Taylorist spokesmen for managerial professionalism by making an implicit deal with the speed-up campaigners, where the latter's demands for norm revision were accepted, but treated as demands for the implementation of scientific methodology in the setting of norms, and for the replacement of 'statistical' norms based on mere observation, by 'technically-grounded' norms based on analyses of work tasks into elementary components. 'Technical' norms could be rightly expected to be higher than 'statistical' ones, but once set, they should be regarded as more or less permanent.

This was to prove a disastrous deal for the forces of managerial rationalism. If the 'absolute truth' claims made by Taylorism for its method of setting output norms were a fiction which could be maintained by shopfloor practice only where there was the high degree of organizational stability afforded by long uninterrupted production runs and secure supplies of standardized inputs, the fiction had to break down in Soviet factories. As we shall see in the next chapter, the preservation of serviceable relations between shopfloor managers and workers within the framework of 'technically grounded norms' required the wholesale fiddling of norm fulfilment accounts. The result was that 'technical' norms appeared to be routinely overfulfilled within a few weeks of their introduction, without any other visible signs of improvement in labour productivity.[58] This generated cynicism about the validity of 'technical norms', against which the defence that conditions did not allow 'technical norm-setting by elements' to be done properly sounded too much like special pleading for an ivory-tower discipline.[59]

Soviet Taylorism got a political boost from the 'great breakthrough' policies as a science that promised unprecedented industrial success by substituting technological rationalism for economistic rationalism, but it was at the same time stopped from giving licence to managers to pursue regularity in shopfloor work-pace as a high priority, medium-term policy objective, in preference to pursuing increments in speed. Articles which showed the benefits for organizational efficiency of, for example, institutionalizing extra breaks or workers to give the foremen a better chance to prevent unscheduled stoppages during the work periods, or of reducing machine speeds for the same reason, disappeared from the pages of the managerial press after 1929, to make only a brief and sporadic reappearance during the interregnum crisis that separated the first two five year plans in 1932–33.[60]

Taylorism was a philosophy of labour management which seemed to express well the aspirations of the movement to replace economic backwardness by 'industrial culture'. It promised to provide the management of the industrialization campaign with a form of rationalism which was consistent with many of the Marxist arguments about the centrality of the 'labour process' and the limitations imposed upon the utilization of advanced technology by market-based criteria of profitability. It also seemed to provide a scientific organizational basis for the values of work discipline, methodicality and efficiency, which were believed to be the essential defining feature of the 'industrial culture' without which there would be no prosperity or international strength. The philosophy, however, failed to resolve the issues of managerial accountability which were posed by the absence of a reliable quantitative measure of production efficiency. On the contrary, it made them worse by assuming that there was no conflict of objectives in the simultaneous pursuit of economy in the expenditure of labour and working at full technological capacity.

Taylorism may have been in theoretical harmony with the idea of industrialization under the auspices of a planned economy, but it was severely at odds with the realities of taut planning. Contrary to the dream of 'mass' or indeed 'continuous' production lines, where work organization could be finely tuned to maximize the economy of time and motion, taut planning brought about an industrial structure which was distinguished by a lack of long and uninterrupted production runs. Although the factories that were built were giants which were clearly meant to be 'large specialist enterprises' manufacturing things in large batches, most of the press reports from the shopfloors described the context of the workplaces there as one of small-batch (*maloseriinoe*) production. This was because production had to be diversified and rescheduled at short notice in response to newly decided priorities. Taylorism was thus denied the high degree of stability in output requirements and input supplies it needed if it were to facilitate a consensual framework for the setting of work performance standards. Its insistence on precise operational methods, timings and the development of elaborate paperwork systems for the monitoring of work performance in fact only multiplied contested issues in shopfloor relations at the same time as it made managers even more vulnerable to charges of 'bureaucratism' than they otherwise would have been. It thus failed to provide a practical longer-term strategy for the pursuit of production efficiency and 'industrial culture', in effect leaving these concerns to the mobilization methods of speed-up campaigning.

'BACKWARD WORKERS'

So far in this chapter I have discussed the relationship between industrial management and the political leadership of the industrialization campaign. The process of raising the efficacy and efficiency standards of work organization in the factories in part involved putting managers and middle-level executives under the pressures of vigilance against 'bureaucratism', in addition to the pressures created by administrative directives and inspections. We have also seen that the industrialization campaign was considered something of a civilizing mission in the course of which the backwardness of peasant Russia was to give way to the prosperous ways of an 'industrial culture', and that this preoccupation helped to create a strongly ambivalent relationship between the managerial philosophy of Taylorism on the one hand, and the political activism of the 'struggle for Bolshevik speeds' on the other hand. Underlying this discussion has been a consistent theme: the overcoming of economic backwardness by the methods of taut planning appeared to require that 'work with the masses' never left its prominent place on the political agenda of industrial issues. This was so not only because 'the masses' were, like managers and executives, perceived to be in need of improvement in respect of their working skills and attitudes, but also because the political leaders felt it necessary to be able to enlist some support 'from below' in their struggles against the much feared stagnation born of managerial incompetence and 'bureaucratism'.

It is interesting therefore to note how 'the masses', i.e. the factory workers, were viewed in the ideological imagery of industrialization politics. 'Backwardness' was inevitably a central concept here. 'Backward workers' (*otstalye rabochie*) were the ones who were illiterate, did not read newspapers, were not interested in political matters, were not even members of the trade unions let alone any other 'social organizations', did not master the skills of industrial work, had no qualifications and did nothing to acquire some, and had yet to be taught the habits and attitudes of 'socialist labour discipline'.[61] Taking care of converting these traits into their opposites was a high-priority task of the trade unions and all the other 'social organizations' whose role in industry was at least in part defined by the proclamation, in 1929, that the trade unions ought to turn their 'face towards production'.

But there was more to 'backwardness' than relatively low levels of education, work performance and participation in organized activities. In the first half of the industrialization decade, the image of worker 'backwardness' was strongly influenced by the anti-peasant stance which the collectivizing militancy of the state shared with the managerialist visions of 'industrial culture'. The fact that Soviet factories were largely filled with immigrants from the peasant countryside commanded much official attention. It was held to be an axiomatic truth that the influx of 'yokels' (*derevenshchiki*) was an unfortunate price that had to be paid for fast industrial expansion, and producing statistics of the influx featured prominently in the routines of explaining industrial failures in the first half of the decade.[62] The kindest thing that was printed about the ex-peasant on the shopfloor was that he was inept, as shown in this example of industrial reportage:

A lathe turner is stooping over a gleaming, gently turning shaft. His jacket is covered in steel dust and flooded with sparks. His face is tense, streams of sweat are mixing with grime and grease. It is difficult to put a finger on it, but there is something distinctively peasant about him. It could be the squat posture, or perhaps the way his elbows wave about when his fingers are at work, and his nose sort of twitches – devil knows what it is![63]

The reporter in this account indeed found that the worker, 'a bright lad of 32', was a peasant who had just spent an hour producing scrap because, in the first place, he had never properly understood the blueprint by which he was working. Not that he had received no training, as he had in fact passed his exams and was now a supposedly skilled-grade machine-operator. It was, however, a typical problem wherever yesterday's peasants took the place of 'old' workers, the skill grades just no longer were in practice what they once had been.[64]

Most of the time, however, ex-peasants in the factories were described in more negative terms than well-meaning ineptitude. Gastev accused the peasant culture 'in our backward country' of the 'uncultured' and 'petty-bourgeois' tendency to alternate periods of 'exhausting hard labour' with prolonged 'resting in complete laziness' or cultivating the artful techniques of 'doing no work without actually running from it.'[65] The 'hooligans, slackers and novices' on the shop-floors were suspect politically, too, according to countless commentaries.[66] Burdened with the habits of thought born of 'petty property-holding', the 'raw workforce' (*syraya rabochaya sila*) was considered to be vulnerable to the 'social-ly alien' influence of 'former people' (*byvshie lyudi*) – former kulaks, officers, priests and traders – who, 'having been derailed and scattered over the face of the USSR, crept into our institutions, factories, waterways and railways' with plans to cause counter-revolutionary mischief by industrial 'wrecking'.[67] The trade unions and other social organizations had an urgent task of 'transforming the brains' (*pererabotka mozgov*) of the new workers.[68]

The media image of the 'old' workers (*starye rabochie*) was more varied. The dominant political view was that the 'old' workers were the sterling stuff of revolution, whose role it now was to educate the 'novices' in selfless work ethic as well as technical skills. The press often gave examples where 'old' workers distinguished themselves by taking up a principled stand against falling standards on the shopfloor, and assumed 'patronage' (*shefstvo*) over errant workers to help them im-prove themselves.[69] It was considered a serious problem that the numerical weight of 'the revolutionary working-class core' among shopfloor workers was radically reduced after 1928, as a result of recruitment campaigns to keep up with the creation of new posts in the party, government and management.[70]

But the positive characterization of factory veterans had to be qualified to some extent. For one thing, it had to be acknowledged that their behaviour on the shopfloor did not always look like a clear expression of selfless devotion to 'socialist construction'. Like the peasant newcomers with their 'petty-property holding' mentality, the veterans of pre-revolutionary industry were sometimes observed to employ their shopfloor knowhow in ways which betrayed a desire 'to give the state less and grab from it more'; they circumvented and abused the rules that governed pay and benefits, indulged in petty cheating and applied various time-honoured techniques of implicit shopfloor bargaining.[71] This 'grabbing' (*rvachestvo*) was, of course, considered to be a habit quite properly acquired in capitalist factories, but unfortunately still persisting in some cases under Soviet conditions, as a leftover from the past.

Another critical view of the older generations on the shopfloors was formed by Soviet Taylorism. As the bearers of 'artisan' or 'craft' customs of work, many of the old workers shared with the peasantry the negative historical qualities to which the ideals of 'industrial culture' efficiency were directly opposed. The kindest way in which the 'craft traditions' were portrayed in the managerial press might feature a myopic old man ('heaven forbid that he mislays his glasses!') who was partial to home-made tipple, and, having trained abroad in younger days, now discharged his foreman's duties in the manner of an old wizard who took technical decisions on the basis of looks and feels, one just had to trust that he knew what he was doing. His devotion above reproach, he never took time off because production in his section could not continue for long without the benefit of his mysterious ministrations. He hated paperwork, needless to say, and had only contempt for the long-winded efforts of polytechnic alumni in a newly established methods section, whose task it was to abolish the mysteries by setting the production process out, down to the last detail and in a manner that made it foolproof to anyone who could read, in written operational instructions.[72]

Less gentle references to 'artisanship' (*kustarshchina*) and 'craft traditions' (*remeslennichestvo*) were more usual in the managerial press, especially during the early years of the decade, before Soviet Taylorism began to be criticized for a 'leftist underestimation of worker initiative'.[73] The alleged conservative ways of industrial artisans and craftsmen, 'the pinnacles of craft wisdom', were declared to be 'petty bourgeois' and a long outdated 'stupidity', full of the 'rotten traditions' of 'systematic grabbing'.[74] In contrast to the rest of the media, the longer articles in the managerial press tended to give more space to the burdens of 'artisanship' than to the assets of 'proletarian consciousness'. Like all Taylorism, its Soviet variety tended to regard most of the historically grown shopfloor customs as almost by definition irrational.

While 'new workers' (*novye rabochie*), who were as yet to be properly 'cooked in the factory pot' (*perevarivat'sya v zavodskom kotle*), were invariably discussed as a temporary but serious problem, 'factory youth' (*zavodskaya molodezh*) was on the whole a positive term denoting a freedom from the conservative attitudes of 'artisanship'. Worker 'youth brigades' were occasionally said to be less prone than their elders to resist time-study by go-slow tactics, more willing to adapt themselves to the discipline demanded by production lines, and in general more willing to cooperate with the 'rationalization' efforts to speed up production and make it more efficient.[75] The problems presented by the 'new workers', however, commanded much more space in the industrial press than the positive characteristics of the 'factory youth'. 'Old workers' (*starye rabochie*), on the other hand, was mostly a term of affectionate respect, as if the veterans had nothing to do with the criticized features of shopfloor behaviour that were known under the headings of 'artisanship' and 'leftovers from the capitalist past'. 'Old workers' mostly denoted an exalted status in the rhetoric of the industrializtion campaign, often interchangeably with the very respectable label 'core worker' (*kadrovyi rabochii*).

It is difficult to refrain from making a comment about the rather obvious similarity between the American 'melting-pot' metaphor for building a nation out of immigrant all comers and the Soviet 'factory pot' metaphor for a cultural transformation of the 'new workers'. The Soviet leaders were rather acutely aware of the peasant backwardness of their nation and also the social problems of the mass-scale uprooting and migration caused by the industrialization campaign. They looked upon the workplaces of the 'socialist construction', and the modern factories in particular, as institutions which had a special importance for the integration of 'the masses' into a new social order that would make the economy strong and the Soviet state at last viable in the face of the 'capitalist encirclement'.

This attribution of an important socializing role to the

factories fitted in with the Soviet leaders' Marxism on two counts. First, productive activity was considered to be the context in which the positive side of 'proletarian consciousness' (positive in the sense of constructing socialism rather than destroying capitalism) would take root in accordance with the 'mode of production' theory of society. And secondly, since industrialization was now the main campaign where the fight for socialism was understood to be taking place, the 'dialectical' vision of social progress by 'class struggle' saw the new 'proletarian consciousness' forming in the context of political mobilizations against the people who appeared to stand in the way of success of the taut plans, 'Bolshevik production speeds' and efficient 'production culture'. A lack of work ethic and all the other manifestations of backwardness in the workers' own midst was one object of the consciousness-forming struggles, but engineers and managers, too, could constitute such an object; I have already noted that the system of 'taut planning' turned concerns for production efficiency into attacks against managerial failures to prevent the various kinds of 'waste' that inevitably made themselves apparent to shopfloor workers as well as visiting inspectors.

'SOCIALIST COMPETITION'

From the vantage point of the political leaders of the industrialization campaign, it seemed that the tasks of creating a new social order, developing a productive 'industrial culture', getting workers to raise their performance standards, increasing organizational efficiency and maintaining momentum despite the tendencies to 'bureaucratism' in executive ranks could be all, to a significant extent, served by persistent 'political work with the masses' on the construction sites and factory shopfloors. This 'political work' gained an institutionalized focus in 'socialist competition'.

Like most important Soviet institutions, 'socialist competition' is said by its Soviet historians to have its roots in Lenin, this time in his appeals, made to the citizens in 1919, to help the civil war economy by voluntary work on Saturdays.

However, the 'socialist competition' that has become a permanent institution came on the scene ten years later as one of the 'great breakthrough' initiatives. Born under the auspices of the party youth organization, the *komsomol*, it quickly became party policy to require all the organizations that existed in industry, from the managerial structures to the trade unions, to keep 'socialist competition' going as a mass movement. Henceforth, the pattern was that the party, and especially the *komsomol*, encouraged its local branches to initiate new forms of 'socialist competition', while the trade unions were charged with the main responsibility for turning these initiatives into mass phenomena.[76]

The initiatives produced a number of honorific titles for workers. The ones that appeared in the early period, from 1929 to 1931, tended to reflect the civil war imagery of the 'great breakthrough' propaganda. The original form of the 'socialist competition' movement were the 'shock brigades', where groups of workers so declared themselves at shopfloor meetings convened to discuss the feasibility of the factory production plans; they did it by undertaking to exceed the production performance that appeared to be assumed by the already taut plans, which then enabled the meetings to issue calls for upward corrections of the factory plans, the so called 'counterplans' (*vstrechnye plany*). The 'shock brigades' thus ensured that factory executives who made known their worries about the feasibility of the taut plans appeared to be quite out of touch with 'the masses'. Another occasion for the birth of 'shock brigades' were meetings convened to discuss imminent failures to fulfil the production plans. 'Shock brigades' would undertake to save the day by 'storming' campaigns of catching up with the plan schedules. Regular bouts of 'storming' (*shturmovshchina*) became known as evidence of faulty management towards the end of the first five year plan, but the 'shock brigades' of workers who offered periods of heroic exertion to compensate for organizational bottlenecks continued to attract official honours.[77]

It is not quite clear when and how a member of a 'shock brigade' gained the title of 'shock worker'. The distinction became important in 1931, when the trade unions began to issue special cards to 'shock workers', which entitled them to various privileges including extra rations. From then on, statistical returns of the 'socialist competition' movement showed an upward tendency, so that nearly three-quarters of all industrial workers were registered as participants, and nearly one-half were registered as 'shock workers' by the beginning of 1935.[78] A good work-performance record, measured in rates of norm-fulfilment where possible, was obviously a relevant criterion, but there were other ones applied alongside with it, such as the discipline record, length of service in the same enterprise (minimum of one year was sometimes required), attendance at night schools, participation in 'social work' activities and class origin ('former people', kulaks and their offspring were supposed to be excluded).[79]

Another contribution to the 'socialist competition' movement were *komsomol*-sponsored 'light cavalry raids' in which groups of young workers sought to prove party leaders right and 'conservative specialists' wrong in their assessment of spare production capacity. The 'cavalry brigades' 'raided' night-shifts to wake up sleeping workers in a blaze of publicity, and factory yards to expose rusting stocks of equipment and raw material.[80] The *komsomol* was also the main sponsor of the short-lived 'brigades of communist labour' which were also called 'communes', because they sought to introduce what were then regarded to be progressive modifications to the relationship between the worker and the factory management. These 'brigades' were on group payment schemes in accordance with their collective performance, adopting their own rules for the distribution of wages to individual members. These rules usually took the skill-grade of an individual worker into account, but on the whole tended to be fairly egalitarian, in some cases even evoking the communist principle of distribution 'according to need', for example by taking into account the number of dependants. It was reported that foremen and skilled workers were often reluctant to join, because they stood to lose out by the adoption of the egalitarian principles. Some of the 'communist labour brigades' also sought to extend their collectivism to the private sphere, by living together in shared housing.[81] The 'communes' lost all official favour in 1931, when the party lead-

ership put its weight behind the principle that each individual
worker should be on strong material incentives to improve his
work skills and increase effort.[82]

In the interregnum years of 1932–33, when there was a
struggle in the party leadership over the future of the taut plan
strategy of industrialization, the favoured form of group
participation in 'socialist competition' appeared to be the so
called 'budget account' (khozraschet) brigades. Here the idea
was to introduce a system of performance accounting and
material rewards which would encourage excellence in reducing production costs as much as in raising the gross output.[83]
This was, however, a difficult idea to implement in the
context of arbitrary prices and unpredictable supplies, so that
the fortunes of this initiative were rather tied to those of
economistic revisionism within the party leadership. Another
product of the interregnum years were 'integrated process
brigades' (skvoznye), which were formed to encourage
workers' initiative in securing coordination between the different parts of production lines.[84] Since this could mean in
practice that the cause of 'socialist competition' might demand downward as well as upward revisions of set production
speeds, the fortunes of the 'integrated process brigades' were
tied to those of the school of management thought which held
that a relatively slow but regular production flow was a
worthier objective than a fast but unreliable one. Both the
'budget account' and 'integrated process' brigades faded from
the propaganda channels of the 'socialist competition' movement soon after the party leadership reaffirmed its commitment to the principles of 'taut planning' at the beginning of
1934.

While striving for the title of 'shock worker' continued to
be promoted throughout the decade, the limelight of the
'socialist competition' publicity belonged to a number of new
movements during the years of the second five year plan. The
practical value of 'shock worker' cards was reduced by the
abolition of rationing, while 'socialist competition' needed
new initiatives to stimulate interest. The collapse of the
movement into mere paperwork routines was frequently
alleged in reports from the factories. New initiatives of
'socialist competition' at least put a pressure on the 'social

organizations' in the factories to do something to show a positive response. Thus 1931 saw the beginning of the Izotov movement, named after a miner who dug five times as much coal as was required by the norm; 1934–35 in many ways belonged to the Menzhikov movement, named after a factory whose workers began to compete in terms of output quality as well as quantity; and August 1935 witnessed the birth of the Stakhanovite movement, named after another miner, who broke production records after insisting on innovation in workplace techniques and organization.[85] Stakhanovism deserves a chapter of its own, because its history was one in which the main trends of the industrialization campaign culminated to leave behind the enduring features of an industrial system. In the pre-Stakhanovite part of the second five year plan, there was a number of new competition movements started, in addition to the ones already mentioned, which received only localized or short-lived publicity. Usually called after the names of workers who reputedly started them, the distinctions between them were fluid and often nominal.

One of the points of widespread agreement among the American engineers who worked in Soviet industry at the time was that the 'great breakthrough' policies of the initial years of the first five year plan enjoyed a strong support among the younger generations of workers.

The thing that impressed me the most was the mass enthusiasm of the people. Even those who had been adversely affected by the regime of the communists seemed to be convinced that something new and better would arise from the tremendous effort that was being expended.[86]

The skilled workers generally took great pride in their work and constantly beseeched the foreign engineers to give them advice, teach them, lecture them and to show them how one man could operate two machines or even quadruple his hourly output. Unskilled workers were largely indifferent and sometimes resented the suggestions for increased output, but the younger generation and the women were just as keen as the skilled mechanics.[87]

Given the young age-profile of the workers in the new factories and on the largest construction projects, this suggests that the 'work with the masses', and 'socialist competition', was to some extent genuinely motivated by ideological appeals. But this was so only in 1929–30. The same set of reports made it clear that popular enthusiasm turned into considerable disillusionment as further exertions continued to be required in the face of falling living standards.

In 1931 (*sic*), when the 'five-year plan in four years' was adopted, imposing still greater sacrifices, much of the enthusiasm disappeared. In 1932, there was no evidence of the spirit with which the Plan had started, and no celebrations marked its completion.[88]

In 1930, all classes of workers were enthusiastic toward their work but at the time of my leaving there, their indifference toward their jobs was very marked; this indifference in some specific instances practically amounted to sabotage.[89]

This in itself poses the question of how the 'work with the masses' was sustained from 1931 on. But there was also another problem which was made evident by the American engineers' reports, only one of which described 'socialist competition' as an unmixed blessing when it came to raising productivity. The evidence provided by the others ranged from saying that 'the only place that socialist competition was paramount was at the meetings',[90] to emphasizing the harmful effects of initiatives which 'diverted attention from the quality of work to the act of heroism'.[91] Positive effects were only temporary, with output tending to 'drop back to previous levels' once the initiatives were 'put back on a regular working basis'.[92] It clearly was not easy to convert ideological attitudes to sustained work motivation:

The ever-present propaganda does mould their (workers') opinions but their work is entirely apart from their beliefs and intentions. This description applies both to the skilled and unskilled workman.[93]

There is a linguistic point to be made about 'socialist competition'. The Russian word for 'competition' in this context is *sorevnovanie*, which even to the untrained eye looks quite different from the word *konkurs* that also means 'competition'. The connotation of the two words was as different as their lexical roots, and it was a serious criticism of a party cell or a trade union branch when it was said that it allowed *sorevnovanie* to degenerate into *konkurs*.[94] The first term recalled the sporting values of striving for excellence and honourable achievement, in the course of which the competitors supported each other by mutual teaching and learning, while the second term had the connotation of one person trying to beat another to a scarce resource. In correspondence with the sporting ideal, press coverage of 'socialist competition' was mainly about workers participating in it, less often about winning, and hardly ever about losing. But if there was a difficulty about converting ideals into sustained work motivation, it would have been surprising if 'socialist competition' had not had in practice to draw upon the motive forces of competition for scarce resources. I have already mentioned that similar motive forces also played their inevitable part in the emergence of the unwritten rules of 'taut plans' management. In short, the ideological terms of the politics of overcoming backwardness gained their practical meaning in the context of relations between managers and groups of workers on factory shopfloors. This is something to be examined in the next chapter.

4 Shopfloor Interactions

INDUSTRIAL WORK AND SHOPFLOOR CULTURE

When asked about the effects of wage incentive schemes on Soviet workers, one of the American engineers who had worked in a Leningrad factory summed up the situation as 'the old story of a "shot in the arm" quickly wearing off';[1] he thus expressed his familiarity with a problem of labour motivation which existed in Soviet factories as well as in American ones. That there are aspects of life in industrial workplaces which assert their presence regardless of difference between nations and their political systems is an intriguing possibility which deserves some exploration. The purpose of this section is therefore to develop an interpretation of factory shopfloor work as a socially organized activity which has a substantial degree of autonomy from political and economic conditions, and to bring into play for comparative consideration the best western studies on this topic.

It is a commonplace observation that industrial production, or 'machinofacture' as Marx aptly called it, typically calls for a greater degree of coordination of activities than the pre-industrial forms of wealth-creation; hence the rise of the management profession and the social sciences. Another commonplace observation is that this coordination relies upon a widespread and acute awareness of the clock. While peasants turn up in the fields to make hay before it rains, workers turn up in their factory because it's 8 a.m. again. As the machines work by the laws of mechanical movement, so people coordinate their activities by the mechanical movement of the clock. While in the pre-industrial age labour took place primarily in response to the cyclical demands of natural conditions, allowing periods of high exertion to be followed by relative ease, industrial labour takes place on the basis of unremitting obeisance to the measured progressions of linear time. An industrial culture is one which upholds time-bound discipline.

This is well illustrated in the following observation of shopfloor behaviour recorded in Ford's Detroit factory in 1920. The observer's eye was caught by a worker who, fifteen minutes before end of shift, made his contribution to a marked slowing-down of the production line by endlessly fumbling with one carburettor, although he could have finished inspecting the whole batch if he had carried on as before. He explained himself with a shopfloor veteran's authority:

Why finish it? It'd do no good. You never get all those boxes cleared off the floor. As soon as you finish one box, they bring another one down. Don't hurry. You never get done anyway.[2]

While to the outsider it seemed natural to want to complete a batch if possible, to the participant member of the production line (who in this instance happened to speak with a Russian accent) it seemed proper to slow down when it was 15 minutes before wash-up time. This particular expression of time-bound discipline was demanded not by the management, but by the workers themselves; learning it was a part of the socialization process whereby novices became members of the industrial culture of their work-group.

Since the cultural aspect of industrialization can be seen in terms of the conceptual contrast between 'task-orientation' and 'time-orientation' at work, it is tempting to ascribe low labour productivity in industrializing countries to a cultural lag on the part of the labour force. I have already mentioned in Chapter 3 that the Soviet industrializers considered the supposed anarchic psychology of ex-peasant workers a serious problem, in which belief they were supported by many of their western advisers:

The attempt to convert an ignorant peasant population into industrial workers in a few years or even in a generation is one of the things the Soviet leaders are finding out cannot be done.[3]

The belief in the importance of the cultural lag is supported by eloquent expressions of aversion to the idea of factory discipline, which are on record from members of peasant cultures round the world: 'How could a man work like that, day after day, without being absent? Would he not die?'[4] Some histories of industrialization, including the history of the famous Ford plant, provide a statistical illustration of the point by showing high absenteeism rates in the early years when the labour force consisted largely of ex-peasant immigrants. The belief is also reinforced by the Protestant Ethic thesis of the rise of industrial capitalism, which has had its influence on western labour historians.

However, a closer look at the evidence concerning the transition from 'task-orientation' to 'time-orientation' in work serves to cast doubt on the contention that a rapid acculturation is not possible. The eloquent expressions of aversion to factory discipline tend to come from peasants who have chosen to stay put, not from the ones who have migrated to industrial employment.[5] Recent studies of migrants in Africa and Latin America have found that the change of behaviour from rural to urban patterns tends to be 'as rapid as the migrant's journey to town':[6]

The values and norms of the village derive from the organisation of life in the village and are not the basis for activities on the shop floor, though the activities may be couched in the *idiom* of village life.[7]

In other words, some of the things factory workers say while at work may show their ethnic backgrounds, but the practical meanings of what they say and do on the shopfloor derive from the organization of life on the shopfloor. The Ford Motor Company took no more than a few years to integrate its unruly immigrants into the production line that became the image of industrial efficiency round the world.[8]

The studies of the acculturation problem show, however, that a rapid success in this respect requires that the following two conditions are met: first, the labour process must be well organized as a set of clearly defined operations, and secondly, it must offer its workers a privileged standard of living compared to other kinds of manual work. The first condition recalls the themes of bureaucracy and Taylorism, about which we now note that this kind of organization serves to 'free' the individual worker from concerns about the effects of his activity on the world outside a clearly delimited sphere. It is almost as if the peasant homestead and village, the boundaries of which demarcate the 'real world' of responsibility from the 'alien world' of indifference, had to be artificially recreated in the new, socially dense and complex urban world. The new 'real world' is a job which is explicitly described by operating procedures and performance standards. The 'reality' of this job world derives from the fact that the operating procedures and performance standards enable one's activities to be acknowledged and rewarded by rendering them 'visible' to others. Responsibility is pinned down to the procedures and standards rather than the practical uses of accomplished tasks.

The second condition of rapid adaptation to factory discipline, that the wages must be good, recalls an important theme that is missing from the Protestant Ethic thesis, i.e. the spirit of consumerism. The ability to adorn oneself with markers of taste, style and social identity by purchasing consumer novelties appears to assume great importance for people once they have entered the urban world. There must be more to life than sheer survival for workers if they are to adopt time-oriented ways beyond the minimum that can be exacted by coercion, and it appears that consumer purchases do provide, at least momentarily, the sought more-than-just-survival satisfactions.[9]

But it would be wrong to deduce from the importance of consumer purchasing power that activities at work are motivated purely by extrinsic rewards. Wages explain why workers turn up at work, and relatively high wages explain why some workers are willing to put up with hitherto unusual rigours of factory discipline. In themselves, however, wages do not explain the manner in which workers pass their time at work, as witnessed by the observations, cited at the beginning of this discussion, of the temporary effects of wage incentive schemes and the ritual slow-downs at certain points in time. Some of the work motivation is intrinsic to the cultural adaptations by workers to their work conditions. While the transition from 'task-orientation' to 'time-orientation' in work does not appear on a closer inspection to be unduly burdened by peasant traditions, it tends to result in the creation of other 'traditions' which are not in every respect identical with a naively conceived work ethic or 'industrial culture'.

The conceptual contrast between 'task-oriented' and 'time-oriented' work suggests a contrast between meaningfulness and meaninglessness. The accomplishment of a task such as the making of hay before the rain comes is something of a 'happy ending' which infuses the activity of haymaking with meaning – because having hay is consensually understood as useful and the difference from not having it compelling. By contrast, 'time-oriented' work on industrial production lines has no such 'happy ending' because, as we have been already informed by the Detroit worker, it never ends. Its purpose is to keep the production line going at some rate measured by output statistics over periods of time. The work is a sort of disciplined marking of time, this perception being only emphasized by the necessary repetitiveness of the actions. The product does not infuse the actions with meaning. The workers may well appreciate their products to be useful or even necessary to society and by that virtue also to themselves, but this understanding is in itself unlikely to motivate a particular level of work performance. The difficulty is that the requirements of industrial coordination define the immediate goals of work activity in terms of production statistics, and statistics are abstract figures which rarely command ready agreement as to their significance. The difference between x units of socially useful factory output per month and $x + dx$ units of socially useful factory output per month can be hardly expected to seem compelling enough to the worker who is at the point of having to motivate himself to repeat the same operation for the umpteenth time.

But it would be too hasty a conclusion to say that, because the product does not provide 'time-oriented' work with a sense of 'happy ending', the work activity becomes meaningless to the worker. It depends on whether there are other interpretative frameworks available to the worker than those of the factory production programme. This is where shopfloor culture comes in. The starting-point of its creation is the sense of endlessness in industrial work. As the purpose is to keep the process of production going, so the work is experienced as a process of keeping going, an activity of overcoming a resistance to itself, i.e making effort. What resistance is being overcome by industrial workers? Here I can draw upon an analysis offered by W.G. Baldamus, where the effort of industrial work is understood to be a combination of three kinds of deprivation.[10] First, there is 'impairment', i.e. the feeling of physical pain and strain; secondly, and especially important in machinofacture, there is 'tedium' – the mental resistance to recommencing the cycles of repetitive work; and finally, 'weariness' – the general fatigue by which the coercive nature of work routines, 'doing time day in day out', makes itself felt.

Each of these deprivations tends to get mitigated, to a varying degree, by a derivative kind of 'relative satisfaction'. The person who knows 'impairment' may also find periods of relief in 'inurement', the agreeable perception of 'getting used' to harsh physiological conditions. The person who has to put up with 'tedium' may be helped along by 'traction', a feeling of being kept going by a momentum that seems inherent within the operational cycles of repetitive work. And, the person who suffers 'weariness' is likely to find periodic refuge in 'contentment', the 'working moods' born of resigning oneself to inescapable necessities. Now comes an important point: it is a prominent feature of the last two kinds of deprivation that the mitigations obtained from 'traction' and 'contentment' are unstable; time drags or flies, oppressive repetition alternates with soothing rhythm, being tired of it all with being in the mood, the acuteness of coercive work realities grows or diminishes without warning or reason. Thus the passing of time-in-work is experienced as effort of fluctuating intensity.[11]

Parting ways with Baldamus to some extent, I note that the fluctuating intensity of effort experience has two consequences. First, if the worker understands his being at work as giving effort to production, his experience of what is being given does not always correspond to the instituted measurements of his work performance (or indeed any other putative measures of energy expenditure). Secondly, if the making of effort is experienced with a fluctuating intensity, the sense of what is being made is quantitative; more or less, so much in the last hour and so much in the hour before, almost as if effort were divisible into precise units of measurement. Although this is not possible, the experience of giving effort needs a quantitative language to be adequately communicated and objectified in social evaluations. The quantitative nature of money therefore makes it peculiarly apposite a form of reward for industrial work.

The intensities of effort experience do not fluctuate in ways which are entirely arbitrary. They are partly patterned by cultural contexts. Monday mornings, for example, are likely to be harder for most workers than Wednesday mornings. What is, however, more important from our point of view is that some work activities come to be known by workers as having objective properties in the sense of requiring consistently more effort than others. In some cases such differences will be known by workers to obtain between jobs which otherwise appear to be very similar to each other. This phenomenon can be illustrated by an experiment in which a job of wrapping chocolates was compared with the job of unwrapping the same chocolates.[12] Although very similar as regards repetitiveness, acheivable speeds and the required skills, the job of unwrapping was regarded by workers as much more tedious than wrapping. This was because sticky paper called for occasional corrections within the cycles of unwrapping. Although not in themselves particularly demanding on time or manual dexterity, having to make the corrections spoiled any momentum that would have otherwise made the act of picking up to unwrap the next chocolate easier. Unwrapping allowed less 'traction' than wrapping and therefore was experienced as more tedious, demanding more effort to carry on with it.

This kind of experience of differences between shopfloor jobs constitutes a major topic in workers' conversations in the course of which the different jobs become known as relatively easy or difficult. The knowledge of 'local conditions' which is thus generated forms the basis for an indigenous shopfloor culture and also a counterpart to the 'official' knowledge which is inscribed in the explicit rules and standards produced by management. The more bureaucratic forms of management such as Taylorism will be especially productive of the shopfloor-cultural sense of difference beween official truths and practical realities. But there is more to shopfloor culture than creating local knowledge. It also creates a human context which makes the endlessness of 'time-oriented' work habitable. This it does by creating a sense of values around the self-consciousness of giving effort. The significance of the local knowledge is in the creation and upholding of the worth of workers' efforts, i.e. the standards of effort value. In this context, it becomes a matter of justice and morality that the conduct of work on the shopfloor is organized according to standards which take into account the local knowledge of effort contents. Thus in the chocolates example, shopfloor opinion would demand either that wrapping is done by seniors and unwrapping by juniors, or that workers of equal status get a fair mixture of both jobs, or that unwrapping is better paid than wrapping, or that it is done at a slower pace; management decisions taken in disregard of these demands would be considered unreasonable and unfair.

Some factory shopfloor cultures have been immortalized in ethnographic studies. The studies of work in a Chicago engineering plant that were carried out by D. Roy in the 1940s are of particular interest because the plant was clearly very similar in its production engineering and organization to many of the production lines that had been set up in the Soviet Union during the previous decade.[13] The studies provide a detailed description of the interactional processes whereby workers evaluated piece-rated jobs in terms of two categories, 'stinkers' and 'gravy', and converted these evaluations into informal but effective standards of performance. 'Stinkers' were subject to a slow-down below the pace which corresponded to the minimum hourly wage while 'gravy' was worked at a premium-earning pace, taking care, however, not to exceed the rates of output which were locally considered to be an invitation to management to revise the piece-rates. It was a matter of pride to be able to earn the full permissible premium on all 'gravy' jobs without undue sweating. This was achieved not only by technical skill but also by the manipulation of accountancy procedures which enabled workers to transfer their time from one job to another without official knowledge. An attempt by management to prevent such cross-bookings by the re-imposition of formal controls over workers' access to tools and set-up gadgets was quickly thwarted by the deliberate creation of organizational bottlenecks. Workers in effect converted the payment-by-results scheme into a process which provided them with a regular weekly pay and at the same time filled the otherwise monotonous work with the interest of a point-scoring game. The dollars-and-cents language of shopfloor talk did not signify an income-maximizing behaviour so much as it served a culture which regulated work performance and generated its own rewards as the playing of a game does.[14]

The same plant became the subject of another ethnographic study 30 years later, by M. Burawoy.[15] Time had not stood still: shopfloor vocabulary changed to some extent, as did some aspects of organization and behaviour; the presence of time-study engineers on the shopfloor was now rare, and workers were more competitive against each other in trying to secure gravy jobs for themselves than they had been in Roy's time. But the essential culture of effort-valuation and performance regulation, or 'the game of making out' in the language learnt by Burawoy, very much remained:

In my own case, it took me some time to understand the shop language, let alone the intricacies of making out. It was a matter of three or four months before I began to make out by using a number of angles and by transferring time from one operation to another. Once I knew I had a chance to make out, the rewards of participating in a game in which the outcomes were uncertain absorbed my attention, and I found myself spontaneously cooperating with management in the production of greater surplus value. Moreover, it was only in this way that I could establish relationships with others on the shop floor. Until I was able to strut around the floor like an experienced operator, as if I had all the time in the world and could still make out, few but the greenest would condescend to engage me in conversation. Thus, it was in terms of the culture of making out that individuals evaluated one another and themselves.[16]

Burawoy's satisfactions in achieving cultural competence

on the shopfloor were very similar to those that had been described by Roy. Burawoy, however, also noticed that the shopfloor culture formed attitudes to managers:

Operators at Allied continually complained about 'being screwed' by the company, and initially I associated this with some vague notion of exploitation. Soon I discovered that such anguish referred to the company's failure to provide the necessary conditions to play the game of making out; for example, drills might have burned up, the blueprint might have disappeared, the machinery might not have been functioning properly, etc. In other words, the management was being accused of 'cheating', of not playing according to the rules of the game; and these accusations served to reassert the legitimacy of the rules and the values of making out.[17]

There is an important deduction to be made from this observation. If such organizational mishaps occur, which they often do especially at busy times, how do shopfloor managers re-establish their reputation for competence and fair play? Even if some may be tough-minded individuals willing to be unpopular, they know workers' ability to turn the production process into an unproductive chaos at the drop of a hat. Shopfloor managers therefore have to secure their workers' cooperation by implicating themselves in the anti-official practices of the making-out game. They help workers to make out by letting them bend some of the formal rules of bureaucratic organization. This aspect of shopfloor management becomes particularly poignant during efficiency drives, which invariably originate above the shopfloor level. Roy's example where the tightening of rules governing workers' access to the tool room was thwarted showed shopfloor managers conniving with the workers' counter-campaign.[18] Burawoy witnessed a more ambitious efficiency drive which likewise failed to make any impression on the actual working standards of shopfloor performance; he was in fact persuaded by what he saw of shop management practice during this episode to conclude that efficiency drives were better viewed as a dynamic of conflict between shop management and higher management than between workers and management.[19] Another industrial sociologist, A. Gouldner, also found the 'indulgency pattern of bureaucracy' at the shopfloor level, and the campaigns from above against it, to be a central theme in shopfloor relations.[20]

This reflects a conflict of managerial objectives which is an unavoidable aspect of industrial organization. The ability to coordinate work so that the production lines keep moving makes the achievement of regular and predictable patterns of workers' performance one important objective. The ability of the organization to adapt itself to a changing environment by raising its levels of performance if necessary is another managerial objective.[21] The achievement of regular patterns of performance requires a sort of equilibrium in shopfloor relations where the work performances are deemed to correspond with 'normal' effort values, which is inevitably disturbed by managerial attempts to intervene in established work practices. Shop managers are primarily responsible for the coordinative aspect of management, i.e. for the predictability of work performances, which they achieve to the extent that they show respect for the 'local knowledge' of work conditions generated by shopfloor cultures. As the people in charge of shopfloor peace, they welcome offences against the cultured sensibilities of shopfloor life no more than the workers in their charge; they therefore discourage rate-busting work and show their distance from the efficiency measures they are asked by their superiors to implement. From the point of view of higher managers, however, the existence of shopfloor 'custom and practice' may look like 'output restriction' and a lack of management control. Burawoy noted about the efficiency drive he witnessed in the Chicago plant that it failed to make any difference to the standards of effort value and work performance on the shopfloor, but it did produce a flutter of administrative activity which served as 'a ritual affirmation of managerial domination'.[22] Such crackdowns were recurrent events the neutralization of which was an integral part of competent practice by shopfloor managers.

If the management of labour requires a show of respect for the rules of the making out game which makes the passing of time in endless industrial work psychologically possible, competent shopfloor management is a cultural accomplishment as much as an application of production engineering science. This brings us back to an aspect of the science of setting objectively valid work methods and performance standards which is the linchpin of the Taylorist vision of rationality in work. The time-study man must be able to persuade the operators that his timings of their operations are practicable. If he fails to persuade them, he will be proven wrong by their results, for they will reduce effort. He must therefore try to set rates that they will find acceptable. We might say that his objective is to set rates at the 'tight' margin of the 'gravy' category, that is, rates which will not be too easy, but will be nevertheless deemed by workers to be worthy of their effort. But since the borderline between 'gravy' and 'stinkers' is negotiated in the process of shopfloor evaluation, the time engineer must have a 'feel' for this process to know what rate to set. That the result of this 'feel' is expressed in scientific-looking artefacts such as fatigue-factor coefficients does not change its source: the cultural competence of anticipating workers' judgements. It could be said that the successful time-study man borrows a watch from the workers to tell them the time.

But the time-study man is usually sent to do his job in the course of raising efficiency standards, which makes it more difficult for him to connive with 'restrictive practice' on the shopfloor than it is for the shop manager. His participation in shopfloor culture is therefore framed within a ritualized game where the measured workers make convincing displays of sweaty brow and he makes a display of his ability to see the reality behind the show. This is where bargaining over the price of a hypothetical unit of effort is most dramatically evident. It would be a war if it was not a game, and a game must give a chance of winning to both sides if it is to be played again. Interestingly, Roy found that just over one-half of the job-batches passing through during his time on the shopfloor were considered to be 'gravy'.[23] Here it is worth recalling that, unlike in football, the results of rate-setting games are the product of post-battle interpretations.

It is possible for the participants in the rate-setting game to show a consciousness of the ritual aspects of their interaction, in which case the conflict of interest over the price of effort could be nicely channelled into humorous variants of the play. The feelings towards the time-study men in Roy's account, however, were mainly hostile, so that it is not surprising that rate-setting was one of the practices that changed by the time Burawoy got to the plant. Rate-setting was now enacted with a minimum of prowling by men with stopwatches, the preferred framework being one of an implicit agreement that some rates would get revised from time to time, but these revisions would be restricted to the rates proven to be 'too loose' by a consistent performance record exceeding 140 per cent of the set rate.[24]

I have already mentioned above that Burawoy did report an efficiency campaign, complete with re-timings and attempted rationalizations of the work methods, the effects of which fell victim to skilful manipulations of administrative accounting by shopfloor managers. This defence of shopfloor custom was successful despite the fact that the efficiency campaign was a response to an economic downturn which threatened redundancies in the company while making the labour markets in general unfavourable to workers. The campaign made a difference to the discipline of coming to work – absenteeism and tardiness decreased substantially – but it was not able to penetrate the activities of the work process itself.[25] The lesson to be drawn must be that the shopfloor culture asserted itself against outside intervention in those areas of activity where a sense of unfairness was keenly felt and a sense of fairness the result of delicate, tacit but practical agreements about two interrelated issues: first, the value of activities in terms of their effort content and secondly, the rules of the game of making out.

To recapitulate: the mass production of things by machinofacture is enabled by a complex coordination of work activities in time, in which context the practical purpose of work appears to be to keep the process of production going at some statistically defined rate of progression. This purpose tends to be experienced as being less real than the effort of serving it. Sociability at work is therefore grounded in the shared experience of effort expenditure in time-disciplined work. It creates a culture of effort valuation which defines justice in terms of effort equity and accordingly organizes members' responses to the official definitions and requirements concerning shopfloor jobs and conditions. Industrial work thus becomes cultured, its practical organization being endowed with an interpretative framework which makes human adaptation to the rigours of factory discipline possible. The framework may resemble the rules of a 'making out' game which channels conflict over the value of effort while providing a scope for individual ingenuity. It creates a sense of distinction between official notions and practical reality in the production process, and cultivates the arts of neutralizing the effects of official interventions in the practical organization of shopfloor work.

In this argument, shopfloor culture is seen as indigenous to *industrial* organization rather than to its political and economic environment. Without wishing to deny the significance of labour markets, trade unions or revolutionary ideologies in workers' lives, my contention is that none of these factors actually defines the social process of working in a factory. Labour markets shape the worker's affairs when he is looking for a job or considering to quit, trade unions may play a part when it is time to negotiate his contractual terms, revolutionary ideology may allocate his place when it is time to stand on barricades. But none of these factors normally determines the structure of passing the time in factory work, not unless the work has stopped. At work time, the source of sociability is the shared experience of time-oriented work. The continued existence of this sociability does not depend on the political fortunes of other working-class institutions such as the trade unions, and it plays an important part in the social order that makes industry possible. Shopfloor culture is the informally organized response of workers to the managerial organization of 'industrial culture'.

It is often argued against the concept of shopfloor culture that it is too narrowly industrial, or too 'technologically deterministic', by creating an unrealistic boundary between the shopfloor and the life in the great world outside the factory gates. It seems plausible that workers remain the same people both in and out of the factory, so that their behaviour at work is influenced by their ethnic background, religious or ideological beliefs, sex, age, marital status and education. Burawoy tested this hypothesis and found that the 'external factors' correlate in fact less closely with work performance than 'internal factors' such as the worker's seniority or position within the division of labour on the shopfloor. The results of regression analysis of work behaviour are supported in this respect by ethnographic studies of 'race relations' on the shopfloor, which show that while ethnic divisions are evident in break-time groupings and conversational banter, they do not affect the practical activities of shopfloor life; whether the banter is humorous or hostile depends on the divisions and alliances which stem from workers' positions in the organization of work rather than from their racial identities.[26] It is not inappropriate therefore to assume that the activities of industrial work have a distinctive cultural aspect of their own, the makings of which might be present in the factories of Stalingrad as well as Chicago.

SOVIET WORKERS AND THE CAMPAIGNS FOR LABOUR DISCIPLINE, 1929–35

A newspaper article published in March 1933 was one of many giving a vivid picture of what the official fight for 'industrial culture' was up against. An iron-smelting plant was producing a metal of faulty quality which was causing breakages in the products made of it. An on-the-spot inspection did not take long to identify one of the causes: a group of workers was feeding a blast furnace with insufficiently refined ore. There was a heap of good-quality ore there, but it was further away for the workers to go to with their wheelbarrows than the low-quality material. The workers could be hardly expected to realize the consequences of taking the raw material from one heap rather than another; 70 per cent of the furnace operators had joined the plant only in the previous six months and they received no training. The latter just seemed too difficult to organize at the prevailing labour turnover rate, especially since what used to be skilled workers were now harassed junior managers desperately chasing after the basic supplies to keep the plant in operation.[27]

In this story, the inconvenient positioning of the good-quality ore suggests that it was supplied more recently than the insufficiently refined material. It would seem then that the workers were either allowed or instructed to use the low-quality material before the arrival of the good ore. If this was so, it would be difficult for the foremen to tell them to stop using it and commence braving the long and obstacle-ridden path to the newly arrived lot, especially if the work was paid by piece-rates, or, as also might have been the case, there were not enough workers to sustain the longer supply route without a drastic increase in effort. The ex-worker foreman was certainly not seen to insist; he was in fact keeping well out of his men's way, sheltering from the winter cold. 'What can you do with them?' he said.[28]

The story illustrates three points which defined Soviet industrial reality in contrast to the clockwork utopia of 'industrial culture'. Taut planning and inexperienced management are two points already familiar from the last chapter. That the wrong heap of supplies was the one in the most convenient position was clearly a phenomenon of misplanning or mismanagement, as was probably the fact that the workers were untrained and unsettled. The third point is that Soviet workers were by all accounts neither meek nor unnaturally obsessive about the rules of factory discipline. The foreman knew better than to interfere with the workers' desire to do a fair day's work on the fairly positioned heap. The workplace chaos that was caused in Soviet industry by the vagaries of taut-plan management was not the context in which managers could easily teach workers the virtues of factory discipline. On the other hand, it was hard for managers to improve organization if they could not rely on workers to turn up in a fit state and do as told.

This was something of a vicious circle that had to be broken if the war 'on the production front' was not to end in defeat. The standards of labour discipline were therefore considered a serious issue for the industrialization campaign, as indicated in this quotation from the pages of the journal for trade unionists:

The discipline of labour is the most important condition of increases in labour productivity. Without making sure of strict socialist work discipline, it is not possible to expect a rise in the productivity of labour, fast economic growth of our country and the strengthening of the dictatorship of the proletariat.[29]

Labour discipline had in fact seldom been off the agenda in Soviet public affairs and it would have been surprising not to find it discussed with renewed verve as the first five year plan got under way. An article published in the journal of the People's Commissariat for Labour itemized 'the strongest forms' of the problem as 'drunkenness, unwarranted absenteeism, hooliganism, tardiness, sleep at work, arguments with and beatings of specialists, deliberate reductions of productivity, absenteeism on religious holidays, thefts and general violations of discipline'.[30]

A special government commission (*kommissiya VSNKh RSFSR*) which was set up at the end of 1928 to investigate the causes of high production costs reported that these problems 'have become normal phenomena' and expressed no doubt that this was due to 'the influx of new, essentially peasant cadres, together with the high turnover caused by them'.[31] Here it is worth noting that 1928 was the year of the Shakhty trial which started the witch-hunt against 'wreckers' in the ranks of 'bourgeois specialist' managers and engineers, who must have been therefore relieved to find that the 'essentially peasant cadres' on the shopfloors were also blamed for industrial problems. Pointing the finger at the yokels (*derevenshchiki*) in manual jobs was a relatively peaceful act in the circumstances, because they knew no better and their misdemeanours were not treated as counter-revolutionary crimes by the organs of proletarian vigilance.

The connection between peasant backgrounds and slack labour discipline was frequently asserted in the managerial press in the first half of the industrialization decade, but the evidence for it was not entirely convincing, even if it were to be accepted that the old 'core' (*kadrovye*) workers were as likely to have their misbehaviour officially recorded as the new 'raw' workers. Statistical breakdowns of recorded offences against factory rules according to the culprits' background tended to omit the data from which it could be seen whether ex-peasant workers in fact accounted for more than their fair share of indiscipline, and, when such data were available, the disproportion in some cases turned out on closer inspection to be a matter of no more than a few per cent.[32] Overall attendance records, which were the most readily available quantitative index of discipline standards, also failed to support the emphasis on the peasant factor. The average industrial worker apparently had eight days of unexcused absence from work on his attendance record for the year 1925/26, compared to six days in 1927/28 and six days in 1931, but the proportion of new workers from the countryside on factory shopfloors had been low in 1925/26 compared to 1927/28 or 1931.[33] Some articles did acknowledge that absenteeism was committed by old 'core' (*kadrovye*) workers and 'shock workers' as well as the young newcomers to industrial work.[34]

It would be wrong to take attendance statistics too literally. It was not uncommon for shopfloor managers to excuse their workers' absences retrospectively, or to regard them as legitimate days off in lieu of overtime, in which case they would not get counted in absence rates at all. In addition, the high rates of labour turnover (in excess of 100 per cent per year during the first five year plan) meant that a high proportion of workers in each factory had been on the payroll for less than a year, creating methodological difficulties for the reliable calculation of average annual absence rates, countering which would have required much more ordered and sophisticated record-keeping than was by all accounts typical. It is possible that absences were on the increase during the first five year plan, but so was the general economic chaos which made unerring attendance in the workplace an unfeasible proposition for most workers. In a situation where production often ground to a halt due to organizational breakdowns and the provision of necessities forced workers to queue outside offices and retail outlets during work hours, it seemed reasonable to workers to expect that if they had to miss one shift they could simply make it up by attending the next one without any disciplinary implications.[35]

Instilling respect for the formal requirements of factory discipline was a theme which had three distinctive peaks during the industrialization decade. One was in the first half of 1929, when two government decrees were issued to entitle managers to sack workers for clear breaches of factory rules without prior warning.[36] The second was in 1932–33, when the main legislative event was a decree which *obliged* managers to sack workers with immediate effect for a single day of unauthorized absence; a late arrival could count as an absence in certain circumstances, according to this decree.[37] The third peak of labour discipline campaigning was in 1938–41, including a decree which made a single day's absence, or indeed reporting to work more than 20 minutes late, an offence punishable by three months in a labour camp.[38] Each of these campaigns was notable for producing an abundance of evidence testifying to a pronounced managerial reluctance to implement these decrees.

The enforcement campaign that took place in 1929 evidently produced numerous reprimands and occasional fines but, by the winter months of that year, sackings for unauthorized absence became, by all accounts, so rare that workers seemed quite indifferent as to whether their absences would be excused. 'Put down "absenteeism" [*progul*] until the 15th, I have to make hay,' a worker said to a shopfloor time-keeper, according to one of hundreds similar reports in the scandalized press.[39] Absenteeism on 'religious holidays' was particularly common according to the press reports during the first five year plan,[40] which was not surprising in the context of 'uninterrupted week' regimes where some working families might have never managed to have a free day together if they had not decided to make a point of it; honouring the occasional Sunday, Christmas and Easter must have seemed a nice thing to do even to workers from atheist backgrounds.

But workers' predilection for taking the occasional extra day off and managers' reluctance to do much about it remained an issue for the industrial campaigners even when 'uninterrupted week' schedules became abandoned in favour of weekly closing days.[41] The unequivocal wording of the decree on absenteeism that was issued in November 1932 clearly meant to put an end to managerial tolerance of attendance indiscipline. Apart from the mandatory sacking for a single day's unjustified absence, the decree required that the sacked workers should return any ration cards that had been issued to them by the factory and vacate 'immediately' their accommodation if it was owned by the factory, 'regardless of the time of year' and whether the worker had anywhere to go. If the worker appealed against the sacking to the factory disputes commission, the appeal was to be ruled on within three days.[42] The decree thus made it theoretically possible for a worker who overslept on Monday to be out of job, without a roof over her head and without any ration cards, before the week's end.[43]

The campaigning press reported the decree to have provoked 'class enemies' to show their colours. The chairmen of factory meetings at which the decree was introduced evidently had the thankless task of coping with comments such as: 'They won't provide you with protective clothing at work, but will evict you from home if you go absent for a day!'; 'They demand discipline but feed you badly'; 'The government does not care about workers – we have to go absent from work to get to the shops to buy necessities.'[44] The bosses on the rostrum were told: 'You live well yourselves, yet you keep hassling workers to give more, more and more'; and, 'Why don't you chain us to the production line, you might as well!'.[45] 'Mass absences from work', to quote the press euphemism for strikes, were organized in reply to delays in the payment of wages (such delays were common occurrence at the time), cows belonging to factory-owned farms were slaughtered by sacked absentees who bore a grudge, personnel offices were looted for attendance records, and, 'fighters against absenteeism' were subjected to treatment ranging from ridicule and ostracism to physical assaults, reported the vigilant press.[46]

A short note of caution deserves to be inserted here. The reports of violent protest against the decree, such as physical assaults, looting and the slaughter of factory-farm livestock, were usually written as illustrations of the general thesis that the decree was particularly disliked by 'class enemies' such as the kulaks (viz. the 'slaughter of cows' stories) who would do anything against the ideals of 'socialist labour discipline', even terrorize other workers and sabotage their sources of food. In other words, stories of violent extremist opposition by alien elements within the new working class were printed to discredit all expressions of opposition by workers against the decree, in which case it would be incautious to interpret them as evidence of a wave of violent protest sweeping across industry. By contrast, vocal expressions of opinion by workers at meetings about their conditions of work and pay, and about productivity measures such as the decrees on discipline, were quite typical, judging by the language of such reports which sometimes conveyed a semi-humorous undertone of familiarity: e.g. 'weavers made a noise' (*tkachi zashumeli*), as a description of workers' response to the introduction of a rationalization measure which initially threatened their ability to make out.[47]

The numerous reports about implementation that filled the pages of the industrial press in the months following the issue of the decree were conspicuous by the absence of a single shining example of a manager who could be seen by all to be implementing the decree in the required uncompromising manner. Evidence of 'liberal-opportunistic attitudes to the decree' by the 'appeasers' in managerial ranks, on the other hand, abounded.[48] Motivated by a desire 'not to damage (shopfloor) relations', shopfloor managers simply classified many absences as legitimate.[49] This was done almost automatically by time-clerks on some shopfloors, while elsewhere it was the foremen who turned absences into 'days off in lieu of overtime' or 'absences for worthy reasons'.[50] Inspections found 'worthy reasons' to include many funerals of semi-distant relatives and many trips to shops and offices on urgent personal business.[51] A 'worthy reason' could be having to stay in bed nursing a hangover inflicted by an earnest attempt to cure a cold by medicinal vodka, let alone having to chase a flat-mate who had absconded with a bag of potatoes.[52] Not surprisingly, statistical counts of attendance discipline registered a sharp drop in unexcused absences and a rise in the 'worthy reason' ones in the months following the issue of the decree, just as they had done during the previous campaign in 1929.[53]

Absences which were classified as illegitimate were referred to senior managers who were supposedly given no choice by the decree but to dismiss the culprits.[54] But this was by no means what always happened, as the counts of guilty absentees matched the counts of sackings only in a minority of factories, according to a survey which found a substantial excess of guilty workers over sacked workers in most factories.[55] The famous Stalingrad Tractor Works, where there was a large castings shop with workers allegedly failing to report to work once a week on average, evidently punished by dismissal only 30 per cent of the absences it classified as illegitimate.[56] Many managers feigned ignorance of the fact that the decree made dismissal a mandatory punishment for a single day's absence, and referred culprits to 'production-comradely courts' that had no powers to inflict 'administrative penalties' such as dismissal.[57] In some cases, managers fired workers for absences, but then tried to arrange their reinstatement via the 'production-comradely courts', although this was not something that the 'courts' were supposed to be able to do, devoid as they were of any legal or administrative powers.[58] Some errant workers were fired and then immediately rehired, in direct contravention of one of the clauses of the decree.[59]

Managers were often reported to admit openly that they were reluctant to implement the decree. Some factories had established their own ways of dealing with the absenteeism problem (deducting double wages for illegitimate absence, awarding monthly bonuses for full attendance record), with which the managers did not want the decree to interfere.[60] Some managers simply pointed out that they could not afford to lose workers and that 'there would be no workers left' if they enforced the decree to the full.[61] It was an interesting feature of the times that the burden of campaigning against the 'liberal-opportunistic sabotage' of the decree by managers fell on the shoulders of trade union officials in the factories whose attempts to do their bit against the 'sabotage' brought them the ultimate indignity of the obvious rebuke from the managers: 'sacking is managers' business and trade unions ought to defend workers, not persecute them'.[62]

Contrary to the letter of the decree, the workers who were sacked on its basis were unlikely to have their ration cards confiscated; only 10 per cent of sacked absentees had to return their factory ration cards, according to a survey carried out in Azerbaidzhan in December 1932.[63] Apart from the fact that getting ration cards back from dismissed workers could not have been easy in any case, some managers had reservations about the wisdom of condemning people to having to find scarce food on the free market and pay unsubsidized prices for it. 'I can't take his ration card from him,' a manager was reported to have said about an absentee who had just been duly fired, 'he is an old worker!'[64] The dismissed workers were even less likely to have to face eviction. Only 0.4 per cent of the dismissed workers were evicted according to the Azerbaidzhan survey, while cases were reported from all corners of the USSR of factory-owned accommodation being still occupied by workers who had been fired. According to a story printed at the beginning of February, a factory housing estate near Moscow included 70 dismissed workers among its inhabitants who were reassured by the 'estate commandant' that their tenancy was secure until May.[65] Although the decree was supposed to override any rights of tenure given to tenants by earlier legislation, it seems that, when managers did try to go into the trouble of enforcing eviction orders on dismissed employees to find accommodation for the deserving ones still in the housing queue, they could not rely on the police to help; this despite the fact that the decree explicitly made the eviction orders subject to police enforcement if necessary.[66] Most managers simply preferred not to know if some dismissed employees remained resident on factory-owned premises.[67]

It also seemed a common practice to enter 'redundancy' in dismissed workers' records, so that there were no implications for length-of-service entitlements and no obstacles to finding another employment within the industrial sector.[68] Conversely, managers showed little prejudice against hiring workers with questionable discipline records: 'Almost all enterprises take on workers dismissed from other enterprises for absenteeism,' complained the trade union journal in 1935.[69] In fact, it did not seem entirely unusual for workers to go absent with the specific aim of getting dismissed, to evade another government decree, according to which workers who left an industrial employer on their own accord for the second time within a year were supposed to come under a six-month ban from factory employment.[70]

It should come as no surprise that lateness was hardly ever registered as absenteeism.[71] And, in general, the decree on absenteeism was implemented in such a way as to enable 'class enemies' to spread false rumours that it had been revoked.[72] But there was a grain of truth in this rumour; the campaign against attendance indiscipline peaked in the winter of 1932–33 and then faded as the focus of media attention moved from the attendance–discipline problem to other labour-productivity issues. Absenteeism and tardiness came back into focus in 1938, when the problem was evidently still there and the government decided to have another go at solving it by edict.[73]

It is not necessary to speculate about compassionate motives managers might have had to account for their less than uncompromising attitude to the enforcement of official labour-discipline rules. Whatever the managers' feelings about their workers, the general state of industrial organization made enforcement zealotry inadvisable. It did not predispose workers to being tolerant when they were asked to work on their free days 'to save the plan'; to put up with erratic production flow which jeopardized their ability to pace themselves and make out; to queue for meagre food and necessities; to work on dirty or dangerous jobs without the prescribed protective clothing and equipment; and to put up with delays in wage payment. Literal implementation of the absenteeism decree could also cause red faces even in times of relative peace on the shopfloors; many of the absentees who were duly dismissed on the fourth day following their absence had to be reinstated when it transpired that it took doctors' notes more than three days to travel from the factory surgery to the personnel office.[74] Insistence on strict labour discipline would have made sense only where work organization was so well tuned that rigid discipline could be seen to have beneficial effects on production results. Where this was not so, 'uncompromising fighters for socialist labour discipline' were liable to be regarded as nasty or mad by shopfloor workers, managers and party members alike.[75]

There was, however, yet another reason to inhibit managers from taking up the disciplinarian mandate. The different branches of the party state did not always see things in the same way. This had been a strong aspect of the labour discipline problem during the first five year plan, when vigilance against 'bourgeois specialists' tended to cast doubt on the rectitude of managers who attempted to penalize indisciplined workers. In these circumstances, dismissed workers who used their rights of appeal often were successful in getting the dismissal quashed by Commissariat for Labour inspectorates or the courts. The press campaign for labour discipline duly included allegations of a 'certain tailism (*khvostism*)' on the part of these organs of the state and the advice to their staff that they should remember to approach problems 'not only from the point of view of defence of guilty workers, but mainly from the point of view of the damage caused by them, including the intangible aspects such as the bad influence of each violation on discipline standards in general'.[76] That 'guilty workers' continued to be reinstated on appeal[77] is perhaps most eloquently testified by the 1932 decree, which was clearly designed to make the offence of unauthorized absence carry the penalty of automatic dismissal without leaving room for managers to respond to pleas of mitigating circumstances.

It is notable therefore that despite its unequivocal wording, many of the workers who were dismissed under the new decree still found it possible to get reinstated on appeal to the courts or the Procuracy while the police did not enforce eviction orders against dismissed workers resident in factory-owned housing. Although witch-hunts of 'bourgeois specialists' were no longer encouraged by official party policy, and despite the fact that the managerial corps were now in large part men from good proletarian backgrounds, many local law-enforcement agencies remained sufficiently preoccupied with suspicions of managerial abuses to be accused by the managerial press of 'disorganizing production'.[78] Managers could not rely on the guardians of law and order to support their point of view in disputes over individual workers' rights; after all, the decree on absenteeism was but one of thousands of legislative expressions of the state's will, many of which were in conflict with one another.

The law was in fact still in two minds as to whether it should judge people by their acts or their class membership and political allegiance. The terms of the labour discipline campaign also stressed the disorganizing role of 'class enemies', although it was often acknowledged that 'good workers', shock workers and *komsomol* members also acted in breach of labour discipline.[79]

The struggles against slackers and go-getters on the shopfloors are now the reflections of the wider class struggle. We can see clearly that slackers and grabbers are not just dark and backward workers, but, not unusually, they are a socially alien and in some cases indeed enemy element in pursuit of exerting anti-proletarian influence in the factory: kulak supporters or indeed kulaks themselves, or former traders etc.

Conflicts arising from labour discipline cases must be approached in a social, class-oriented manner, not in a limited, formally judicial manner.[80]

If ordinary ex-peasants or indeed 'core' workers indulged in absenteeism and other acts of indiscipline, this was taken as a sign that management and the mobilizing agencies in the factory were failing in their 'work with the masses', in which case a simple application of administrative penalties was not the answer. It was less controversial to dismiss the culprits if they happened to be people whose class allegiance could be shown to be suspect. That 'many managers and administrators often dismissed good employees on the basis of formal records such as social origins, court sentences served, etc.' was something that the Commission for Soviet Control would make a point of criticizing in 1936.[81]

The decree on absenteeism was followed by a reduction in the statistics of days lost to illegitimate absences from six in 1932 to less than one in the following years.[82] The total number of days off work, however, did not seem to be falling. In Leningrad heavy industry, where the situation may well have been better than in less privileged sectors, absence statistics showed a rise from 5.3 per cent of total working time in 1932 to 5.7 per cent in 1934, representing some 17 days spent off work by the average worker.[83] The single most important item in these losses was illness. According to a survey carried out in heavy industry in 1936, sickness benefit was paid to cover 874 days per 100 insured employees in 1929, 715 days in 1933, 1056 days in 1934 and 1130 days per 100 insured workers in 1935.[84] The upward trend evidently continued in 1936.[85] Not all workers were insured, since not all were members of trade unions, and those who were did not get sickness payments on every occasion they fell ill.[86] The quoted figures are therefore smaller than the actual average numbers of days lost to illness.

It is difficult to judge whether the absences due to illness were excessive. The age profile of the labour force could have given grounds for optimism as to its general health, but nutrition was low in 1932–33, accommodation was overcrowded, heating was often inadequate and so were the standards of sanitation. There were epidemics of malaria and influenza, and it is worth remembering that antibiotics including penicillin were still unknown to medical science.[87] Industrial injuries, too, were adding to the toll. According to the survey of sickness payments in heavy industry, the average worker spent two days per year recovering from industrial injuries.[88] Accident rates varied widely between industries, ranging from 53 accidents (necessitating a sick leave) per 1000 workers in a typical textile mill to 260 accidents per 1000 workers in an automobile plant.[89] However, it seemed plausible to suspicious minds that crackdowns on illegitimate absenteeism encouraged some workers to give themselves extra days off by a bit of sick-role playing. The activities reported from 'the-fight-against-absenteeism front' occasionally included spot checks on sick workers to catch malingerers,[90] but the pressure was directed mainly against doctors who were said to be prone to 'giving away sickness certificates as if they were not financial documents'.[91] Clinics in neighbouring factories were compared for average length of prescribed sick-leave, as were individual doctors, many of whom came under criticism for diagnostic habits which were thought to be costly in lost work-days.[92] There is little evidence as to what effect this campaign had on the general work-attendance rate.

Overall, most workers needed the wages and it is unlikely that they were quite as anarchic in their approach to attendance discipline as was indicated by the most alarmist reports in the campaigning press. The problems of labour discipline and efficiency, however, only began when the shopfloor time-keepers did their roll-calls and found the workers to be present. To start with, there was the behaviour categorized as 'technological indiscipline', which constituted a frequent topic in the campaigning media from the beginning of the first five year plan until the summer of 1935. The industrial press was full of alarming reports from factories said to be coming to a standstill with broken-down machines 'which had suffered a barbaric treatment'.[93] The Stalingrad Tractor Works appeared in need of 'not medium but capital repairs' on its machinery after two years of operation; an open-hearth furnace managed on average less than 200 smelting cycles between major repairs instead of the normal 350–400 cycles; the equipment of a coke plant had to be scrapped entirely after a mere 14 months of operation.[94] And, when the expensive imported machinery was working, the goods at the end of the production line were often found to be of substandard quality. Collective farm fields were reported littered with immobile tractors, in some sections of a new automobile truck works shoddy output amounted to between one-half and three-quarters of the total, while 'most production' of an equally new and American-equipped cotton mill was said to be defective in quality.[95]

At the initial stages of the first five year plan, reports on this theme sometimes included examples of wilful sabotage, such as the introduction of large nails or indeed shot-gun cartridges into the raw material to wreck the processing machinery.[96] Some of the reports by western workers and engineers also alleged that deliberate sabotage was a frequent occurrence, although others thought that the 'wrecking' motive was overplayed in the press and good direct evidence of it was hard to come by.[97] In any case, 'wrecking' in the sense of a politically motivated action was considered by the organs of revolutionary vigilance to be something that few manual workers would want to indulge in. Thus, according to a western memoir of working in a Leningrad factory, a party investigation of a wrecked machine immediately sought to clarify the matter by attempting to find out if there was a kulak's son among the people who had access to the machine. This is how the plant party secretary explained his class-based vision of the likely suspect:

Who else? It couldn't possibly be a workman, and one of the poor peasants would not do such a thing, no, not even if he was religious and refused to work on a collective farm. His class instinct is too strong to let him contemplate sabotage.[98]

An authoritative article in the managerial press on the subject concurred with this line of thought, but at the same time took care to indicate that workers were in fact to blame for equipment breakdowns which were not always caused by accidents occasioned by poor management.

We assume that, given the presence in our factories of many 'former people', it is possible to explain some of the wrecking in terms of counter-revolutionary motivation, but such cases are not numerous.
A study of data collected in the Moscow region gives grounds for believing that, essentially, the wrecking that has been taking place in our factories is the consequence of: (1) hooligan motivation on part of irresponsible workers; (2) resentment at the establishment of new, at times less advantageous, conditions governing wage earnings; (3) wishes to take it easy and enjoy additional periods of rest; and (4) protests against rationalisation, the tightening of the workday etc.[99]

This type of 'hooligan', i.e. 'not counter-revolutionary', motivation was said to be behind even the blatant cases of wilful damage, such as when the cause was someone having emptied a packet of large nails into the raw material. When such 'hooligan motivation' could be proved, dismissal seemed to be the most usual penalty, evidently without any prejudice to the dismissed worker's chances of finding a job in another factory.[100] Some of the more extreme cases were prosecuted in the courts as 'production hooliganism'.[101]

But the large majority of cases of excessive wear and tear on equipment, and of shoddy output, could not be seen to be due to wilful damage. Rather, the problem was believed to be largely due to generally slack standards of 'technological discipline', i.e. workers' failure to follow the prescribed operational procedures, if such were indeed available for the workers to follow. The enforcement of 'technological discipline' was therefore considered an integral part of the drive for industrial efficiency. Factory rules provided for the usual range of 'administrative penalties' from reprimands and warnings to deductions from wages and dismissal.[102] Alternatively, offenders could be referred to the 'production-comradely courts' which were empowered to impose small fines (up to 10 roubles) and payments for damages (up to 50 roubles), or to make recommendations to the management of more severe penalties.[103] The main function of the 'courts', however, was to deter workers from indiscipline by creating adverse publicity for offenders. The 'courts' organized special exhibits at works entrances where pictures of offenders and graphic illustrations of the damage they had caused were displayed: the offenders might be 'sentenced' by the 'courts' to being present at the exhibitions during rush-hour periods, or to broadcasting over the works loudspeakers what they had done and how it would never happen again.[104]

An uncompromising 'fight for technological discipline' was liable to run into the usual difficulties born of the general chaos that appeared to rule on the shopfloors, especially during the first five year plan. Thus a lathe operator whose cutting tools lasted on average one hour instead of the supposed six hours, causing him to spend 80 minutes per shift in queues for replacement tools,[105] might have been able effectively to defend himself by alleging a substandard quality of the tools (especially if they were Soviet-made), or inappropriate quality of the worked-on metal (raw material was known to vary in quality), or he might admit that he had reset the lathe to work at unauthorized high speeds but argue that this was necessary if he was to make a living on the piece-rates, given the prevalent work conditions. Since any one of these arguments would have had a good chance of sounding plausible to fellow workers, it was not easy for managers, or the organizers of 'production-comradely courts', to find clear-cut cases of 'technological indiscipline' suitable for exemplary punishment. This point was well illustrated by a survey of seven large factories in Leningrad, in which an attempt was made to cost the losses due to shoddy output, and to divide these costs into those caused by workers, foremen and production engineers respectively. Workers were found to be responsible for 37 per cent of the damage overall, but this percentage ranged from 4 to 69 per cent in the answers given by individual factories.[106] I believe that this disparity reflected the ambiguities involved in attributing responsibility for shoddy production, because the actual behaviour of workers in neighbouring factories was unlikely to be so radically different. Shopfloor managers were sometimes explicitly accused by the press of being prone to classifying breakdowns and shoddy production as due to other reasons than shoddy work by their own workers, 'to avoid arguments and keep good relations'.[107]

Press reports about 'the strengthening of technological discipline' were certainly similar to those about the absenteeism problem in supplying abundant evidence of managerial inaction. The lathe operator who blunted six cutting tools within the time envisaged for blunting just one evidently was not bothered by anyone for getting through them so fast, and it was very unusual for workers to incur financial penalties for causing breakdowns or making shoddy products.[108] When financial responsibility of this kind was introduced in some factories as a special feature of 'cost accounting' (*khozraschet*), it proved impossible to implement and had to be withdrawn in the interest of 'workplace atmosphere'.[109] It was found in fact that not even a 50 per cent rate of shoddy output necessarily disqualified a worker from being declared a 'hero of the five year plan', while in some factories the party organization was reduced to trying to improve the situation by getting one-half of the workers to be 'good-quality producers', thus effectively giving up altogether on the other half.[110]

Like the campaign against absenteeism, the campaign for a 'precise and regular utilization of equipment' reached its peak in 1933.[111] Workers were asked to learn 'forethought, no panic and a creative approach to work' from foreign technicians so that the 'beautiful' foreign machines were given a chance.[112] While the campaign for labour discipline had always had its place alongside a campaign for better management on the shopfloor, in 1934 the attention shifted perceptibly from workers' behaviour to the organizational conditions provided by management. Longer-lasting machinery and better-quality product were to be obtained by organizational improvements to make sure that all workers were properly trained in the use of their equipment, which should be supplied with regular maintenance schedules and clearly written operational procedures.[113] The abandonment of the 'uninterrupted week' regime in favour of weekly closing days was to help the cause of preventive maintenance and make it easier to attribute responsibility for production damage, as it would enable machine operators to be assigned to specific machines on a more permanent basis.[114] The emphasis on 'technological discipline' in the sense of making machine operators follow prescribed operational procedures, however, would be challenged by the advent of the Stakhanovite movement in autumn 1935.

Of the other types of behaviour criticized under the heading of 'labour discipline', rowdy aggression against managers was reported in tones in the managerial press which, in the initial stages of the first five year plan, amounted to a veritable moral panic. This is how a lengthy article on the subject described the situation in a Ukrainian factory:

All technical personnel and most cultured and active workers live under the threat of physical violence. All cultural work has been stopped. There are areas in the plant which it is possible to enter only at the risk of getting beaten up. This hooligan terror inevitably leads to a general weakening of labour discipline. It is common for workers to arrive drunk and carry on drinking at their machines. The hooligans are beginning to feel themselves the real masters in the plant as well as in the streets. The morale of technical personnel is depressed.[115]

Evidently it was not just 'technical personnel' of the lower ranks who came into direct contact with expressions of proletarian displeasure. One press report from a large Moscow factory described a shopfloor scene, witnessed by a crowd of 'several hundred', in which the director was himself personally informed by a worker of her intention 'to re-arrange his face so his wife and children would not recognize him'.[116] This was only a verbal attack, but a number of physical assaults on shopfloor managers and time-study engineers were also reported in the press, with the additional message that the culprits tended to remain unpunished as they enjoyed the protection of party and trade union organizers in their factories.[117]

'Hooligan walkouts and refusals to carry out management orders on a mass scale'[118] were also reported. In one such case, which occurred more than one year after Stalin de-

nounced 'specialist baiting' in the well-publicized 'six conditions' speech, a maintenance worker who caused extensive
damage by refusing a manager's order to repair a failing
machine was dismissed, but promptly reinstated by the
intervention of a Procuracy official who chose instead to
prosecute the dismissing manager for being 'a Ford and an
oppressor of the working class'; the latter was sentenced to
three months of corrective labour with a 25 per cent deduction from wages to compensate the reinstated maintenance
worker for lost pay.[119]

That managers and officials could not count on being able
to preserve decorum at formally convened meetings has
already been indicated in the discussion of the decree on
absenteeism. Similar meetings had been apparently even
more eventful during the first five year plan. Some were
reported to be occasions for much 'chest-thumping' and
rhetorical questions of the 'what have we fought for?'
variety;[120] some voted to decline invitations to volunteer
extra work to mark special Soviet days;[121] in others, guns
were brandished and murder threats uttered to intimidate
time-engineers and shopfloor managers;[122] there were also
meetings where officials with Jewish accents were barracked
and 'USSR without Communists or Jews' called for.[123]
Again, these were probably exceptional cases which were
reported to prove the presence of ideological adversaries in
the factories. But the managerial press also showed explicit
awareness that, in the main, vocal protests and serious
breaches of labour discipline took place in contexts of shopfloor bargaining over work-performance standards and the
conditions of work and pay. 'It works, they get their way,' was
the wistful verdict of an article about discipline problems in
Leningrad industry.[124]

In 1934, the campaigning press on the whole stopped
discussing blatant breaches of labour discipline such as rowdiness, wilful damage to machinery and absenteeism. Instead,
it now turned its attention to allegedly slack working standards, which it discussed in terms of faults in work organization and the structure of pay rewards rather than in terms of
'hooligan' or 'class-alien' influence. A well-publicized survey
revealed that the seven-hour day was in the practice of most

shopfloors reduced to 4–5½ hours of actual working.[125] Managers were asked by their commissariats to make sure that workers arrived on time and stopped leaving early, and to ban from the shopfloors all those who had no business there, including activists seeking to sell lottery tickets and do all manner of 'social work' during work-hours.[126] The theme was picked up by Molotov in his speech at the 17th Party Congress, which was followed by a spate of press reports of on-the-spot checks.[127] Shopfloors were shown to be places where the unison of all machines working could not be heard until some 90 minutes after the time-bell, and where arriving late and going early seemed as normal as was work rhythm liberally interspersed with informal smoking breaks and walks to far and near corners of the factory on non-work business or simply to chat with friends.[128] One time-study of a group of four lathe operators recorded 66 visitors calling by within four hours, not counting the work-connected visits.[129]

Some of the 'time waste' was acknowledged to be due to features of Soviet life which were beyond the workers' control. Public transport frequently faltered, canteen queues were longer than the time allowed for meal-breaks, while opening times and queues made it sometimes impossible to make a necessary purchase, obtain an official stamp or get a personal hearing from a welfare officer in off-the-job times.[130] Some work-time was lost to party, *komsomol* and trade union activism. At a conference convened at a Moscow factory (during work hours?) to discuss the problem, a worker-delegate drew laughter from his audience by this contribution:

A social organisation comes to a worker during work hours to agitate against time-wasting. Yes, that is so. They come while he is busy at work and commence their agitation: 'And do you know comrade, that we now have a campaign for the tightening of the working day?'[131]

The practice of carrying out 'social work' duties in work time was specifically banned by a joint decree of party and government in 1931 and then again by a commissariat directive in 1933.[132] The factory meeting at which the above-quoted remark was heard in 1934 also passed a unanimous resolution abolishing the practice. None of these bans had more than a transitory effect and the looseness of controls over workers' comings and goings apparently remained a feature of shop-floor life throughout the decade.[133]

WAGE INCENTIVES AND THE CAMPAIGNS FOR PERFORMANCE STANDARDS, 1933–35

One of the points made in Chapter 3 was that there was a difference between the first and second five year plans in regard to the emphasis placed by industrialization policy on the goal of production efficiency. Whereas the first five year plan was dominated by large construction investment projects and the struggle for their completion, the second five year plan was to see the expensively acquired technology justify itself in well-running production lines where 'waste' of all kinds was minimized and labour productivity maximized, to form the basis of 'industrial culture'. Whereas the first five year plan envisaged inspirational goals for labour in the form of spectacular transformations of the Russian skyline (viz. the brightly coloured posters of toiling heroes in front of gigantic dams and power stations), the second five year plan envisaged cultured masters of machines in endless search of time-oriented perfection for the sake of regular upward-sloping production graphs. The second five year plan had the problem of motivating as well as organizing efficient industrial work on its historical agenda.

While the setting of production quotas or 'norms' for individual operations had been an undisputed centrepiece of the Soviet vision of good work organization right from the inception of the industrialization drive, thinking about the mysteries of work motivation was no clearer than what western management philosophy had to offer on this subject. A debate on the relative merits of basic pay and performance-linked incentives did take up some space on the pages of the managerial press, but its development was limited as the protagonists tended simply to state what their favourite schemes were and support them with arguments which took little care to consider the arguments advanced in favour of other views. Interestingly, the leading professors of Soviet Taylorism tended to favour time-payment schemes over piece-rates.[134]

It was easier to learn about the reasons for workers' disaffection than what motivated good work, and the reason sometimes advanced by skilled workers was that the egalitarian attitudes of initiatives such as the 'communist labour movement' spelled poor rewards for their skills.[135] At the same time, investigations of industrial difficulties drew attention to the problems of work organization which depersonalized responsibility for results (*obezlichka*). In response, Stalin's 'six conditions' speech criticized 'petty bourgeois levelling' and emphasized the virtues of workplace organization which promoted a sense of personal responsibility and the awareness of production costs.[136] The speech considered the 'levelling' problem to be one of inadequate pay differentials which caused high labour turnover and skill shortage; a skilled worker should be paid more than an unskilled worker and it was wrong when 'a rolling-mill worker earned no more than a sweeper . . . intolerable when a locomotive driver earned only as much as a copy clerk'. This may have sounded like an advocacy of greater differences between occupational pay-scales on a skill-graded basis rather than an advocacy of wages based on piece-rates, but the industrial policy that took shape under the banner of the 'six conditions' speech quickly became marked by an obsession with performance incentives in general and piece-rates in particular. The percentage of man-hours paid for by piece-rates almost became another statistical indicator of industrial progress, which put managers under a constant pressure to see to it that payment by piece-rates spread through all the branches of production. The proportion of workers on piece-rates evidently increased from 58 per cent in 1928 to 70 per cent in 1935.[137]

There seemed a fair degree of consensus about the wisdom of performance-related pay, but in practice there was also considerable controversy as to when the pay should be linked to the collective results of small groups of workers ('brigades') and when it should be linked to the performance of individuals. The militants of the anti-levelling campaign demanded individual piece-rates, while collective piece-rates were often preferred in the factories. Collective incentive schemes were comparatively simple to administer, in addition to which they were often preferred by the workers themselves, some of whom may have recognized working in a brigade led by one of its working members, and paid on a collective-result basis, as similar to what they knew as the traditional organization prevalent among migrant peasant labourers.[138] The brigade system thus seemed rooted in peasant traditions while being ideologically suitable for socialist factories. After all, the collectivization campaign in the countryside had just been experienced as a forceful action under an egalitarian banner. Ex-peasant workers were liable to perceive individual piece-rates as reminiscent of the invitation to individual self-enrichment that had been issued to them in 1926:

They wanted us to work individually in the village, and look what happened – in the Solovki [forced labour camps] many have been taken. I don't want to earn more than anyone else. They will only dekulakise you when you get home.[139]

However, the virtues of individual piece-rates were constantly propagated in the press throughout the second five year plan, even for production lines which did not lend themselves to detailed individual job demarcation and called for disciplined teamwork rather than individually maximized effort. It was repeatedly confirmed that not only workers operating their own machines, but also those working on conveyer belts, maintenance workers, tool-setters and all kinds of auxiliary workers should be put on individual piece-rate schemes.[140] The reason for this lack of moderation was clear from the context in which it was expressed: simpler and older forms of wage-payment were slow to disappear and managers were suspected of turning technological conditions into spurious excuses for covering up 'levelling tendencies'.[141]

The piece-rates were of course linked to the output norms of which, as we have seen in Chapter 3, there were two kinds. 'Experiential-statistical norms' were set on the basis of actual performance while 'technically-founded norms' were said to be determined on the basis of a scientific analysis of productive capacity, to be 'at the head, not at the tail of the

movement for the mastery of technology'.[142] But the setting
of any norms is a scientific process only in the never-never
land of pure 'scientific management'. In the social practice of
effort valuation and bargaining over fair performance standards, 'technically-founded norms' were a euphemism for
relatively tight norms. It was not surprising that managers
often found their claims about how many of the norms in their
factories were 'technically-founded' contradicted by inspections, organized by higher party or trade union committees,
which found a proportion of these norms to be 'in fact
experiential'.[143] These claims and counter-claims were the
product of periodic campaigns of norm revision, of which the
norms that were labelled 'statistical-experiential' were a more
legitimate target than the 'technical' ones.

Norm-setting must have involved a great volume of work,
given the number of new production lines that were being set
up, the policy of increasing the proportion of jobs worked on
individual piece-rates and the almost annual campaigns of
norm revision. In one Moscow engineering plant alone, the
number of norms to be reviewed in the course of the campaign that took place in the early months of 1933 amounted to
85,000.[144] It was not clear how many staff were available for
this task, although it was noted in the critical press that only
four of them had any engineering qualifications.[145] Most
norm-setters were trained on the job with the aid of crash
courses. Graduate engineers knew little about technical
norm-setting if they did not come from one of the few
institutes where it was included in the curriculum, and considered it a job for economists rather than engineers.[146] Being
an 'economist' was low in the scale of values of the industrialization campaign; it smacked of Menshevism, 'rightist
opportunism' and narrow-minded wage-clerks. While the
propaganda promoting 'technically founded norms' held that
they were to be set by persons of high technical expertise, real
engineers knew better: norm-setting was a matter of haggling
rather than technology. In any case, the sheer number of
norms to be set and revised within short periods of time made
a mockery of any pretence to science; as the campaigning
press often complained, norms were set 'bureaucratically' in
offices or 'by the eye' on the shopfloors.[147]

It was not always clear exactly who had the final authority over the validity of a norm. Under the 'functionalist' system of management which was considered the progressive form during the first five year plan, formal authority over norm-setting must have been vested in the norm-setting departments (*TNB*), but then all norms also had to be ratified by the factory commissions for settling disputes, with the factory trade union committees as courts of appeal.[148] At the end of the first five year plan, 'line systems' of management came to be favoured rather than 'functionalist' ones, which meant that the specialized branches of management became more clearly subordinated to general managers, i.e. either to all-factory chief engineers or to the heads of individual production units. (Many Soviet factories were very large, so that a single production unit or shop – *tsekh* – could have up to several thousand employees.) The *TNB*s in particular were reorganized along these lines after a special conference in 1932, which only encouraged the already common practice of unilateral decisions by foremen and shop managers to amend norms that caused trouble with workers.[149] This practice was to some extent formally legitimated in 1934, when shopfloor managers were empowered by a commissariat directive to modify norms or piece-rates in cases where this was warranted by unavoidable 'technological deviations' in shopfloor practice.[150] In the same year, the disputes commissions had their powers restricted to complaints brought by individual workers.[151] They remained busy, but now as before, the most popular avenue of redress by workers against contentious norms consisted in 'the running after and having rows with norm-setters and foremen'.[152]

The clarity of jurisdiction over the norms was not helped by the review campaigns which demanded involvement from labour mobilization agencies such as the trade unions. Thus the campaigns during the first five year plan and then up to 1934 were usually organized in the form of activists proposing tighter norms (*vstrechnye normy*) at shopfloor meetings and having themselves appointed to shock workers' commissions for the review of norms.[153] At the same time, the trade union, party and *komsomol* organizations in the factories kept being asked by all voices of party–state authority not to meddle with 'one-man management'.[154] In 1935, the norm review cam-

paign was organized by industrial commissariat directives
making factory managers responsible for the progress and
outcome, which formally transferred the campaign from the
jurisdiction of 'social organizations' to the jurisdiction of state
administration and management.[155] But the functionaries of
'social organizations' including the trade unions were still told
that they had a 'stronger responsibility for the prevention and
liquidation of any stalling tricks and tailism by managers'.[156]
After all, it was often observed that shopfloor managers'
interest in changing the norms lay in loosening the tight ones
but leaving the loose ones alone.[157]

The confusion over authority in regard to the norms, and
the generally low status of the time-study men in the factories,
was perhaps at odds with the fact that the norms were
accorded a central place within the wage-labour organization.
But this was a state of affairs which allowed the norms,
inherently contentious artefacts that they were, to be contested without a direct challenge to the ideological notion that
the 'who does what for how much?' issues should be settled
by a higher principle than the anarchy of conflicting self-
interests. Thus nobody needed to challenge the assumption
that workers should work to full capacity and that this meant
work performance standards which were objectively right
and reasonable; rather, the underqualified bureaucrats in
charge of setting the norms often happened to be wrong and
should be corrected. Thus bargaining over the value of labour
could take place, but within the 'informal' confines of 'formal'
bureaucracy, so that it did not get staged as a conflict between
labour and the state.

So norm-setters were frequently criticized, appealed
against and corrected. Neither qualified engineers nor high-
powered managers, the norm-setters nevertheless worked in
offices, which made them vulnerable to being denounced as
'bureaucrats'. They had to be literate and numerate, so their
class background tended to be suspect. They were admirably
suited for the role of fall-guy in the dramas of shopfloor
bargaining. Thus a letter could be printed in the trade union
daily 2½ years after the party expressed its displeasure at
'specialist-baiting', in which a worker concluded his complaints about the injustices of the norms and wage-incentives

in his workplace by raising the pointed question of whether this might have been due to the fact that the norm-setter was the son of a former manager who used to own 90 acres and 100 horses.[158] During the Stakhanovite days of 1935–36, norm-setters were exposed to charges of 'technical conservatism' if they showed caution in tightening the norms, but also to charges of 'sabotage of the Stakhanovite movement' if they tightened a well-overfulfilled norm during its supposed lifetime.[159]

From time to time, norms were criticized by the campaigning press and the party authorities for being unrealistically tight. Such criticisms could be heard particularly often in the winter 1932–33 when there was a movement afoot in governmental circles to slacken the pace of industrialization. Norms 'set on the assumption of ideal technological conditions and consequently impossible to fulfil' were blamed for the high labour turnover rates;[160] some were said to be tighter than their American cousins, and some were loosened by the shock workers' commissions which were set up in some factories for the purposes of norm review in 1933.[161] Inappropriately tight (*skvernoe*) norm-setting was cited among the causes of low living standards by a regional party boss in a special circular to factory officials in February 1935 (a few weeks before the joint party–government decree announcing the norm-tightening campaign for that year).[162] Even in the Stakhanovite heydays of the following year would there be criticisms in the press that some norms were too tight, having been set on the assumption of technological improvements which were never carried out.[163]

But the most frequent criticism levelled at the norms was that they were too slack. 'Experiential norms' were said to be too loose because they had been set without the benefit of proper work-method study, while 'technical norms' were allegedly becoming outdated by improvements in technology and workers' skills. High rates of over-fulfilment were usually quoted as the proof that a norm was too low.[164] These criticisms were made in the course of the norm review campaigns whereby the party leaders hoped to make industrial labour productivity grow substantially faster than industrial wages.[165] Success was mixed. Labour productivity did grow at the rate of about 11 per cent per year during the second five year plan,[166] as it indeed should given the heavy investment in new plant; but nominal wages grew twice as fast again,[167] which they should not have done, given that ever more workers were earning their money on piece-rates which were subject to annual tightening campaigns.

Shopfloor implementation of the norm review campaigns was subject to the same conditions as the implementation of the campaigns for labour discipline. The unsmooth running of production meant that workers were seldom afforded the satisfaction of finding a work rhythm which would enable them to earn their money without feeling frustrated by adverse circumstances beyond their control. Having to stop working on a job at unpredictable intervals, being transferred to different jobs mid-shift, and having to work with substandard tools or raw materials were aggravations which were felt by the production workers on piece-rates in particular.[168] Even earning a modest wage by achieving modest levels of productivity must have seemed to require undue effort in circumstances which, while not allowing 'tedium' to be alleviated by 'traction', filled the worker's day with the irritations of being 'pushed around' and the sense that his earning ability was limited by mismanagement. This was in addition to the other grievances which have been already mentioned in the context of the labour-discipline problems, plus the fact that the complexities of wage-calculation, with the confusion of authority over norms, piece-rates and special incentive schemes, often led to unpleasant surprises at what was in fact found in the wage-packets. (Alleged wage underpayments were the subject of yet another set of high-powered government edicts, procuracy instructions to prosecute errant managers, and a sustained press campaign.[169])

If they wanted to preserve a semblance of shopfloor peace and performance stability, managers were well advised to be flexible about implementing the norms and tariffs which assumed unrealistic production flows without bottlenecks and thus threatened the workers' ability to make out. Foremen took full advantage of the 'technological deviations' clause which enabled them to relax again freshly tightened norms even before the current norm review campaign was over;[170] they arranged full wages for stoppage time, although the rules said that workers on halted lines should be paid only half the basic time-rate for idle hours;[171] and they helped piece-rate workers to make out by aiding and abetting a rich variety of shopfloor fiddles, of which more will be said in the next section. Shop managers sometimes indulged in 'tariff indiscipline' such as upward revisions of the official wage-scales issued by the industrial commissariats, or the establishment of 'fictitious bonus systems' for workers whose earnings were threatened by tightened norms, while factory directors did their best to provide room for this kind of flexibility by manipulating the planning organs into the provision of good wage budget allocations.[172] If they were not successful, the wage budget was simply overspent, in spite of the government decrees that were issued to stop this inflationary practice.[173]

In truth, there could not be many people in the factories who were interested in raising labour productivity by tightening work norms. The trade union journal boasted that the main burden of the 1933 campaign had to be carried by the trade unions because managers 'underestimated its importance or indeed opposed it'.[174] But the trade union officials and activists in the factories could not have been much keener for, if they had been, the formal responsibilities for norm review would not have been transferred to the managerial hierarchy in 1935. Party activists in the factories were also less than zealous in this respect. This fact came up for some scrutiny in the course of the party purge in 1933, when many of the expulsions were on the grounds of alleged opposition to norm review campaigns and refusals to see the issue in 'class struggle' terms.[175]

Shopfloor organization in Soviet factories was no different from others round the world in tending to promote stability in work relations by upholding performance standards which fell short of the expectations generated by technological investment. The stimulus for raising performance standards had to come from the outside, which, in the absence of market conditions, took the form of political campaigns for stricter discipline and tighter output norms. These campaigns were political in a dual sense. One was the obvious fact that they were instigated and carried out by the party state with its language of 'class struggle' and 'socialist construction'. But this was not a cloak for a simple terror to make people work harder. Some such terror was applied to managers, at some times in a greater degree than in others, but 'slackers' and 'discipline violators' in workers' ranks were not among the categories recommended for police action. The success of the efficiency campaigns largely depended on other forms of penetration into shopfloor practice. Here we come to the other sense in which the efficiency campaigns were political. A clue to it is given by the fact that the terms of the efficiency campaigns demanded that 'technical norms', the rules governing wage payments for idle periods, enforcement of discipline etc. assumed a continuous improvement in the organization of the production process. Managers came under criticism in the campaigning press if they simply issued directives requesting a stricter enforcement of the rules, 'thinking that that was their bit done, while on the shopfloors attitudes to the official rules and punishments clearly lack seriousness'. They certainly were asked to apply the rules, but:

At the same time, Soviet society and workers must again focus attention on the necessity for the speediest possible removal of production irregularities consequent upon carelessness, or indeed criminal negligence on the part of the managerial personnel in some enterprises. We must not forget that the absence of clarity, precision and regularity in the work of the productive organism inevitably leads to violations of labour discipline.[176]

This was as if to agree with workers who said, as many did in factory meetings, that they would gladly work more productively if only managers provided the conditions for it. The terms of the efficiency campaigns had a strong overtone of encouragement to workers to channel their resentments of managers into intolerance of mismanagement. This aspect of 'the struggle for Bolshevik speeds' is the theme of the next section.

MANAGERIAL AUTHORITY AND SHOPFLOOR POLITICS, 1929–1935

There is a sense in which it would be possible to write the

history of industrialization as a story of the changing fortunes of foremen. In Britain and USA, for example, the story would start with the foreman being not a company employee as he is now, but an entrepreneurial subcontractor who supplied and organized factory labour. Having negotiated a contract for a batch of production, the foreman hired and fired labour, paid wages out of his own pocket as it were, and took full responsibility for the division of tasks and their allocation to individual workers. Since then, there has been a long and protracted process of bureaucratization, in which all aspects of labour management came under company control. The story involved the rise of the trade unions in which the foremen played a key part, especially in USA, and bitter confrontations between the traditional powers of foremen on the one hand, and the brave new world of 'scientific management' on the other hand. The foreman used to be a subcontractor of factory labour also in Japan, where his authority over workers was further ramified by the traditions of noblemen status.[177]

It seems that in Russia, too, the foreman used to be a figure of great authority on the shopfloor, who hired and fired his workers, determined their wages and conditions of payment, and told them what to do.[178] On the shopfloor he was the *master*, which is what he is still called. The Revolution brought about a radical change in this respect, in that conditions of employment became subject to extensive legislation, while authority on the shopfloor was to some extent divided between managers, party cells and trade union committees. And from 1926, the foreman's powers became subject to further limitations by the introduction of 'functional' management structures.[179]

When the show trials with Donbass engineers started a movement of 'class vigilance' against 'bourgeois specialists', some foremen lost their jobs and new appointments were made by popular vote, in disregard of the rights of appointment supposedly held by higher-ranking managers. Furthermore, the newly appointed foremen, norm-setters, etc. were sometimes held accountable to their electors at subsequent meetings, which made all aspects of the 'managerial prerogative', including the authority to define and allocate work tasks, conditional upon workers' approval.[180]

These developments caused much alarm among industrial managers, including those at the top policy-making levels. The trade union organizations and party cells in the factories were obliged to convene special meetings for workers during the first half of 1930, at which the excesses of 'electivity' and 'specialist-baiting' were denounced, and the hierarchical principles of authoritative management, or 'one-man management', were reaffirmed.[181] This was a difficult campaign, by all accounts. The 'taut industrialization' policy was making itself felt on the shopfloors, with the conditions of work and pay getting adversely affected by organizational breakdowns which must have sometimes looked to workers like blatant mismanagement. The party policy was therefore not unequivocal in its backing of managerial authority, in that it still insisted on 'self-criticism' and political vigilance against 'wrecking' by managers and engineers. The latter were instruments of political mobilization, without which, thought the party leaders, the industrialization campaign was liable to lose the momentum that was needed to overcome the legacy of economic and cultural backwardness. The meetings were rowdy affairs which reflected the frustrations that were mounting on the shopfloors, and they did not put an end to a situation where higher-ranking managers felt undermined by wholesale replacements of foremen which were taking place on political initiatives exercised at shopfloor level; this situation continued for at least another year.[182]

The thousands of new foremen had impeccable working-class backgrounds which made them politically more secure than the 'bourgeois specialists' who remained in factory offices. The manner in which they got their promotions from the work-bench was liable to confuse their sense of accountability; it was noted in the managerial press that the new foremen were 'great social workers' who, however, in many cases did their new jobs without any idea about how they were to fit into the management structure.[183] They had practical experience, but no wider technical training; many were hardly more than semi-literate.[184] And we have seen in Chapter 3 that they seemed backward in the perspective of 'industrial culture', in need of a 'reconstruction of the senses' if they were to play a positive role in making technological industry efficient.[185] All these observations must have looked like good reasons for the 'functionalist' structure of management which promised to transfer power from shopfloor managers to specialized offices of 'intra-enterprise planning'.

'Functionalism' was the ruling principle of industrial organization until 1933. It was meant to limit the foreman's job to instructing workers in the operational procedures that were laid down in written instructions, filling forms to supply necessary information to the specialist offices, and occasional troubleshooting which might be made necessary by unpredicted circumstances.[186] The decisions that made up the conditions of work were to be taken elsewhere. Work procedures were to be determined in the offices of 'technological planning', performance standards in the 'bureaux of technical norm-setting' (TNB), day-to-day allocation of jobs to individual workplaces in the 'bureaux of allocation and scheduling'. Foremen had no funds at their disposal to offer extra incentives to workers, while the skill-grading and disciplining of workers was in the hands of the factory 'departments of labour' whose policies were under the jurisdiction of a different branch of government than the policies of the rest of factory management.[187] The maintenance of machines, the sharpening of tools, the storage and supplies of blueprints and equipment fixtures, all these things were organized by separate centralized branches of management. Innovations were the responsibility of 'rationalization bureaux', quality control at all stages of the production process was in the hands of the quality inspectorate. If the conditions of work caused any grievances among workers, 'functionalism' in effect meant that it was not the foreman who was to blame, nor indeed the foreman's superiors in the hierarchy of shopfloor management.

I have already made the point in Chapter 3 that the 'scientific management' philosophy of Taylorism which prescribed the 'functional' structure of authority was ill-suited to the dynamism that was demanded by the implementation of 'taut industrialization' strategy. Even if the foremen had been given the time to study organizational charts and think about their role on the shopfloor, it is unlikely that this would have

done much to reduce the chaos in which they found themselves. The following description is reminiscent of the tale
from Chicago in Chapter 3, in pointing at the destabilizing
effects of overheated economy on shopfloor organization:

'Come on, come on!' shouted an engineer, sweaty and bedraggled as he
was running from one machine to another.
'Come on, come on!' repeated after him equally hot and bothered
technicians and foremen.
One was chasing a product from one machine to the next, another was
himself operating a machine in place of an incompetent worker, the third
manager was searching for a tool, the fourth one was dragging some fittings
along, while two were engaged in a hysterical row over some raw material.
They all interfered with each other's jobs, gave conflicting orders, tried to
persuade, appeal, reassure, threaten . . .
Today the whole section is mobilised for one order, which will be
abandoned tomorrow when another customer pulls his weight somewhere
high up and the whole factory is mobilised for shock-work fulfilment of his
order. Day after tomorrow, that order will be abandoned, too, to make way
for yet another priority . . .
Even the factory director was on the shopfloor, running from one
machine to the next, chasing particular orders, as if to make sure that there
was not even a suggestion of planning left in the shopfloor process.[188]

This situation, to the description of which must be added
chronic problems with all manner of supplies, was not one
with which the 'functional' organization of management
could cope. Disruptions, crossed-wires and process breakdowns were the order of the day. In this situation, the
trouble-shooting role that the foremen had in the work
process grew well beyond what was envisaged by the 'functionalist' structures of authority. The foremen were constantly called upon by workers to sort out problems for which
neither the worker nor the foreman, but managers located in
offices outside of the shopfloor, could be held responsible.[189]
The foreman could always promise the bemused worker that
he would do his best to help, but never guarantee results,
because they depended on factors beyond his control, such as
the good will or intelligence of the office-based staff. It was
natural for foremen to keep workers' frustrations at bay by
presenting themselves to workers as their allies in their
struggles to earn a living despite the obstacles put in their way
by inept or negligent pen-pushers. Foremen were always

chasing after all manner of inputs for their workers, from breakfasts to blueprints.[190] They allocated jobs as circumstances rendered the 'allocation bureaux' schedules inappropriate, and perhaps also modified the operational procedures prescribed by the technological planners, to make up for inferior quality of raw material, or the fact that it was more convenient to use different equipment than that envisaged by the production engineers.[191] Then they spent much time negotiating with workers how to make sure that the modifications did not take their toll in piece-rate earnings.[192] The latter problem was constantly on the agenda, thanks to the conflict between 'scientific management' assumptions and shopfloor realities.

In this context, their working-class backgrounds provided the foremen with handy expertise. They were experienced in the arts of the shopfloor fiddle, whereby workers in all corners of the world turn the struggles for 'making out' into an important source of job satisfaction.[193] What was peculiar about the Soviet factories was not that the arts of outwitting management controls flourished, but that it was the foremen who used them, often in deliberate display in front of their workers, to turn the frustrations visited upon the shopfloors by the disharmonies of Taylorism and 'taut speeds' into an atmosphere of shared mirth and snatched justice. They would make fools of quality inspectors by a range of techniques which might include skilful cover-up jobs, or clandestine adjustments to calibrating instruments.[194] They would modify work accountancy systems to help workers make sure of their earnings[195] and, on night shifts especially, protected a person's natural rights to a few hours of undisturbed sleep, if the nine-to-five office staff failed to facilitate a stoppage-free production flow.[196] But above all, they would assume a leading role in the struggle with norm-setters. They flooded the 'bureaux of technical norm-setting' with claims of unavoidable 'deviations in technological conditions' which rendered their output norms inapplicable,[197] contested the validity of tight norms and proved their point with the aid of time-wasting tricks,[198] and sometimes engaged in 'hostile campaigns' which discouraged norm-setters from setting foot on the shopfloor.[199]

In some western ethnographies of 'shopfloor culture', the process of bargaining between workers and time-study engineers over performance standards tends to be described as a self-conscious and ritualized sort of gamesmanship.[200] The impression given by the pronouncements of foremen on the subject of 'technical norm-setting' in the Soviet managerial press was, however, quite wholeheartedly hostile. The political thirst for 'Bolshevik speeds' required 'technical norm-setting' to assume away any obstacles to full-capacity work, with a view to putting shopfloor managers under pressure from their workers to strive for organizational improvements which would enable workers to make out even on tightened norms. The shopfloor conditions, however, were such as to make it more realistic for foremen to turn the norm-setters into derided outsiders, by making it obvious that 'the office technicians of technical norm-setting are helpless when it comes to correct evaluation of the highly complicated process called production'.[201]

The functionalist structure of management left the foremen with few formal powers, but it was the foremen who were the first port of call for workers' frequent grievances about the actual conditions of work and pay. This was a stressful situation, in which the foremen considered themselves, in common with the workers, the victims rather than perpetrators of mismanagement. They handled it by showing the workers that they were on their side against the inept pen-pushers who expected miracles while causing chaos. Since the sense of fairness kept being offended by constant disturbances in the equations between effort and earnings, which is what the norm review campaigns and constant changes in production-line set-ups amounted to from the shopfloor point of view, it is understandable that the foremen should worry about pacifying workers more than efficiency. Efficiency, after all, was not their problem in the 'functionalist' management organizations. There is no reason to disbelieve an American specialist who compared his experiences of working as a foreman in USA and USSR; after a long litany of the frustrations of powerlessness amidst disorganization, there was one thing to be said for the Soviet experience: 'workers' attitudes to the foreman are comradely and trusting, while in

America the foreman is a scarecrow.'[202]

It did not take long for the party leaders to realize that the foreman was playing a peculiarly influential role on the shopfloor, while the organizational structure enabled him to evade managerial responsibility for labour productivity. The foreman's reluctance to enforce labour discipline, and his inclination to plead powerlessness on this issue while being in fact 'the soul of the shopfloor',[203], began to be frequently mentioned in 1932, and this developed into a reversal of government policy on management 'functionalism' in the following year. Politbureau member Postyshev put on record his view that it was urgent 'to increase the role of the foreman, give him rights and responsibility, and thus fundamentally change the state of affairs where the foreman gives information, but avoids taking responsible decisions and weakly organizes work.'[204] A party resolution on industrial problems in the Donbass region singled out bureaucratic buck-passing for attention as the major sickness there, and ordered a management reorganization which would transfer power from specialist offices to shopfloor managers.[205] This became policy for industry in general at the beginning of 1934.[206]

Foremen received increasing attention from the press as the reorganization in factories got under way. Their resentments were given a voice, and also, it seemed, some approval. The staff of specialist offices were often acknowledged to be better educated than foremen, but now it was also said that they tended to be less useful in practice than foremen.[207] It was also repeatedly alleged that the specialist offices were staffed primarily by people who had proved themselves useless in shopfloor management, and sometimes it was insinuated that these people were too partial to their desks and comfortable office hours to care about the problems of production, especially those that occurred on night-shifts.[208] The staff of 'rationalization bureaux' and 'technical norm-setting bureaux' were singled out for the most unpleasant characterizations and charges of parasitic uselessness.[209] This coincided with a wider campaign against 'soul-less bureaucrats'.[210]

Foremen were also given a strong backing in their resentment of paperwork. The managerial journals that had given an enormous amount of space to the administrative systems of data-collection required by 'scientific management', and kept emphasizing the importance of work performance accountancy for good labour management, now spared no sarcasm in relation to the paperwork aspect of Taylorism.

Whole institutions sit over the creation of more forms and questionnaires. There has arisen a distinct type of 'specialist' for the creation of paperwork systems, for whom this is the main content of his wisdom; and there have arisen ideologues of the scribing who elevate it to the status of scientific theory, and accuse of heresy any living thought that is directed against the bureaucratic method of management.[211]

This was a campaign which the foremen relished as much as the criticisms of norm-setters. After all, a large part of the paperwork was intended to stop shopfloor fiddling in reporting stoppages and work done. Foremen were now given support when they used the framework of 'socialist competition' to demand a substantial simplification of the paperwork,[212] and space in the printed media for acerbic statements on the subject of the 'various office creators of "methods" and "systems" of accounting'.[213]

The greatest blow to 'scientific management', however, came when the criticisms of norm-setters escalated into radical attacks on the principles of 'technical norm-setting' themselves. The foremen who voiced their scepticism about the claims that the techniques of 'technical norm-setting' could guarantee valid performance standards had their view confirmed in a theoretical attack on what had been the basic orthodoxy of Soviet Taylorism. It was now claimed that there was in fact no basis for the belief that the analytical method was the way to identify the most efficient work procedures and set objective performance standards for them. Creative experimentation and comparative records of performance were now declared to be the best strategy for improving efficiency, in contrast to 'office academicism' and 'monopolistic-science method'.[214] In November 1935, this view was endorsed by Stalin himself:

Scientific knowledge always has been subject to testing by practice and experience. Science which has torn itself from practice and experience –

what sort of science is that? If science had been the way it is imagined by our conservative comrades, it would have been long dead for humanity. Science is what it is because it has no place for fetish, and because it does not fear contact with what is vital in the old, it listens carefully to the voice of experience and practice.[215]

The foremen were clearly wooed to cross the lines and employ their shopfloor skills on behalf of the managerial concern with efficiency. Numerous articles were published advocating substantial enlargements of foreman authority.[216] Some of these arguments had a distinctive 'put the goat in charge of cabbage' flavour. Norm-setters, quality inspectors, wage-accountants, toolmakers, maintenance workers, store-keepers and scheduling clerks would be all relocated to shopfloor sections and made answerable to the foremen, who would also have wage budgets to dispose of as they saw fit, if all of these proposals were put together and implemented. It was believed that if the foremen were given wide organizational powers within their sections, they would assume responsibility for efficiency.

In reality, however, the reorganization in the factories did not bring many new powers to the foremen. It is unlikely that the party leadership was entirely serious about the rejection of functionalism; after all, if managerial control really had been transferred to the shopfloor, the latter would have been even better able to abuse the producer's position in an economy which put the 'consumer sovereignty' principle right on its head. Besides, autonomous control in the hands of shopfloor managers would have enabled them to resist government sponsored campaigns for 'Bolshevik speeds' in production. Be this as it may, the 'functionalist' lines of authority were disappearing only slowly. One of the anecdotes told by the American foreman mentioned above had him wasting a long time arguing with a scheduling clerk who had his own firm views as to which machine a particular piece of work ought to be done on, and the power to stop the foreman who thought otherwise; this was some nine months after the supposed abandonment of 'functionalism'.[217] And by 1937, the foremen's enemies in the 'technical norm-setting bureaux' began to receive some sympathetic attention to their problems in the press.[218]

It is doubtful that the foremen ever wanted the responsibility that seemed to be on offer in 1935–36. There was a catch. The party seemed to share the foremen's dislike of office-based managers, with their claims to superior managerial expertise, and their insatiable thirst for foreman-filled forms, but it did so in the context of a speed-up campaign. The political leadership of industrialization was disappointed in the results of the norm review campaign that took place in the spring of 1935, and a few months later started the Stakhanovite movement, which was not an altogether new but a more concentrated attempt to inject innovative and efficiency-oriented dynamism into the factories, by methods of political mobilization. Taking advantage of the animosities that had developed in the factories between offices and shopfloors was a part of these methods.

However, the foremen would have needed very strong incentives to cooperate with the speed-up campaigns. In the division of managerial objectives between the regularity of work-pace on the one hand, and the speed of it on the other hand, the managers on the shopfloor favour regularity, because the achievement of regularity is much more consistent with peace, while speed-up campaigns mean trouble in shopfloor relations. The foremen were no keener on 'socialist competition' for 'Bolshevik speeds' than the professors of Soviet Taylorism. As the Stakhanovite movement got under way, it was the foremen in fact who often featured in stories of shopfloor resistance to the movement.[219] The foremen continued to play their role in the way they had played it under 'functionalism', as powerless but fair organisers who helped their workers to make out. They did not take responsibility for efficiency, realistic concerns for which they considered to be out of their hands.

The foremen tended to be the bearers of a shopfloor culture the rise of which was heralded by press reports of 'organized cheating'. During the first five year plan, the customs of shopfloor fiddle were alleged by the campaigning press to be rooted in the practices of maintenance crews in particular. There was evidence that the sorry state of production equipment was in part due to the maintenance workers' ways of increasing their earnings by creating favourable conditions for the negotiation of, for example, premium-paying overtime work. If the management tried to retrieve the situation by transferring some of the maintenance duties to other groups of workers, the maintenance workers' grievance became promptly evident in sudden breakdowns of key equipment.[220] Since 'maintenance brigades' consisted of skilled workers, the militant extremes of restrictive practice which were reported by the alarmed press had been committed not by anarchic-minded ex-peasants but by 'old workers' who were protecting their earnings from the general fall of real wages that was taking place in the early years of the industrialization drive.

Otherwise, both 'old workers' and 'new workers' had the traditions of migrant labour to evoke in response to grievances against the work conditions in which they were to earn their living: to quit and move on, or use their willingness to do so as a bargaining counter. This changed during the second five year plan. Labour turnover rates dropped to double figures while the time-honoured arts of shopfloor fiddle became the common property of the new workers on the production lines as well as of the old workers in maintenance crews.

There is a lot of tendency among the work-force to use rip-off tricks. The grabber [*rvach*] now uses different methods than, say, in 1931 when he kept threatening to quit. There is a return to old and well-tested methods of grabbing [*rvachestvo*] which are more difficult to fight than those prevalent in 1931.[221]

The difficulty faced by the outside campaigners for higher productivity standards was not so much that some work-cheating was artful to the point of being hard to detect, but that it was 'organized cheating' under the connivance or indeed encouragement of shopfloor management.

Some of these practices were strikingly similar to those described by western ethnographers. For example, the custom of cross-booking piece-rated jobs, i.e. arranging the issue of job-order slips in such a way as to enable the worker to get some jobs done at a rate-busting speed without the norm-setter ever getting to know, and perhaps to use the saved time for earning a premium on another job where the norm was tighter. While the official rules of piece-rate accountancy usually attempted to prevent this practice by demanding that only one job-order slip could be in the worker's possession at a time, and with it only the tools and blueprints prescribed by the single job-order, it was evidently very common for workers to be able to have a number of job-order slips in hand and misreport the actual times of commencing and completing jobs. Since this involved also the circumvention of rules governing the supply of tools, cribs, jigs, blueprints and raw material, the cross-booking by production workers on piece-rates was taking place with the cooperation of foremen, clerks, store-keepers, progress-chasers and machine fitters, who tended to see it as a reasonable way of cutting red tape.[222]

Another accountancy custom whereby foremen in effect instructed wage-clerks to help workers regulate their earnings was to let them be paid for jobs which they had not yet done.[223] This practice is worthy of a special note not only because it has been likewise reported to play an important part in the informal relations of a western factory,[224] but also because the Soviet reports of it throw a new light on the perennial issue of 'storming' (*shturmovshchina*). There can be no doubt that the production flow was typically irregular, but factory output statistics may have exaggerated the effect if they were based on shopfloor records which could enter next month's work in this month's accomplishments. In other words, production was further behind schedule than was suggested by monthly plan-fulfilment figures, but the differences in work-pace between slack and 'storming' periods could well have been less extreme than the often quoted statistics according to which most of a month's production happened just before the month's end.

Similarly as western reports of 'goldbricking' tactics whereby workers tried to persuade time-study engineers to set relatively loose norms, the Soviet press described a variety of 'tricks known to every machine-operator worth his salt' which were deployed in the struggles with the norm-setters and were 'so frequent in our factories that they can be observed almost every day'.[225] The only difference was that the Soviet reports included some particularly blatant tricks of the trade, such as the deliberate mis-setting of machine tools to cause vibration, overheating and shoddy production, to persuade the norm-setters that the cutting speeds prescribed in their norms were too high.[226] That the leading part in particularly daring displays of shopfloor cunning was sometimes played by fore-men has already been mentioned.

Other kinds of shopfloor fiddle had a more specifically Soviet flavour, in that they reflected the mixing of public and private aims which have been mentioned in the discussion of *blat* networks in Chapter 2. For example, machine operators were reported to obtain high-specification tools on the black market, which enabled them to set their machines to work at higher speeds than those envisaged by the norm-setters on the basis of the low-specification tools provided by the factory toolroom. Again, shopfloor managers apparently turned a blind eye to this practice, on the grounds that the workers were entitled to earn piece-rate premiums on operations for which they invested in better tools out of their own pockets.[227] The obverse side of this coin was also reported; good-quality tools, machine parts, materials etc. somehow had to find their way from factory storerooms into the *blat* networks, and the pilfering of such things was evidently commonplace.[228]

And finally, to make one more return to the theme of work accounting, the blatant fiddle of obtaining wage-payments by filling job-order slips with inspired fictions (*pripiski*) re-portedly assumed large proportions in factories where the work accountancy systems were particularly inadequate to the complexities of working arrangements that had to be made to keep production lines going. An inspection experi-ment carried out in the Gorkii automobile works in the middle of 1934, i.e. some two years after the new production line was set into motion, revealed that only one out of 26 foremen refused to sign job-cards according to which workers carried out tasks such as 'assemble a perfect woman' and 'grind his head off' at wage costs running into thousands of roubles. Foremen evidently routinely signed fictitious job descriptions for workers who were idle due to production stoppages 'to avoid arguments'.[229]

But were the shopfloor cultures in Soviet factories similar

to the outlines developed by the argument in the first section of this chapter? According to these outlines, the central characteristic of shopfloor culture is that it has ways of attributing 'real' effort content to the various jobs of the production process, in contrast to the effort contents assumed by official performance norms, and handling the issues of justice that arise from the awareness of comparative effort-expenditures necessary for earning a 'living wage' on the various jobs. Members know advantageous jobs from disadvantageous ones, and share a sense of implications of this knowledge for the moral regulation of shopfloor behaviour. This is not to say that they always agree with each other in their evaluations of behaviour, only that they share a knowledge of the important issues there are to argue about: the sorting of jobs into good and bad, the distribution of thus labelled jobs among shopfloor members, the fairness of the conditions of making out, the appropriate methods of restoring justice where it fails, and of protecting the custom and practice that develops on this basis from outside interventions. The vitality of the last three issues in factory affairs has been already demonstrated in the evidence concerning the shopfloor fiddle and the responses to the labour-productivity campaigns. The other two issues – the classification of jobs in terms of effort value and their allocation to individual workers – were also reflected in the press reports from the 'labour-productivity front'. They upbraided norm-setters for causing heated arguments about 'advantageous' and 'disadvantageous' norms by their inaccuracies, criticized or praised managers for responding to the problem by pay-rises for 'disadvantageous' jobs, and noted the contests between 'allocation bureaux', foremen and workers' collectives over the rights of job allocation.[230]

The conceptions of shopfloor justice became particularly important in the context where individual piece-rates were introduced into the sort of work organization where supplies were running out, equipment was breaking down and jobs had to be changed mid-stream. In this situation, skill and hard work were not enough to enable a worker to earn above-average wages on piece-rates. To sustain a high level of earnings, she needed her ambitions to find a cooperative response from foremen, machine-setters, store-keepers and auxiliary workers, all of whom had to be careful about whom they were seen to grace with preferential treatment.

The same Ivan Gudov who arrived in a Moscow railway station at the beginning of Chapter 2 and sang a happy tune at the end of it also has had events on this theme to recall in his memoirs. He started in his machine-tool factory as an auxiliary labourer responsible for the transport of raw-material supplies to machine-operators. He found that they cultivated his favours, because his decisions of what to fetch next could be important to them. Then he acquired the qualifications of a milling machine operator in the factory night school. On his appointment to a milling machine as its proud operator, his wages dropped from the levels to which he had been accustomed as an unskilled auxiliary labourer. This was because, he soon learned, as a novice he got landed with having to work piece-rates on a disadvantageous job with a tight norm. Eventually he also realized that his senior colleagues perhaps helped themselves to their norm-exceeding achievements by a bit of judicious tampering with their machine set-ups.

Whatever it was that Gudov did in response to these discoveries, that it did not win him friends in the right places became obvious when his own unauthorized experiments with machine set-ups caused some damage for which he incurred the unusually hard punishment of having to pay the costs. He nevertheless persevered with his experiments, and found himself further at odds with the people who mattered when he found ways of overfulfilling the norms by substantial margins. He volunteered a 'socialist competition' undertaking to do his jobs at the rate of 175 per cent of the norm, but the factory magazine reported this as 115 per cent. When he tried to prove his point by meeting his output targets twice over, his supplies ran out and his demands for work fell on deaf ears: 'You have earned enough already,' the foreman told him. 'It won't do you any harm to take it easy for a few days.' To this the hot-tempered Gudov responded by a blustering attempt to obtain his supplies regardless of the foreman's judgement, with the result that the shopfloor collective framed him for rowdy behaviour and got him dismissed.[231]

Gudov's experience with 'socialist competition' is a cue to resume the discussion of the movement, which was suspended at the end of Chapter 3 by the observation that it was sometimes criticized for being contaminated by the capitalist spirit of *konkurs*, i.e. anarchic strivings for private gain at the expense of others. It is not difficult to see the point. If the shopfloor reality was one in which supplies kept running out and work-orders kept getting changed, the earning ability of workers on piece-rates and other performance-linked schemes depended on the extent to which their ambitions enjoyed the goodwill of others on the shopfloor. The limits of this scarce resource, the cooperative goodwill and organizational effectiveness without which it was not possible to make out, were determined by shopfloor-cultural conceptions of equity, which tended to favour skilled or senior workers and disfavour novices while upholding parity between individual workers of equal status.

'Socialist competition' initiatives, where groups of workers undertook to increase their productivity standards on the condition that the management facilitated the increase by making sure of the necessary supply allocations, were bids to change the prevalent conceptions of shopfloor equity to make them more favourable to the 'shock workers'. Managers were under a political pressure to support the campaign for 'Bolshevik speeds' by signing such agreements with the 'shock brigades', but they were not in fact able to guarantee better supplies when these often dried up because of general misplanning rather than because of internal factory mismanagement. Supporting the 'shock workers' therefore meant offending others on the shopfloor, whose conditions of making out worsened. The leaders of the industrialization campaign clearly hoped that the need to restore workable peace in labour relations would concentrate the managers' minds on finding innovative ways of solving the supplies problems and extending the advantages of 'shock work' status to more workers.

The official struggle for 'Bolshevik speeds' was thus translated into a practical struggle for the control of allocation on the shopfloor. Some 'shock brigades' set up their own 'operative planning' groups to deal with supply bottlenecks and

circumvent unsympathetic foremen.[232] Some 'shock brigades' also demanded the simplification of work accountancy
and product-quality controls, to the extent that the industrial
press eventually criticized 'budget-account (*khozraschet*) brigades' which were 'in fact no-account systems' but the means
of drawing wages for fictitious work.[233] There were also
'shock brigades' which attempted to help their cause by
inviting high-ranking managers to become members.[234] And
finally, the 'brigades of communist labour' and 'living communes', which won much acclaim in the heady days of 1929
for wishing to extend their togetherness from the workplace
into the home, also happened to be organized means of
jumping the housing queue, for surely the factory ought to
support them by special allocations.[235] (Collective living, it
should be remembered here, did not need ideological motivation, for shared accommodation was the only kind available
in any case.)

It is not surprising that managers were often found to be
less than enthusiastic supporters of 'socialist competition'
initiatives, as in the following press report.

Tens of thousands of proletarian shock workers in the Urals throw themselves into the battle for new work speeds and the fulfilment of the five-year
plan within four years. They demanded that the shopfloor managers give
them technical assistance, and the sort of decisive leadership that is
appropriate to one-man management. The shock workers' demands,
however, are left pending and all too often encounter open resistance. In
one plant, an engineer answered the shock workers in these words: 'What a
tiresome business, this socialist competition; since you have undertaken the
extra work, why don't you see it through yourselves?' . . . One shop
manager refused point blank to sign an agreement, proposed by shock
workers, according to which the shock workers would eliminate all
absenteeism and stoppages on their part if the management agreed to
reciprocate by guaranteeing timely supplies of raw material.[236]

Managers were said to adopt 'book-keeper–bureaucratic attitudes' to the movement and quoted to answer requests for
special attention with irony: 'You are communards, surely
you can work better anyhow.'[237] They complained of the
disruptive effects of speed-up initiatives on the production
flow and sometimes vented their bemusement in public: 'It's
just as well that what the "socialist competition" is doing on

the shopfloors has nothing to do with us', proclaimed a steel-industry engineer in a speech to a 'congress of rationalizers.'[238]

They were not entirely without public support. The managerial press acknowledged that the demands made by 'socialist competition' initiatives were not always legitimate (hence the observations about *konkurs*), and backed the principle of 'one-man management' against the more blatant claims of shopfloor authority by the leaders of the 'communist-labour brigades'.[239] But on the whole, managers had to be very careful in their methods of reconciling the interests of work-flow regularity and shopfloor peace with the 'socialist competition' initiatives. Being seen to resist the movement or trying to undermine it (e.g. by taking speed-ups at face value and reducing manpower where they took place[240]) could expose managers to charges of 'wrecking', of which they were reminded by the occasional show trial such as the one which involved two quality inspectors who were sentenced to four years in prison for frustrating a 'shock brigade' by failing to pass its products.[241]

The expedient solution to the problems posed by 'socialist competition' initiatives was similar to the one employed in response to the government campaigns for labour discipline and norm-tightening, i.e. to minimize its disruptive effects on the shopfloor status quo by what the campaigning media called 'bureaucratic formalism' and corruption by 'tailist grabbing'.[242] Managers, together with the party and trade union establishments within the factories, encouraged 'shock work brigades' to help get the plan up to schedule by spurts of intensive work when necessary, in return for a flexible approach to wage-accounting procedures during slack periods.[243] And they encouraged senior workers to join 'socialist competition' and become 'shock workers', making the act of joining more a matter of formal registration than an actual change of working practice. Unlike the novices in the youth brigades, the established workers were no rate-busters and shared the foremen's interest in protecting the shopfloor ways from the intrusions of speed-up campaigns.[244] They also shared background experience with the foremen, and the bemusement of shopfloor veterans at the influx of new workers who had yet to be socialized into the civilized ways of shopfloor culture. They were 'shock workers' who helped shopfloor managers to channel into workable routines the intended shocks of outsiders' demands for 'Bolshevik speeds'. That is why the earnest Gudov found his '175 per cent' undertaking publicized as mere '115 per cent' and received no support for his insistence on proving his prowess.

The movement that was started by youth brigades under *komsomol* auspices thus quickly became dominated by 'old workers'. Almost one-half of the delegates at the Congress of Shock Workers at the end of 1929 had work experience exceeding ten years, making it a senior gathering indeed compared with the profile of the industrial workforce as a whole.[245] In the factories, the patterns of recruitment into the movement reflected traditional status hierarchies on the shopfloors. A textile mill where one-half of the workforce were registered 'shock workers' at the end of 1933 had nearly all skilled workers on the honorific register but only one-quarter of the weavers and virtually none of the auxiliary labourers;[246] and the automobile plant in Gorkii had almost three-quarters of its men workers registered in the 'shock work movement' at the beginning of 1933 but less than half of its women workers, although the women had a better discipline record than the men.[247] In Soviet Industry as a whole, the proportion of workers who were on 'socialist competition' registers approached two-thirds in 1931 and three-quarters in 1935, while between one-third and one-half of all workers were officially recognized as 'shock workers' by their trade unions.[248]

Another factor which helped to absorb the impact of 'shock work' initiatives on management–labour practices was ironically brought about by the very forces of political mobilization that had promoted the movement in the first place. The combative hearts felt a calling on many fronts, and they saw activists of the 'shock work' movement as the cadres on which they could rely to win battles in the countryside, the state administration and the cultural fields. In the early years of the first five year plan, many young 'shock workers' quickly found themselves seconded or transferred into jobs well removed from their shopfloors or indeed industrial work.[249]

The other side of the coin must have been also true: some of the *komsomol* members started 'shock brigades' in the hope of getting a job in the political apparat and did not much care if work relations and processes on the shopfloor remained unaffected while the 'shock work movement' became 'formalized'.

This is not to say that the working establishment in the factories could have it all its own way against the campaigners for 'Bolshevik speeds'. The radical mobilizers were well aware of the capacities of 'bureaucratic formalism', and they had potential allies on the shopfloors because low wages and the erratic conditions of making out could make the status distinctions between 'old workers' and 'new workers' keenly felt by ambitious newcomers. Who was granted 'shock worker' status and what this meant was a contested issue. The campaigning press frequently criticized the phenomenon of 'phoney shock work' (*lzheudarnichestvo*) and reported meetings in the factories where 'good shock workers' made loud protests about bonuses which went to undeserving protégés of the factory establishment;[250] it reported inspections which found the phoney variety to account for a substantial majority of the 'shock workers' in some districts,[251] cases where workers could become 'shock workers' only if they paid some money into a kitty, and also cases where 'shock workers' were created on paper without the individuals even knowing.[252] Some trade union branches were criticized for allowing 'former people' who had been deprived of citizenship rights, including deportees, to join the ranks of 'shock workers';[253] others for excluding good workers who were not 'social work' activists.[254] In any case, whether one was or was not a 'shock worker' did not necessarily amount to a great difference in terms of extra rewards; only 12 per cent of 'shock workers' received any substantial bonus payment, according to a survey carried out in 1933.[255] The main point about being a 'shock worker' was that young workers who had the title could expect to be treated as well as the 'old workers' in the shopfloor allocations of the conditions for making out.

It should be obvious by now that 'socialist competition' for 'Bolshevik speeds' was not something that necessarily divided workers who were party members from those who were not.

The factory branches of the party were frequently criticized by the campaigning media for lukewarm responses to 'socialist competition' initiatives, allowing the majority of their members to abstain from joining the movement or making them do so only as a formality.[256] The *komsomol* was perhaps a more willing Trojan horse in the factories for the speed-up campaigns, but its branch officials were junior in status to the factory 'triads' of managing directors, party secretaries and trade union chairmen who were keener to hoard productive resources than to give in to the pressure for tauter plan targets.[257] On the shopfloors, the sparse party membership (about one-tenth were members) must have been closer to the foremen and 'old workers' than to aspiring rate-busters.

Work in Soviet factories shared many of the characteristics of industrial shopfloor culture outlined in the first part of this chapter. Its processes were regulated by standards of effort value in the face of outside pressures for better performance. Labour productivity was rising as the Soviet economy emerged from its chaotic state, but perhaps not to the extent envisaged by optimistic notions of 'industrial culture' and technological capacity. The special feature of the campaigns for improving industrial efficiency consisted in combining administrative requests for discipline and speed-ups with political methods of channelling shopfloor conflicts into actions against established practices. It was only a partial success.

5 Stakhanovite Politics

STAKHANOVISM AND AFTER

In 1935, the balance of opinion in the party leadership evidently shifted in favour of those who thought that the various forms of 'bureaucratism' were going too far in stifling 'mass mobilization' and sacrificing progress to the welfare of self-interested cliques. The verification of party documents was turned into an attempt to purge party officialdom with the help of rank-and-file participation at general meetings at which the virtues of 'criticism and self-criticism' were to be exercised to the detriment of 'family-mindedness', i.e. the inclinations of officials to protect one another from what seemed to them unfair and uninformed criticisms.[1]

The trade unions also came under pressure to put their house in order, and at the same time do something about the habits of 'suppression of criticism' in their ranks. It was not right, claimed the critical press, when trade union officials in the factories levelled 'class enemy' accusations against anyone who crossed them at meetings, or browbeat workers who insisted on their rights with remarks about 'unconscious burghers' (*nesoznatel'nye obyvateli*).[2] They ought not to be forgetful of their duties to defend workers against managerial abuses and it was a 'gross suppression of self-criticism' when they accused people who pointed this out to them of being 'Shlyapnikov-type worker oppositionists' (allusion to a minority movement within the party which had been defeated by the ban on factions in 1921).[3] Furthermore, the trade unions were upbraided for appointing their officials without proper elections, the principles of 'democracy' and 'electivity' being important not only because they were a safeguard against corrupt bosses, but also because they were in keeping with the spirit of the new Soviet Constitution that was at its draft stage.[4]

Allegations of failings in respect of 'accountability, electivity, bonds with the masses and control from below' remained prominent in the mutual recriminations between trade union officials that were vented in the press during the next three years.[5] The rediscovery of the defensive function was a less consistent theme, as the exercise of 'self-criticism' also included calls to 'unmask and destroy the remnants of trade unionism (*tred unionism*)' in the work of trade unions.[6] Many contradictory views were stated on the subject of exactly what functions the trade unions should concentrate on; 'they are living through a peculiar crisis',[7] Stalin said, although this was true of other institutions, too, in the three years that followed summer 1935. The trade unions were advised to concentrate on 'cultural and living conditions' (rather than 'production problems'); support the Stakhanovite movement; organize more production conferences on the shopfloors; do a lot of 'mass inspection', including the inspections of wage-packet accounts as workers often complained that their earnings were smaller than expected on the basis of one or another performance-incentive scheme; they were urged to improve their responsiveness to workers' complaints against managerial abuses, and to refrain from encroaching on the prerogatives of 'one-man management'.[8]

In the summer of 1935, the media became discernibly more populist in their tones. The trade union daily, for example, raised the case of a technical college student who committed suicide after she, the daughter of poor peasants, had been getting bad grades from her insensitive teachers of Russian and geography, one an ex-priest and the other an expelled party member, while her fellow students from kulak backgrounds had been getting good enough grades to earn state grants.[9] The teachers were duly dismissed, as was the college principal who also received a party reprimand. The emphasis on class origins in this story was incidentally at odds with the official rules which had nothing against students from kulak backgrounds earning their grants by good grades, and with a new anti-discriminatory trend in judicial policy that was evident in reports of numerous court decisions to reinstate in their jobs people who had been dismissed on the no-longer adequate grounds of wrong class background.[10]

The landmark event in the theme of caring for 'living people' in the face of 'soul-less bureaucrats' was Stalin's speech to Army Academy graduates in May 1935, which made it clear that this policy was to further the cause of raising industrial performance. He reaffirmed commitment to the 'taut plan' strategy by recalling that the success of the industrialization drive had been achieved against the opposition of party leaders who shrank from difficulties, 'preferred what they saw under their noses to the vision of the future', wanted a shift of emphasis back to consumer goods industries, 'some of them threatening insurrection against the central committee, and even bulllets'. This allusion was juxtaposing opponents of the 'taut plan' strategy with supposed accomplices of the assassin who had shot the Leningrad party leader Kirov six months earlier, which could not have been very encouraging to those who were now pressing for moderation in plan targets and speed-up campaigns. But there was another interesting point made in Stalin's speech; for whereas formerly the conditions had been ones of a 'technological famine' which made it appropriate to say that 'technology is everything', now the main shortage was in people who were able to 'harness technology', so the appropriate saying was that 'cadres decide everything'. Too many managers and leaders treated people as pawns and valued machines above people, just as the bosses he had known during his Siberian exile who had valued horses above people.[11]

The phrase 'harness technology' (*osedlyat' tekhniku*) was an interesting variation on the earlier emphasis on 'mastering technology' (*osvoenie tekhniki*), in that it made a metaphorical allusion to peasant skills. This was something that was not lost on the soon-to-be hero Gudov when he saw the speech posted on a factory notice board, according to his memoirs. Having himself self-consciously learned to grapple with the reactions of his milling-machine to various types of strain by comparing them to the responses of load-pulling horses which he understood well, Stalin's talk about horses and harnessing made him, the ex-peasant Gudov, feel less silly and out of place in his efforts to become a real machine operator.[12]

Furthermore, Stalin's ridicule of bosses who valued machines more than people foreshadowed a particular campaign for change in managerial policy at shopfloor level. In discussing the issue of 'technological discipline' in Chapter 4, we have seen that, in 1933–35, there was a considerable emphasis placed by the campaigning media on the necessity to protect machines from the 'barbaric' carelessness and ineptitude of new workers; managers were asked to set up operational cards for machines with clearly prescribed procedures and to enforce their observance by imposing fines. There was also an emphasis on improving the quality of production, managers having been made liable to severe court sentences for shoddy production by a decree issued in December 1933,[13] which was another reason why the development and enforcement of detailed operational prescriptions was good management, in addition to the fact that it fitted in with the Taylorist image of rational organization. Actual enforcement on the shopfloor was, of course, modified by the practical conceptions of fairness prevalent there, but we have already seen on Gudov's example in Chapter 4 that novice workers could expect worse than raised eyebrows if they were found to have set their machines at higher speeds or greater loads than those prescribed in operational cards. Gudov was humiliated by a foreman who called him by a pejorative name for peasants (*lapotnik*) on the first occasion, while the second occasion on which he was caught earned him a ban from night shifts and a fine.[14]

Things changed in the summer that followed 'cadres decide everything'. In Gudov's machine-tools factory, many managers and the party branch secretary were replaced, and one of their decisions was to reinstate Gudov following his dismissal for rowdiness as a result of conflict with his shopfloor collective. Now the reinstated Gudov enjoyed a growing support for his experiments with machine set-ups and double-rate performance, thanks to the new party secretary and senior management. After all, it was becoming clear why

well-motivated workers should want to deviate from
'technological discipline'; the officially prescribed operational procedures had been set by overrated foreign engineers
with anti-Soviet prejudices, some of whom were even spies,
Gudov assures us, or how else could it have happened that a
German engineer knew where a blue-print was filed when his
Soviet colleagues did not?[15]

The mobilizing spirit of 'cadres decide everything' thus also
challenged the general attitude, common among Soviet engineers as well as their western colleagues, that Soviet workers were a backward lot. This is another one of Gudov's
comments on the 'cadres decide everything' times:

> Such attitudes were widespread among the engineering staff of the Ordzho-
> nikidze factory. The old managers carried on about the shortage of skilled
> workers as an excuse for their own bad work. They relied on the foreigners
> not all of whom were marvellous, that was quite clear. I am not talking
> about the fact that some of them actually were trying to slow us down . . .
> Anyway, when the workers themselves made attempts to implement new
> norms which were higher than the deliberately lowered German ones, our
> technical personnel felt flustered . . . The remarkable growth of skill and
> culture on the part cf Soviet workers escaped the perceptions of some of
> our engineers.[16]

So Gudov, reassured that he had nothing to be ashamed of
if he applied peasant common sense to the mysteries of new
technology, and supported in his ambitions against the established shopfloor rules of making out by a new set of senior
managers, was encouraged in his search for new angles on
piece-rated jobs. In keeping with the new disdain for 'office
management' and excessive reliance on 'foreign methods',
engineers were assigned to the production-lines to pool their
skills with machine operators, to whose norm-fulfilment rates
their salary premiums were pegged. This was in the aftermath
of the campaign of norm revision that had been decreed for
1935. Its implementation evidently caused many difficulties;
'relationships with foremen became complicated', as workers
were refusing to work a new breed of unfavourable norms,
demanding that job allocations in fairness take into account
the new distinctions between good and bad jobs. Stoppages of
the production flow also multiplied, as the changed conditions of making out led to unexpected misalignments in the

work speeds of different sections.[17]

To this situation shopfloor cultures could be expected to adapt with the help of the counter-official practices discussed in Chapter 4. But that was exactly what the mobilizing intentions of 'cadres decide everything' sought to prevent. Ambitious new workers like Gudov, who had been kept in their place by shopfloor custom and practice, were in effect asked to show that they were not backward even if they still spoke in peasant accents. They were the 'living people' to whom the 'taut plan' mobilizers turned to help overcome 'technological conservatism' and 'formalistic' responses to efficiency campaigns. One day, Gudov was prevailed upon to do a rush job at a schedule which he could never meet without unorthodox methods. He made it. The following night, the factory director's chauffeur got him out of bed and brought him to a top management meeting. Gudov explained his success on the rush job which, it was worked out, he accomplished at a rate of 410 per cent of the norm. This record was declared a dignified answer to Alexei Stakhanov's coal-digging feat that had been proclaimed in the press five days earlier. Posters were immediately painted and telegrams sent. 'All Soviet industry switched to the second cosmic speed,' recalled the much celebrated hero. He got the next day off on the director's orders.[18]

Stakhanovism differed in some of its ways from the previous forms of 'socialist competition', including the 'shock brigades' in their militant days six years earlier. The first difference was that, whereas the 'shock work' movement had been started by the komsomol as an appeal to urban youth in particular, Stakhanovism was an appeal to the majority ex-peasant element within the new working class. The photographs of Stakhanovite heroes such as Gudov showed them sometimes in their workers' overalls, sometimes in their new western-style suits, and sometimes in the embroidered shirts of traditional Russia underneath their tailored jackets.[19] Stalin made a point of proclaiming that 'a son is not responsible for his father', and 'social organizations' within industry were encouraged to welcome people from 'class enemy' backgrounds if they earned the honour by good work performance.[20] Class relations were now considered to be different from what they had been at the beginning of the first five year plan.

Secondly, Gudov's recollections show that the Stakhanovite mood had a touch of xenophobia about it, in contrast to the earlier enthusiasts of 'technological mastery' who identified the path to 'industrial culture' with learning the best from the West. The *komsomol* activist whom we have witnessed (in Chapter 3) saying that 'we Russians are very far behind and very, very stupid' spoke these words in 1933; she would be unlikely to repeat them in her talks with fellow railway passengers during the Stakhanovite years. Soviet professors of 'organisation of production' certainly came under a criticism for construing their science as 'an application of foreign methods and principles to the conditions of socialist production' and failing to develop a 'proper scientific methodology for the study of socialist enterprises'.[21]

Thirdly, the wider political context of Stakhanovite struggles tended to be described in the mobilization calls as one in which the enemy to overcome were bureaucrats who had 'separated themselves from the masses' rather than 'former people' such as 'bourgeois specialists'. 'Bureaucratism' was a dominant theme of criticism in the 'cadres decide everything' summer of 1935, and, after the trial of Zinoviev, Kamenev and other 'left' Bolshevik leaders a year later, it became frequently identified as the condition which made it possible for foreign or exiled counter-revolutionary agents to hatch their subversive plots. Along with the charges of Menshevism and Trotskyism which now became a currency of political vigilance, accusations of 'bureaucratism' could be levelled against people in positions of managerial and administrative authority even if they had the credentials of sound working-class background. This made it more difficult for the ex-proletarian managers and 'old workers' on factory shopfloors to protect established custom and practice from the incursions of ex-peasant rate-busters like Gudov.

The fourth point to mention has already been made in the discussion of foremen in Chapter 4. Taylorism and the methods of 'technical norm-setting' came under criticism for reflecting the evils of 'bureaucratism', not just in the shortcomings of underqualified norm-setters and methods engineers, but in the assumptions which equated productive efficiency with rigid distinctions between manual and mental labour. One of the ideological claims of Stakhanovism was that it was advancing socialism by the promotion of innovative cooperation and mutual learning between managers, engineers and advanced workers, which served to break down the distinctions between manual and mental labour. However, this claim should not be confused with a demand to reduce the division of labour on the shopfloors; on the contrary, the well-publicized innovations of Stakhanov and his emulators tended to increase the division of labour between machine-operators and various types of auxiliary worker. The breakdown of the distinctions between manual and mental labour consisted in engineers being seen on the shopfloors to consult the advanced workers who were themselves increasing their technical qualifications in evening classes so as to support their practical intuitions about possibilities of faster work by a broader-based knowledge; and secondly, leading Stakhanovites like Gudov spent a substantial proportion of their working days away from their machines, on lecture tours, in conferences with engineering scientists and innovators, and as resident instructors of other workers. Many were of course promoted to managerial jobs, just as the pioneering 'shock workers' had been earlier on.[22]

The fifth point of difference between Stakhanovism and the earlier 'shock worker' movement could be perhaps discerned with the help of the distinctions, discussed in Chapters 3 and 4, between the managerial goals of effectiveness and efficiency, and between 'task-oriented' and 'time-oriented' work. This was the more general historical distinction between the first and second five year plans. The latter increased an emphasis on efficiency, which was understood as working to technological capacity without any 'waste'. The awareness of the necessity to promote 'time-orientation' in industrial work, which had been earlier exemplified by the pronouncements of the Taylorist philosophers, was now shown in Stalin's description of the ideal Stakhanovite, at a Kremlin conference of the movement in November 1935, as someone who is 'in the habit of counting minutes and seconds'.[23] The Stakhanovite propaganda included a survey which showed Stakhanovites to be in markedly better health than other workers, with the explanation that they enjoyed the benefits of 'rational organization' which made their work well routinized and therefore relatively free of stress or fatigue.[24]

Like the 'shock work' movement, Stakhanovism was pitted against the 'technological conservatism of some engineers'. In the earlier campaign, this was understood to consist largely in the pessimistic reluctance of technical staff to promise the delivery of 'taut plans' by adopting the up-to-date methods of Taylorist production engineering. The Stakhanovite movement still identified 'rational organization' with a fine division of labour on the shopfloor, but it also urged wide experimentation and innovative search for more productive methods by equipping machines with specially adapted gadgets to make possible greater loads and faster set-ups. As we have seen on the example of Gudov's factory, Stakhanovism sought to make workers' ingenuity in finding new angles on their jobs available for the benefit of productivity standards in general.

And finally, Stakhanovism differed from the earlier movements of 'socialist competition' in its very strong emphasis on individual self-motivation, the material rewards of excellent work and the upward social mobility that could be achieved by new workers who took up their opportunities. Spectacular monthly earnings of leading Stakhanovites on progressive piece-rates were widely publicized, as was the theme of self-transformation from poor ignorant ex-peasants into a radiant elite that was repeated in speech after speech at the Kremlin conference of Stakhanovites.[25]

In the main, however, Stakhanovism very much displayed the same characterisics of 'socialist competition' as have been already discussed in Chapters 3 and 4. First of all, it was a political method of mobilization which interpreted existing production practices as intolerable and sought to inspire radical change in this respect by holding up the spectacular achievements of mobilized workers for others to emulate. In Stakhanovite publicity, bad situations were made good by the transformatory powers of conscientious heroes who shook their workplaces up and proved their point by world production records and by the highest standards of 'production culture'.

The situations that were defined as intolerable were basically ones of mismanagement. Mobilized workers were supposed to show up incompetence or corruption in managerial practice and make managers accountable with the help of political campaigns against the 'saboteurs of socialist competition' in managerial ranks. This is how a machine-operator from a Kharkov machine-tools factory explained what was stopping him from working as well as he could:

The factory has been working badly in recent months. They try to explain it by bad supplies of castings, but that is not the only reason. The point is that they don't want to organise work properly here, and so to speak, spurn Stakhanovite work. In our section there are 20 machines and in each shift there is the shift manager, the section manager, the shift foreman, the planner and the job allocator. On the day shift there is also the deputy shop manager and another one of the shop office staff. There is plenty of management [*nachal'stva mnogo*] but no proper one-man management.[26]

There followed a description of a 'typical working day' in which the Stakhanovite did not know what he was to work on until some 30 minutes after the beginning of shift, and then was constantly interrupted by a succession of stoppages due to organizational bottlenecks which the numerous managers tried to overcome by methods of direct intervention that caused much ill-tempered confusion.

At a preliminary session of the Kremlin conference of Stakhanovites with party leaders, Gudov was interrupted in his speech by Ordzhonikidze, the commissar for heavy industry, who requested him to tell everyone about how he had been nearly dismissed from his factory as a result of his efforts to overfulfil production quotas. When the story was told, Ordzhonikidze proceeded to interrogate Gudov's factory director for the benefit of the assembled conference delegates:

'What are you going to do with the saboteurs? It's no good dandling them. You are a Bolshevik! You have trained in the red academy, you must know what's what. Saboteurs must be taken down! He who stands in our way must be swept away! Without mercy!'[27]

Being denounced as a saboteur of any kind could be quite ominous for any manager by the following summer, when the vigilance against 'bureaucratism' and foreign agents was gathering momentum. The managers assembled at another conference therefore must have been relieved to be chided for incompetence by the heavy industry commissar, rather than charged with wrecking intentions:

'Managers and engineers must be at the head of the Stakhanovite movement, otherwise the movement will dissipate. Most managers and engineers have failed to assume leadership as yet . . .

Some say this is due to saboteurs among managers and engineers. This is nonsense. We have educated thousands of new engineers and re-educated the old ones . . . They are honest and patriotic, would give their lives for their country, they are no saboteurs. [Here the speech was interrupted by a burst of applause.] The fact is, they don't know how to lead the movement. Stakhanovite methods require innovation in the organisation of work. Otherwise, it simply means imbalances where the earnings of one worker are made while other workers cannot earn very much because the flow of production is not as it should be.'[28]

'Socialist competition' was a form of political pressure on managers to increase their standards in keeping with the 'taut plans' demands on 'production culture'.

The third aspect of Stakhanovism was that, like some of the earlier forms of 'socialist competition', it was a rate-busting movement to help the government campaigns of norm revision on the basis of which the 'taut plans' could be made tauter. In winter 1935–36 the press was replete with quotations from Stakhanovites' pronouncements at factory meetings on the subject of loose norms:

'On the E-21 detail, at first I was giving 227% of the norm; after a few days, 280%; then after a while, 365%, then 540%, now 714%, and I am confident that I will be giving even more. What sort of technically founded norm is it when I increase its overfulfilment almost day after day?'[29]

Not surprisingly, the party central committee met to discuss the lessons of the Stakhanovite movement and decreed that the industrial commissariats should carry out another norm-revision campaign the following spring. That the new norms should be somewhere between the old ones and the

Stakhanovite standards, was Stalin's advice.[30] Wage funds were also to be increased, so that workers' earnings would not have to suffer a drop as a result of working tighter norms.[31]

Sectoral conferences were duly convened by the industrial commissariats in the next few months, which set norm review deadlines, targets of average percentage by which output norms should be increased, increases in wage-funds made available for this purpose, progressive piece-rate schemes and various other rules, such as that the new norms should be immune from further revisions until the end of the year. The exact targets varied between the sectors, but not very much; on the whole, norms were to be increased by some 25 per cent and wage budgets by just over 10 per cent.[32] No sector got away with limiting its norm increases to single figures. The rule of thumb seemed to be to set the new norms at levels which were close to average actual performance in December. The presence of Stakhanovite records apart, December performance figures were bound to be above normal because this was the month when most plants were 'storming' to catch up on their annual plan targets. The exercise was repeated in 1937, only this time it was possible for at least some of the factories to moderate their tightening targets down to single figures.[33] As in previous years, the norm review campaigns were difficult to carry out without the help of much criticized 'office methods', given the number of norms that were to be revised; e.g. 55,000 norms were under review in the Stalingrad tractor works in spring 1937.[34]

The fourth aspect in which the Stakhanovite campaign confirmed the 'socialist competition' pattern discussed in Chapter 4 was that it made use of the animosities and conflicts of interest on the shopfloors. It coincided with the attack on 'bureaucratic' norm-setters and encouraged workers who were kept by established shopfloor hegemonies from enjoying the cooperation necessary for making good wages on piece-rates to get patronage from senior managers and party officials to improve their position. Gudov himself was, of course, a case in point, but the press was full of similar triumphs where 'social organizations' intervened to enable 'chronic underfulfillers' to become Stakhanovites by getting hitherto neglectful tool-setters, store-keepers and foremen to look after them better.[35]

Fifthly, the Stakhanovite campaign only accentuated the contradiction between the goal of 'industrial culture' based on well routinized, methodical and regular time-oriented work and the heroic mode of the mobilizing appeals which inevitably tended to put emphasis on spectacular achievements. Efficient industrial work is essentially routine and in that sense unheroic. The plethora of record-breaking production feats in the last months of 1935 took place in the context of 'storming' on hot jobs that had to be done to meet the plan fulfilment targets for that year, which was something that was understood to be in fact quite the opposite to the ideals of 'industrial culture'. The justification for putting energy into setting up production records was that such activities served to 'shake up' existing practices and showed what could be done by animating the spirit of innovation, but the triumphs of spectacular record-breaking were actually ones of task-oriented rather than time-oriented work. Leading Stakhanovites like Gudov made their records to celebrate special occasions after which they went absent from their workplaces to collect their laurels or simply to have a rest on the director's orders, which separated them from those who had to keep production going day after day. The workers and managers who were left within the confines of normal shopfloor work could have been excused for thinking that their own jobs were quite properly not the same as the jobs of preparing and achieving world records.

So, like the previous forms of 'socialist competition', Stakhanovism became something that everyone ostensibly approved of to avoid the risk of seeming to oppose the party line, but what was or was not in the true spirit of the movement became another publicly contested issue between the opposing viewpoints of labour-mobilizing political radicalism and managerialist rationalism (see Chapter 3), i.e. another form of contest between the motive forces of the 'taut plans' strategy on the one side and 'industrial culture' on the other side. Since either of these viewpoints inevitably had its extremist and moderate viewers, Stakhanovism was open to conflicts of interpretation along these lines as well. (It would be a simplification to identify managerialist rationalism with moderation; e.g. such leading lights of Soviet Taylorism as Alexei Gastev, who had been prominent during the first five year plan, were visionary extremists in some respects rather than pragmatic moderates.[36])

The record mania of early Stakhanovism soon came under attack in the managerial press, amidst reports of the damage to equipment which was the result of machine operators chasing norm-fulfilment targets at the expense of maintenance schedules.[37] Instead of one-shift records, the movement was encouraged to organize Stakhanovite 'five-days' or 'ten-days' in spring 1936. These were widely criticized for being a flop, because they showed the record-making approach to be ineffective if it did not tackle fundamental issues of intra-enterprise, and indeed supra-enterprise, planning. Planning authorities were criticized for sending their officials to the factories to make sure that the ranks of Stakhanovites multiplied within weeks but failing to improve supplies to the enterprises under their control.[38] This was an interesting counter-offensive by the managerialist spokesmen, because one of the traditional points of 'socialist competition' initiatives had been to focus attention on spare capacities in the factories to discourage managers from complaining about unfeasible plan targets. But the 'month of Stakhanovite study' organized among the managerial corps in summer 1936 under Ordzhonikidze's patronage and the slogan of 'learn to work in a Stakhanovite fashion day after day' increased its criticism of making up for lack of balance in plan targets by shopfloor 'stormings', whether or not these were wrapped up in the Stakhanovite banner.

We must finish once for all with the ideology that prevailed at the beginning of the first five-year plan when, in our efforts to teach enterprise managers plan discipline, and to make them accept that plan targets were not negotiable, we rejected all requests by enterprise managers to the higher organs for the provision of more favourable conditions in which to seek the fulfilment of plans. Now it is necessary to engage very seriously with the methodology of planning, beginning with shopfloor planning and ending with inter-industry planning; here too, there is much more precision and perfecting needed. Decrees regulating the economy of industrial enterprises must be revised – too much has happened since 1929–1930 for all the rules governing enterprise management to remain the same.[39]

This plea for planning and organization was not quite compatible with the early celebrations of Stakhanovite spontaneity. Ordzhonikidze's injunction to managers that they should learn how to lead the movement, which was also made in the summer 1936, could well have been taken to mean that managers should not give up their prerogatives and the concern for their craft in the face of pressures to be seen to mobilize. The early Stakhanovite attack on 'foreign methods' was also countered. The managerial journal continued to propagate them, albeit under the heading of 'foreign experience – to Stakhanovite hands'.[40] In summer 1937, a certain 'Trotskyist' came under a bitter criticism for having forced Leningrad polytechnics to drop the science of 'technical norm-setting' from their syllabuses in the previous year, and a call was made to factory managers to stop neglecting 'the norm-setting work and its cadres'.[41] The point was followed up by a story which showed indifference to the welfare of norm-setters to have affected also police and procuracy officers who could not be bothered to press charges against a pair of disgruntled blacksmiths who had caused a norm-setter grievous bodily harm.[42]

The divisive nature of Stakhanovite elitism was also noticed in summer 1936, when the press criticized factory officials for lavishing care and consideration on selected Stakhanovites at the expense of others. Calls were made in the press to extend due care to mere 'shock workers', and indeed to the workers who did not fulfil their norms at all.[43] It was pointed out that not everyone could be a Stakhanovite, because not everyone could be getting the requisite organizational support under the prevalent conditions.[44] In fact, the emphasis should be not on Stakhanovite individuals at all, but on promoting 'Stakhanovite enterprises' where 'virtually all employees are assured the sort of workplace organisation that has been provided for individual Stakhanovites'.[45] The setting-up of 'integrated process (*skvoznye*) Stakhanovite brigades' received a favourable mention in the press, although the implicit logic of such brigades counselled speed-downs as well as speed-ups to make sure of perfect coordination.[46] 'Integrated process brigades' had made their appearance under the 'shock work' banner in 1932, but had disappeared from public view after the reaffirmation of the 'taut planning' principle in 1934. Another aspect in which the Stakhanovite mantle came to be claimed by managerial policies which had been often pronounced to be unsound were collective piece-work schemes. They were still attacked in some articles for being less 'anti-levelling' in character than individual piece-rates,[47] but defended in other ones, on the general grounds that blanket pressure to individualize incentives were in many cases quite unreasonable.[48] The famous Gorkii automobile works installed collective piece-rates on a large scale, together with a comprehensive and detailed managerial–administrative system undisguisedly imported from Ford's Detroit plant; this was late in 1935, when the individualist, anti-paperwork and anti-foreign themes of Stakhanovite propaganda were at their shrillest.[49]

Here it is worth pausing to note that the political and centralized nature of the industrialization campaign leadership in fact coexisted with a considerable variation in managerial policy between enterprises, even where these belonged to the same industrial commissariat and used the same technology.[50] This phenomenon was also reinforced by the Stakhanovite movement with its emphasis on innovation and experimentation. Some factories remained more 'functionalist' in their management structures than others even after 'functionalism' appeared to fall out of favour,[51] and in some ways the 'anti-functionalist' emphasis on the 'one-man management' powers of foremen and shop heads, supported as it was by party leaders' pronouncements,[52] was equivocated by press articles praising the virtues of installing on the shop-floor specialized progress chasers (*dispetcheri*) empowered to reallocate jobs.[53] A wide range of managerial issues were bitterly contested in individual factories, often with the lethal aid of political denunciations in 1936–38, but the outcome of these contests was not always predetermined by what sort of managerial policy was currently favoured by the party leaders and the media.

To return to the mobilization-*vs.*-managerialism theme, we have seen on Gudov's example that the Stakhanovite movement was sometimes hatched at midnight meetings which were, incidentally, in keeping with the famed observation that the lights in Kremlin offices shone nightly until the small hours. Under the title 'learn to value time', the managerial press made a point of praising a factory director who campaigned against all out-of-hours work, and criticizing those managers who were under the spell of the prevalent ethos to be seen still at work long after dark. 'What do they do during the day?', the article asked, and went on to denounce the nocturnal shows of dedication as cover-ups for a damaging lack of care for rational organization which, among other things, caused grievance among workers who were likewise expected to make up for mismanagement by 'storming' sessions on their free days.[54]

Not only managerial issues, but wider economic issues, too, were contested in the polemics over what constituted a proper support for the Stakhanovite movement and what amounted to its sabotage. The role of financial discipline and the banks, for example: should managers be able to pursue Stakhanovite innovations unconstrained by the 'bureaucratic' attitudes of the banks to budgetary discipline?[55] Again, here was an echo of the debates about the 'taut planning' strategy that had taken place during the 'great breakthrough' period. I have already mentioned in Chapter 1 the wide-ranging dispute over economic policies between the directors of two steel corporations that was pursued all the way, until it ended in one set of the protagonists being consigned to labour camps in 1937. The centralized political system of the industrialization campaign made managers and officials accountable for their actions by the processes of 'criticism, self-criticism and class vigilance against bureaucratism', without being constant in its insistence on the implementation of particular policies. This was perhaps in keeping with the Marxist dictum that the future was properly shaped by the dialectics of struggle rather than the logic of a coherent blueprint.

The Stakhanovite movement certainly animated plenty of dialectic on the shopfloors, just like the previous forms of 'socialist competition'. In its early period, incensed reports of 'sabotage' of the movement railed against senior workers who tried to dissuade their colleagues from rate-busting and foremen who simply tried to ban Stakhanovite initiatives from their shopfloors on the grounds that coal-digging feats were not suitable for emulation in more sophisticated industries.[56] Some managers tried to calm things down by the historically plausible observation that Stakhanovism was just another wind that would blow itself out,[57] some argued that Stakhanovite claims of excellence were invalid if their norms were not 'technically-based' ones to begin with.[58] Self-declared Stakhanovites who insisted on the special considerations due to their new status were rebuked by their foremen for being 'speculators' and ostracized by shopfloor collectives that became suddenly keen on proper rule enforcement when a Stakhanovite went wrong.[59] Some earnest Stakhanovites who advanced their claims to special status by informing meetings about other workers' discipline transgressions found themselves the subject of prolonged vendettas that drove them out of their Stakhanovite apartments, without being able to count on local officials to defend them.[60]

Foremen denied Stakhanovites the advantages of cross-booking and made them wait for the next order;[61] quality inspectors failed their output;[62] some managers simply imposed low ceilings on Stakhanovite earnings, so that wage-budgets would not be overspent;[63] norm-setters were quick to tighten the norms that were overfulfilled by Stakhanovites;[64] shop managers were unexpectedly eager to accept Stakhanovite claims about the efficiency of their methods, and to reduce manpower in the Stakhanovite workplaces accordingly;[65] and foremen refused to authorize payments for stoppage periods to Stakhanovites whose speed-ups they believed to have had disruptive effects on the production flow.[66]

All of these and many other acts that caused grievance to Stakhanovites were discussed at meetings and reported in the press as instances of 'sabotage of the movement'. Appeals were sent to the party central committee to send plenipotentiaries to sort out the 'saboteurs',[67] and the 'saboteurs' and their defenders were demoted or dismissed from their jobs, expelled from the party and their trade unions, and sometimes referred to the courts.[68] Factory managers and officials had to be seen to be for the movement; so, they set up great production feats in aid of the 'storming' that was necessary to meet the 1935 plan targets, apart from which they made sure that the numbers of workers registered as Stakhanovites showed a healthy upward trend. This they did by the well-tried methods that were often criticized as 'bureaucratic formalism', i.e. by the wholesale registration of skilled workers and production-line workers with above-average records of norm-fulfilment as Stakhanovites.[69] In Gudov's factory, for example, 34 per cent of all workers were registered Stakhanovites by the end of 1936, comprising 50 per cent of all workers who were on progressive piece-rates, 39 per cent of workers on ordinary piece-rates and 8 per cent of time-paid workers.[70] Unskilled auxiliary labourers tended to be left out, as Stakhanovism was considered suitable mainly for the 'leading professions' on the factory shopfloors.[71] Like the previous 'socialist competition' movements, Stakhanovism was 'formalized' to become compatible with the interests of shopfloor peace, i.e. to fit in with the prevalent conceptions of shopfloor hierarchy and effort equity.

The initial Stakhanovites saw their earnings reduced to markedly more moderate levels as the record mania blew over and shopfloor managers observed again the precepts of shopfloor justice in regard to the allocation of favourable jobs and the provision of support for above-average piecework performance. 'You are not doing so badly – didn't you have 148 per cent norm-fulfilment and 640 roubles made in February? What more do you want?' said a shop manager to an aggrieved Stakhanovite.[72] Some Stakhanovites found themselves the immediate victim of other people's speed-ups, as the quality of their raw material got worse;[73] some found their earnings halved to below-average levels on being transferred to rickety machines;[74] and many had to take their fair share of the difficulties with supplies.[75] 'Everyone seems to have got used to this, no one seems bothered,' said a report from Gudov's factory.[76] Insistent Stakhanovites were known as people who shout too much to divert attention from their failings, and forced back to normal ways of working.[77] Some found themselves banned from taking liberties with their machine set-ups.[78] They were allowed to voice their grievances at factory meetings and in the press, but no action

followed.[79] 'Social organizations' tended to drop allegations
of 'sabotage of the movement' from their committee agendas
by spring 1936,[80] by which time, as we have seen, the press
was giving space to a variety of conflicting viewpoints as to
what was compatible or not with the true spirit of the movement. It was perhaps a sign of the progress of normalization
on the shopfloors that some of the 'Stakhanovite five-days'
that were organized in spring 1936 evidently took place with
some of the night-shift workers still finding time to sleep on
the job.[81]

The norm review campaign of 1935, which had taken place
before the advent of Stakhanovism and was therefore subsequently criticized for the inadequacies of its 'office
methods', in fact left in its wake many workers whose piecework performance stayed below the levels dictated by the
tightened norms. The proportion of 'non-fulfillers' varied
between industries and plants to the extent of exceeding
one-half of the total in some factories.[82] This did not always
mean that these workers were particularly badly off, as some
may have been the beneficiaries of various supplementary
payments to make up for enforced stoppages, etc. Prior to the
Stakhanovite movement, some managers may have favoured
those methods of norm-fulfilment accountancy which showed
the norms to be tight rather than loose, if they still could pay
just enough wages to the 'non-fulfillers' to keep enough of
them from seeking better employment elsewhere, remembering the prevalent shortage-of-labour conditions. The
Stakhanovite movement, however, put a lot of emphasis on
norm-fulfilment records in general, while the growing number of Stakhanovites had to be shown as substantial 'over-
fulfillers'. The statistical records of norm-fulfilment therefore
tended to show only between 10 and 20 per cent of workers to
be 'non-fulfillers', which was a smaller minority than the
workers who were classed as Stakhanovites with appropriate-
ly impressive over-fulfilment records, after the norm review
campaign supposedly took its course in spring 1936.[83] This
must have been partly due to a change in accountancy
methods to make the results suit the requirements of the
times, and partly to the fact that much of the norm-tightening
was done on the basis of technological improvements which

were projected rather than actual, so that workers subsequently got many of the tightened norms loosened again on
the grounds of 'non-implementation of organizational-
technical measures' or 'technological deviation'.[84]

This did not mean that the norm revision campaign itself
was a cosy process. There was a lot of confusion among
managers as to how seriously they should be taking their
wage-spending limits, i.e. they did not know how much
money they had available to pacify workers by extra payments for stoppages etc., and by letting them earn their wages
on better piece-rates than those envisaged by the tightened
norms. However, they soon found that it was better to
overspend on wages, because not doing so spelled trouble not
only from aggrieved workers but also from some of the higher
authorities who considered it a sign of bad management when
workers' wages dropped.[85] Managers duly got reprimands
from the industrial commissariats for overspending on wages
in the following autumn,[86] but this was something that many
of them had been quite used to. The pattern was followed in
1937. There was a lot of confusion and shopfloor unrest
involved in the norm revision, with the new relativities between favourable and unfavourable norms being contested by
aggrieved workers and subsequently smoothed over with the
help of managerial rule-bending in regard to wage-
payments.[87] This was, again, in accordance with the pattern
discussed in Chapter 4, the persistence of which was apparent
even when its inflationary aspects became usable as incriminating evidence against 'Trotskyist bandits' in the ranks of
senior managers; e.g. in the case of the managers of the
Rostov plant for agricultural machinery where labour productivity rose by 5 per cent but wage expenditure allegedly by
42 per cent between March 1935 and November 1936, during
which period two annual campaigns of norm revision took
their course.[88]

The process of post-Stakhanovite normalization on the
shopfloors could not be a linear one, for the forces of political
mobilization always had enough space in the campaigning
media to fight their corner against managerialist interpretations and 'formalist' practices that sought to neutralize the
pressures of 'socialist competition'. While some articles

emphasized the importance of accuracy and coherence in the process of planning at all levels, other ones were more concerned about the 'profound damage' inflicted by those who interpreted planning and management as 'a sort of peculiar function the discharge of which should be a monopoly of special functionaries, inaccessible to "ordinary" mortals'.[89] There was a concerted effort to revive the radical-mobilizing spirit of Stakhanovism evident in the early months of 1937, when the press carried banner headlines announcing that 'a new wave of the Stakhanovite movement is rising'.[90] Denunciations of 'saboteurs of the movement' appeared again, which were more ominous now than they had been in autumn 1935, for now they were mixed in with accusations of intentional wrecking of machines to cause Stakhanovite initiatives to fail, and hints about 'Trotskyist' malevolents.[91] The secret police was becoming hyperactive under its new chief Ezhov and such denunciations were a grist to its mills. The Stakhanovite 'new wave' may have been also occasioned by a shift in the balance of power among the leaders of industrialization consequent upon Ordzhonikidze's death in February.

Stories about managers looking after their own in the distribution of bonuses and trying to suppress Stakhanovite criticism thereof, about the general decline of 'political work' in the factories and the necessity to resist 'petty bourgeois talk (*obyvatel'skie razgovory*) that still goes on here and there' were printed amidst reports of shopfloor meetings which criticized slack norms.[92] According to a report from Gudov's factory,

1–1½ years ago, people were promoted into heroes quickly and not always with enough thought. Some got a bit dizzy from it. Now managers blow on cold spoonfuls, having burnt themselves on hot ones. They all too often talk of certain Stakhanovites' conceit and all too rarely give any help.[93]

But this did not amount to a sustained revival of Stakhanovism. Not much was heard about technological innovation by the joint efforts of workers and engineers or about specific proposals advanced by workers to improve the efficiency of shopfloor organization, by reducing the 'office methods' of management. The charges against 'unmasked Trotskyists' concerned a whole range of managerial sins including over-spending of wage-budgets, 'abuse of progressive piece-rate systems', 'speculation on labour productivity indices', delaying the introduction of new products, 'spoiling the rhythm of production', 'making workers angry', 'conspiring to dissociate wages from output', transferring workers from one shop to another, and pampering a small group of Stakhanovites too much while keeping other workers short of supplies.[94] Even if it had been clear from these accusations as to what practical lessons to draw from them for shopfloor management policy, the frenetic denunciation contests and police terror were now causing so much havoc in the ranks of management and officialdom as to leave them in no condition to pursue any particular policy on the shopfloors at all. Production lines continued to work in the frenzy of the purges thanks to the autopilot of established custom and practice.

Charges of mismanagement by corrupt 'bureaucrats' were a consistent theme in the violent 'who gets whom' of 1937–38, while consensus over what constituted sound management of industrial labour was more than ever lacking. The dominant definition of industrial efficiency was that everything should be working to full capacity, which was an impossible goal of a naively conceived industrial utopia. It only produced an acute awareness of 'waste', the many varieties of which were the object of countless battles and few clear victories in the struggle for a prosperous 'industrial culture'. The Stakhanovite campaign was an offensive of mobilization that was clearly meant to have a strategic significance in this respect. It did not, however, solve the problem of industrial accountability to provide a consensual framework in which achievements could be seen as clearly valid and important and it could not escape the fate of the previous campaigns of 'socialist competition', i.e. its routinization within the very forms of industrial organization that seemed to harbour slack standards. The intensity of the offensive only revitalized disagreements as to what it was about the industrial organization that was particularly anti-efficient and needed changing the most. Stakhanovism therefore produced few victories which had their value unchallenged. It became one of the phenomena in Soviet public life to be consensually acclaimed in name while few of the things done in their name remained untarnished by suspicions of corrupt purpose.

Even plan-fulfilment was in doubt as a worthy practical aim of the Stakhanovite 'new wave' in early 1937. These were the conclusions drawn by a revitalized Stakhanovite from the trial of Pyatakov, until recently one of Ordzhonikidze's deputies in the heavy industry commissariat, and other senior 'Trotskyists':

> The situation is such that workers' activity cannot be judged simply by plan-fulfilment. We understand productive activity to mean the widest participation in all the life of the shopfloor and the enterprise, Bolshevik criticism regardless of individuals.[95]

She did not elaborate what this meant in work-day practice, in conformity with the general failure of the 'new wave' to gain a distinct shape in the deluge of anti-bureaucratic, anti-Trotskyist and anti-Menshevik denunciations that filled the channels of public life.

There was no government campaign of norm revision announced for 1938, when industry had to cope with the combined effects of the purges that were depleting managerial ranks and the war preparations that were draining the workforce into army call-ups. In 1939, when the purges were called off, the secret police chief Ezhov was removed from office to death row and the corps of administrators and managers was made relatively secure from the caprices of 'class vigilance'. Developments in Soviet industrial life then confirmed the pattern that had been established in the first half of the decade; there was another round of norm revision, and a new campaign for the tightening of labour discipline, announced by a new decree on absenteeism and tardiness in December 1938, which was not dissimilar from the one issued six years earlier.[96] It was only stricter, in the sense that it made failures of punctuality more explicitly classifiable as unauthorized absence to be punished by immediate dismissal (20 minutes late was absenteeism and so was repeated lesser lateness), and in that it made managerial failures to enforce the provisions of the decree explicitly liable to prosecution in the courts. The decree was supported by the issue of labour books to workers, in which the circumstances of employment contract termination were to be recorded to discourage the hire of dismissed workers and to make dismissed workers, and those who left an employment without proper notice, liable to a loss of social insurance entitlements. In this respect, too, the new labour legislation was reminiscent of 1932, when the absenteeism decree coincided with the issue of passports to urban residents to discourage casual migration.

The most interesting similarity, however, was that the campaigning press gave publicity to a hundred ways in which the enforcement of the decree was evaded by the collusive responses of workers and managers in 1939, just as it had done in 1933. The new norm revision campaign was also by all accounts true to form; norms were again much tightened and on average overfulfilled, while recorded overall increments in actual output were modest by comparison, because tightened norms in fact tended to be subject to subsequent shopfloor renegotiation on the particularistic grounds of 'technological deviation'. The next step of the government was to strengthen its legislation on labour discipline by another decree, issued in June 1940, which made absenteeism and quitting without due notice subject to court sentences of up to six months of 'corrective labour at the normal place of employment' (meaning a 25 per cent deduction from pay), or up to four months in labour camps. Enforcement was, again, less than uncompromising.[97] But the war was approaching, and with it another chapter in Soviet history. Let it just be said now that the punitive labour law was well known to be dead letter when it was officially repealed in 1956.

INDUSTRIALIZATION AND THE PURGES

The above observations about the pattern of political initiative and industrial response in the campaigning for labour efficiency conclude this study of the labour–management aspect of Soviet industrialization in the 1930s. What follows is a brief exploration of the implications this study may have for interpretative ideas concerning the purges and especially the police terror in 1936–38. The argument can be summarized as being in favour of these views: (1) that the purges were in part fuelled by an escalation of conflict over issues of policy concerning the conduct of the industrialization campaign; (2) that the mobilization policies of the industrialization campaign based their appeals to workers on conflicts of shopfloor interest, and on the whole did not resort to using police terror against manual workers to make them work harder; and (3) that the social conditions created by the industrialization campaign were not conducive to a collective outrage by industrial workers at the repressive actions of the police.

One divisive issue was posed by the tasks and failings of administrative control: how could the proponents of radical policies be satisfied that policy failures were not caused by sloppy or corrupt administration? Some sort of periodic purge of administrators, albeit not necessarily one involving the secret police, seemed to many an appropriate additional institution of executive accountability in contexts where the normal administrative means of assessing the performance of executives could not be trusted. We have seen in Chapter 3 that many of the western engineers working on contracts in the Soviet Union at the time thought that periodic purges of managers and government officials in principle could have been a good idea. But what should be done if it appeared that some sets of party and state administrators were able to arrange for the purges to lose their bite where it mattered, thus in effect making themselves unaccountable to the central policy-makers and decentralizing the state? This was a difficult problem for the 'revolution from above'. The policies of the first five year plan in particular created a migrant and hungry society which would have been awkward to control in any case, and there was far too much evidence of chaos on the ground to suggest that the policy-makers could trust their hastily constructed instruments of executive control. The normal issues of policy administration – centralization vs. decentralization, radicalism vs. moderation, and the prevention of corruption – thus became a central battleground of the 'revolution from above'.[98] The 'struggle against bureaucratism' certainly had something to do with issues of policy not all of which could be put down simply to Stalin's personal strivings.

Another policy problem that was in all probability a constant source of conflicting attitudes among the officialdom was how 'taut' the 'taut plans' should be. The radical thinking that stemmed from a faith in the transformatory powers of political mobilization required the plan targets to be spectacular enough to serve as inspirational symbols of 'overcoming backwardness', and it perceived scepticism about the feasibility of the 'Bolshevik speeds' of development as amounting to a dangerous 'demoralizing tendency'. The costs of failures to keep to schedule, on the other hand, were all too apparent in wasteful breakdowns of coordination, making the case for greater caution in target-setting especially strong as the first five year plan headed for the economic crisis of 1932–33. The subsequent appearance of articles advocating a pro-market reform of the economic system; Stalin's observation that it was 'obviously' no longer necessary 'to whip the country and drive it on' (*podkhlestyvat' i podgonyat' stranu*); the year-long delay in adopting the second five year plan; the public show of disagreement between Molotov and Ordzhonikidze over the second five year plan at the 'congress of victors'; the controversy among steel-industry chiefs over the value of a *khozraschet* experiment that was vented on the pages of the industrial press – these are just some of the facts in favour of the hypothesis that the 'taut plans' strategy remained a contested issue at the top of political agendas, despite the united chorus of agreement on the wisdom of the leader and his 'general line'.[99]

The industrialization campaign created a hastily grown army of managers facing intractable problems of labour motivation and administrative coordination, while the system of 'taut planning' failed to provide any reliable criteria for the evaluation of managerial performance. Were industrial failures due to slacking managers or to overtaut targets not allowing enough slack for the achievement of coordinated schedules? This was a question to which no facts could provide an answer, for they had to be interpreted in the light of a decision as to which logic should be given the benefit of doubt – the do-or-die logic of 'mass mobilization' or the managerialist perceptions of objective circumstance. 'Bureaucratism' thus meant two things in the context of arguments over plan targets: on the one hand, the misuse of political pressures for the making of unrealistic demands and promises, and on the other hand, the misuse of administrative accountancy for cover-ups and the pursuit of corrupt self-interest. In either case, the term also encoded the fear of a collapse of party–state authority due to the 'divorce from the masses' consequent upon abuses of office. Moderation in target-setting could be seen as desirable for allowing a more peaceful and better organized progress, or it could be seen as a licence for the 'creative potential of the masses' to be smothered by administrators' inadequacies. Both sides of this argument could produce evidence in their support, and both saw the other as potentially disastrous for the success of the industrialization campaign.

That the logic of industrialization by mass mobilization should lead to a widespread use of 'terror' to keep 'demobilization tendencies' at bay is a plausible enough observation, but it may well be historically inaccurate if 'terror' in this context is taken to mean a socially or politically indiscriminate use of coercion to motivate hard work throughout the 'atomized mass' of working population. This would suggest no other links between 'the regime' and 'the masses' than those of mutual fear, the political mobilization ironically ending in the extinction of all politics, as indiscriminate coercion rendered impossible any attempts to influence behaviour by appeals to social divisions and group interests – there are no social divisions or group interests within a thoroughly terrorized and atomized population.[100] A closer attention to the mobilization propaganda, however, suggests that the industrialization campaign did involve a lot of appealing to social divisions and group interests. The attack on the 'bourgeois specialists', for example, carried the message to industrial workers that the rises of productivity envisaged by the 'great breakthrough' would be a different and less disagreeable process than the 'rationalization' campaigns that had been carried out by the 'bourgeois specialists', at the cost of much worker resentment, since the mid-1920s. 'Specialist-baiting' had its shopfloor appeal, and the 'great-breakthrough' period indeed was one of considerable ferment in the relations between workers and managers.

The 'socialist competition' movements provide another example where the politics of 'mass mobilization' drew some practical energy from conflicts of interest on the shopfloor. Both the 'shock work' and Stakhanovite movements involved a discernible element of spontaneity, because they were a form of arm twisting which could force managers to reallocate organizational resources in favour of the younger workers' interest in being enabled to earn good wages where only 'old' workers had enjoyed an effective degree of managerial coop-eration before. In other words, the movements were political opportunities for 'new workers' to break the shopfloor hege-mony of 'old workers'. 'Socialist competition' initiatives thus exerted 'from below' pressures on managers to improve their practices so that more workers had their earning powers unhampered by organizational difficulties or adverse techni-cal conditions.

Another example where 'work with the masses on the labour productivity front' could involve the practical politics of taking advantage of existing inter-group relations within industry is the endorsements by leaders of the industrializa-tion campaign of the animosities felt by shopfloor workers against time-study engineers. The reorganization of 'norm-setting' that was decreed after the party conference in 1932 clearly implied that the practice was imbued more with 'office methods' than with technological knowledge, and the attack on 'technical norm-setting' developed into an unequivocal condemnation of its scientific pretensions and 'bureaucratic' practices in 1935. While workers were asked to put up with annual norm-tightening throughout the industrialization de-cade, their contempt for the norm-setters was available to be used as a political asset by both line managers and party agitators.

The industrialization campaign combined a complex prac-tice of labour–management politics with a division of policy-making opinion over the issues of 'taut planning' and 'bureaucratism'. The escalation of the purges into the *ezhov-shchina* of 1937–38 coincided with an offensive by mass mobilizers against managerialists, by means of the Stakhan-ovite movement, and with managerialist efforts to interpret the movement in their own way. The fight over productivity standards was thus intensified but its violent potential was channelled largely into a battlefield defined by the 'bureaucratism' issue, where ordinary workers were markedly less vulnerable than their bosses. Within the context of the purges, the issue of 'bureaucratism' became one of whether certain types of administrative practice could have made even those administrators who had impeccable working-class backgrounds a proper object of 'revolutionary vigilance'.[101] Within contexts of shopfloor conflict, sections of 'new workers' could advance their interests and feel reassured by the new constitution as well as party leaders' pronouncements that suspect class origins or ex-peasant status now mattered less than work performance.

If there was a lot of conflict on the shopfloors, and if workers were less vulnerable to the purges than their bosses, it is possible that workers were not always outraged by police interventions in factory life. This observation is reinforced by circumstantial evidence of workers' perceptions of state repression, which has been discussed in Chapter 2.

First, the labour camps were not necessarily known in the 1930s to be as bad as the post-war ones portrayed by Alexander Solzhenitsyn in *One Day in the Life of Ivan Denisovich*. The new workers often had come into contact with forced labourers on construction sites during the first five year plan. Judging by reports from western witnesses, there was not always much difference between free and imprisoned workers in their provisions and work conditions. The two sets of workers sometimes came together in the same collectives and prisoners sometimes had managerial authority over free workers. Many of the free workers were probably quite aware that the 'kulak' prisoners as well as the 'bourgeois specialist' ones had been on the receiving end of rough justice, but the nature of their predicament possibly did not seem much different in kind from military conscription, which was a traditional hazard of peasant life.

Secondly, we have seen in Chapter 2 that workers usually came into first-hand contact with the police on charges of hooliganism, and the evidence concerning court administration in this respect, at least in the first half of the decade, suggests that the punitive agencies were inefficient and could be evaded, often by the simple device of giving a false address and moving on. USSR was a society of migrants many of whom were able to equip themselves with new identities, even after the introduction of passports.

And thirdly, competition for scarce resources with the help of *blat* networks was a fact of life which brought individual workers and party–state officials with their political powers into the same cliques, and which made real or bluff claims and counter-claims of privileged access to coercive agencies a normal currency of negotiation. This was a skill which the western experts learned to use just as swiftly as the natives. Fears that a rival clique might not be bluffing in having a repressive agency of the state on its side was thus combined with hopes that state coercion could be also manipulated by friendly strings.

The political processes of the industrialization campaign were reducible neither to communist fanaticism, nor to Russian traditions, nor to Stalin's caprice, nor to the needs of 'primitive socialist accumulation'. They perhaps reflected the fact that the new traditions of the revolutionary state had yet to establish peaceful means of conflict resolution. They combined the practical politics of industrial bargaining with a deep conflict between the roles and attitudes shaped by the administration of 'taut plans'. And they possibly diffused a popular revolt by drawing the violent energies of social strife into a fight over 'bureaucratism'. From this vantage point, the purges appear to be not unlike a civil war by proxy.

Notes

CHAPTER 1

1. Davies, R.W., *The Socialist Offensive: The Collectivisation of Soviet Agriculture*, 1929–1930 (Macmillan, London, 1980), pp. 39–41.
2. Lewin, M., *The Making of the Soviet System: Essays in the Social History of Interwar Russia* (Methuen, London 1985), Chapter 4.
3. Davies, *op.cit.*, esp. Chapters 4–5.
4. See the story of Lida's father in Strøm, A., *Uncle Give Us Bread* (Allen & Unwin, London, 1936).
5. See Shabkov's story in Scott, J., *Behind the Urals* (Cambridge, Mass., 1942), pp. 17 ff.
6. Davies, *op.cit.*, Chapters 6–9.
7. Lewin, *op.cit.*, Chapter 7.
8. Drobizhev, V. and Lel'chuk, V., *Ocherki po istoriografii sovetskogo obshchestva* (Moscow, 1967), pp. 104–34.
9. Quoted in Lewin, *op.cit.*, Chapter 7.
10. *Ibid.*, p. 179.
11. *Voprosy profdvizheniya* 1936, No.5, pp. 86–9, and No.8, pp. 28–32.
12. Based on data provided by Wheatcroft, S.G., 'A re-evaluation of Soviet agricultural production', in Stuart, R.C. (ed.), *The Soviet Rural Economy* (Rowman & Allenheld, Totowa, NJ, 1983), pp. 32–62.
13. *Ibid.*
14. Khrushchev, N.S., *Khrushchev Remembers* (Penguin, Harmondsworth, 1977), p. 83.
15. See Wheatcroft, S.G., *The Soviet Economic Crisis of 1932: the crisis in agriculture*, Paper presented to the Soviet Industrialisation Project Seminar at the Centre for Russian and East European Studies, University of Birmingham, January 1985, Appendix 1.
16. Churchill, W.S., *The Second World War* (London, 1951), vol. IV, p. 447.
17. I am indebted to Professor R.W. Davies for the last point.
18. Carr, E.H. and Davies, R.W., *The Foundations of a Planned Economy 1926–1929* (Macmillan, London, 1969), vol. 1, Part I.

19. Ward, C.E., *Russian Cotton Workers and the NEP*, (PhD thesis, University of Essex, 1985), Chapters 10 and 12.
20. Carr and Davies, *op.cit.*
21. The reference is to Preobrazhenski, E., *The New Economics* (Oxford University Press, 1965). Originally published as *Novaya ekonomika* (Moscow, 1923). Preobrazhenski assumed a continuation of the NEP.
22. Hoover Archive, AER collection, file D.M.F.; also W.L. Gorton collection.
23. Wheatcroft, S.G., Davies and Cooper, 'Soviet industrialisation reconsidered: some preliminary conclusions about economic developments between 1926 and 1941', *Economic History Review*, (May 1986).
24. Stalin, J.V., *Collected Works*, vol. 13 (Moscow, 1955), pp. 53–82. First published in *Pravda*, 5 July 1931.
25. Davies, R.W., *The Soviet Economic Crisis of 1932: the crisis in the towns*, Paper presented to annual conference of National Association of Soviet and East European Studies, March 1985.
26. *Ibid.*
27. Wheatcroft, *op.cit.*, Appendix 1.
28. Davies, *op.cit.*
29. Strøm, *op.cit.*
30. Davies, R.W., 'The socialist market: a debate in Soviet industry, 1932–1933', *Slavic Review*, vol.42 (1984), pp. 201–23.
31. Lewin, M., *Political Undercurrents in Soviet Economic Debates* (Princeton University Press, New York, 1974)
32. *Materialy ob˝edinennogo plenuma TsK i TsKK VKP(b), 7–12go yanvarya 1933g* (Moscow: Partizdat, 1933).
33. Getty, J. Arch, *Origins of the Great Purges: the Soviet Communist Party Reconsidered, 1933–1938* (Cambridge University Press, 1985), p. 16.
34. My calculations, based on data provided by Davies, R.W., 'Soviet industrial production, 1928–1937: the rival estimates', *CREES Discussion Papers*, SIPS No.18 (Centre for Russian and East European Studies, University of Birmingham, 1979).
35. e.g. *Voprosy profdvizheniya* 1934, No.7, pp. 41–51.
36. Wheatcroft, S.G., *Changes in the Pattern of Employment in the USSR, 1926–1939* (Paper Presented at SSRC Conference on Soviet Economic Development in the 1930s, University of Birmingham, June 1982), Appendix 3.
37. Benvenuti, F., 'La "lotta per la redditivita" ' nell'industria sovietica (1935–1936)', *Studi Storici* 1984, No.2, pp. 461–510.
38. *Ibid.*
39. Based on Davies, 'Soviet industrial production, 1928–1937', *op.cit.*
40. Lampert, N., *The Technical Intelligentsia and the Soviet State* (Macmillan, London, 1979), esp. Chapter 3.
41. Smith, S.A., *Red Petrograd: Revolution in the Factories, 1917–1918* (Cambridge University Press, 1985), pp. 193–9.
42. Fitzpatrick, S. (ed.), *Cultural Revolution in Russia, 1928–1931* (Indiana University Press, Bloomington and London, 1978), pp. 8–40.

43. Lampert, *op.cit.*, Chapters 3 and 6.
44. Fitzpatrick, *op.cit.*, p. 22.
45. *Ibid.*, pp. 8–40.
46. *Ibid.*, p. 11.
47. Clark, K. in Fitzpatrick (ed.), *op.cit.* pp. 189–206.
48. Lapidus, G.W., 'Educational strategies and cultural revolution', in Fitzpatrick (ed.), *op.cit.*, p. 92.
49. Sharlet, R., 'Pashukanis and the withering of the law in the USSR', in Fitzpatrick (ed.), *op.cit.*, pp. 169–88.
50. *Ibid.*
51. Körber, L., *Life in a Soviet Factory* (London, 1933), p. 45.
52. Lewin, M., *The Making of the Soviet System: Essays in the Social History of Interwar Russia* (Methuen, London, 1985), p. 239.
53. *Ibid.*, pp. 234–6.
54. Sharlet, *op.cit.*
55. Estrin, A., 'O vine i ugolovnoi otvetstvennosti v sovetskom prave', *Sovetskoe gosudarstvo i pravo* 1935, No.1–2, pp. 108–25. A conflict of opinion between the procuracy and the secret police over jurisdiction and the scope of law did not remain below the surface. See Vyshinskii, A.Ya., 'Nashi zadachi', *Sotsialisticheskaya zakonnost'* (1935), No.5, pp. 1–16, and esp. pp. 13–15.
56. Getty, J.A., *Origins of the Great Purges: the Soviet Communist Party Reconsidered, 1933–1938* (Cambridge University Press, 1985).
57. *Ibid.*, pp. 51–61.
58. *Ibid.*, pp. 87–90.
59. Kravchenko, V., I *Chose Freedom: the personal and political life of a Soviet official* (Readers Union and Robert Hale Ltd, London, 1949), Chapter 17.
60. The reference is to A.Ya. Vyshinskii. For his defence of due process of the law see, e.g., 'O nekotorykh voprosakh organizatsii sovetskoi yustitsii', *Sovetskoe gosudarstvo i pravo* (1935), No.5, pp. 22 ff., and 'Nashi zadachi', *Sotsialisticheskaya zakonnost'* (1935), No.5, pp. 1–16.
61. See the discussions of A. Zhdanov's role in the party purges in Getty, *op.cit.*
62. Lewin duly notes this phenomenon and gives it a special name, *la démesure*. See his discussion of it in *op.cit.*, pp. 26–30.
63. Wheatcroft, S.G., 'On assessing the size of forced concentration camp labour in the Soviet Union, 1929–1956', *Soviet Studies*, vol.33, No.2, pp. 265–95.
64. Wheatcroft, S.G., 'Towards a thorough analysis of Soviet forced labour statistics', *Soviet Studies*, vol.35, No.2, pp. 223–37.
65. Wheatcroft, S.G., 'A note on Steven Rosefielde's calculation of excess mortality in the USSR, 1929–1949', *Soviet Studies*, vol.36, No.2, pp. 277–81. For higher estimates see Conquest, R., *The Great Terror* (Macmillan, London, 1968), Appendix; and 'Forced labour statistics: some comments', *Soviet Studies* vol.34 No.3. Also see Rosefielde, S., 'An assessment of the sources and uses of forced labour, 1929–1956', *Soviet Studies*, vol.33, No.1; and 'Excess mortality in the Soviet Union:

a reconsideration of the demographic consequences of forced industrialization 1929–1949', *Soviet Studies*, vol.35, No.3, pp. 385–409.
66. Conquest, *The Great Terror, op.cit.*
67. Wheatcroft, 'Towards a thorough analysis . . .', *op.cit.*

CHAPTER 2

1. Gudov, I., *Sud'ba rabochego* (Politizdat, Moscow, 1970).
2. Strøm, A., *Uncle Give us Bread* (Allen & Unwin, London 1936), pp. 31 and 119.
3. Lida's story in Strom, *op.cit.*
4. *Za industrializatsiyu*, 10 July 1932, p. 2.
5. 1.5 million were called up in January 1938. See Drobizhev, V. and Vdovin, A., *Rost rabochego klassa v SSSR* (Moscow 1976), p. 123.
6. Pisarev, M.I., *Naselenie i trud v SSSR* (Moscow 1966).
7. Lewin, M., *The Making of the Soviet System: essays in the social history of interwar Russia* (Methuen, London 1985), pp. 219–20.
8. Wheatcroft, S.G., *Changes in the Pattern of Employment in the USSR, 1926–1939* (Paper presented to SSRC Conference on Soviet Economic Development in the 1930s, at the Centre for Russian and East European Studies, University of Birmingham, June 1982).
9. Shiokawa, N., 'Labor turnover in the USSR, 1929–1933: a sectoral analysis', *Annals of the Institute of Social Science*, No.23 (University of Tokyo, 1982).
10. Wheatcroft, *op.cit.*, provides detailed statistics of the growth of the whole range of occupational categories over the 12 years between the censuses.
11. *Ocherki po istoriografii sovetskogo obshchestva* (Moscow, 1967), article by V. Drobizhev and V. Lel'chuk, pp. 104–34.
12. *Za industrializatsiyu*, 25 November 1930, p. 4; and 2 February 1931, p. 5; *Trud* 9 January 1933; *Voprosy profdvizheniya* 1933, No.5, p. 44.
13. *Za industrializatsiyu* 12 July 1931, p. 3; 28 July 1931 p. 3; *Trud*, 7 January 1933.
14. Drobizhev, and Vdovin, *op.cit.*, p. 97.
15. *Ibid.*, p. 106.
16. *Voprosy profdvizheniya* 1933, No.3, pp. 37–51; *Predpriyatie* 1932, No.15, pp. 1–3.
17. My calculations based on data provided by Drobizhev and Vdovin, *op.cit.*
18. Drobizhev and Vdovin, *op.cit.*, p. 119.
19. *Ibid.*, p. 130.
20. *Voprosy truda* 1933, No.8–9, pp. 106–10.
21. In 1929–32, more than one-half of all newcomers to the non-agrarian sector of the economy were peasant men; another one-sixth were peasant women, one-fifth were urban women and one-tenth were urban men. In 1933–37, out of every ten newcomers to the non-agrarian sector of the economy three were peasant men, the rest being

more or less equally divided between peasant women, urban women and urban men. These proportions are calculated on the basis of the data provided in Drobizhev and Vdovin, *op.cit.*, pp. 116 and 130–32; and Wheatcroft, *op.cit.*, p. 51.

22. Drobizhev and Vdovin, *op.cit.*, p. 134.
23. *Voprosy truda* 1933, No.8–9, pp. 106–10.
24. Drobizhev and Vdovin, *op.cit.*, p. 138.
25. Wheatcroft, S.G., 'Famine and factors affecting mortality in the USSR: the demographic crises of 1914–1922 and 1930–1933'; *CREES Discussion Papers SIPS*, No.20 (Centre for Russian and East European Studies, University of Birmingham), p. 24.
26. According to Gudov, *op.cit.*, it was a retort sometimes heard at meetings called to encourage workers to emulate a miner called Izotov in his feat of 500 per cent output quota fulfilment (in 1932), that production increases would be gladly offered if miners' food rations were extended to other workers. For the opinion that factories outside the cities were better off for food because of their farms see Hoover Archive, Zawodny Interviews, II/13.
27. Hoover Archive, American Engineers in Russia collection, G.A. Burrell, 'Life in a Soviet town'.
28. Hoover Archive, J.K. Zawodny Interviews.
29. Hoover Archive, AER collection, Questionnaire J.K.J.: 'Frequently Russian workers were classed as lazy and indifferent, but it is the writer's opinion that they did well when their food supply was considered.'
30. *Voprosy profdvizheniya*, 1933, No.13, p.20; *Za industrializatsiyu*, 2 January 1933.
31. *Trud*, 2–5 October 1934.
32. *Voprosy profdvizheniya*, 1933, No.3, pp.37–51.
33. *Voprosy profdvizheniya*, 1933, No.12, pp. 24–34.
34. *Predpriyatie*, 1935, No.8, pp. 4–5.
35. Hoover Archive, J.K. Zawodny Interviews, II/26.
36. *Voprosy profdvizheniya*, 1935, No.2–3, pp. 29–35.
37. *Trud*, 15 March 1934 and 10 October 1934.
38. *Za industrializatsiyu*, 27 September 1933; *Trud*, 21 February 1935.
39. *Trud*, 20 February 1935.
40. *Predpriyatie*, 1935, No.17–18, pp. 2–3.
41. *Pravda*, 22 November 1935.
42. *Predpriyatie*, 1935, No.17–18, pp. 2–3; *Voprosy profdvizheniya*, 1936, No.7, pp. 11–15.
43. Smolensk Archive, WKP 189, letter from Rumyantsev, 16 February 1935.
44. *Za industrializatsiyu*, 14 November 1930, p. 3; 23 September 1932, p. 3.
45. Gudov, *op.cit.*, p. 62.
46. For statistics see Barber, J., *Housing Conditions of Soviet industrial workers 1928–1941* (Paper presented to the West European Conference on Soviety Industry and the Working Class in the Inter-War

Years, University of Birmingham, June 1981), pp. 3 and 8–9.
47. Scott, J., *Behind the Urals* (Cambridge, Mass., 1942). This information relates to 1938.
48. See the story of a suspected police informer in Hoover Archive, Zawodny Interviews II/24.
49. Smith, A., *I Was a Soviet Worker* (London, 1937), pp. 44 ff.; Shvernik, in *Devyatyi vsesoyuzni se˝zd professional'nykh soyuzov SSSR* (Moscow, 1933), p. 103.
50. Barber, *op.cit.*, pp. 6–7, provides figures suggesting *that* per capita average of housing space for workers was in the region of 4 square metres.
51. *Predpriyatie*, 1935, No.10, pp. 39–41.
52. Smith, *op.cit.*, describes a barrack belonging to one of the large electrical engineering plants in Leningrad (*Elektrozavod*) as consisting of a wooden structure about 800 feet long and 15 feet wide, containing about 500 narrow beds covered with mattresses filled with straw and dried leaves.
53. *Trud*, 20 December 1933; *Trud*, 5 January 1934; *Za industrializatsiyu*, 14 November 1930, p. 3.
54. *Trud*, 20 December 1933; *Za industrializatsiyu*, 8 January 1934; *Voprosy profdvizheniya*, 1933, No.3, p. 39.
55. *Predpriyatie*, 1934, No.19, pp. 1–3.
56. Barber, *op.cit.*
57. *Ibid.*
58. Hoover Archive, AER collection, Questionnaire J.B.B.
59. Hoover Archive, AER collection, Questionnaire M.K.
60. *Trud*, 20 December 1933, gives an example of a single room of 13 square metres costing 6 roubles 55 kopek per month, which was about a half of what was paid by people renting barrack beds.
61. Drobizhev, V.Z. and Lel'chuk, V.S., in *Ocherki po istoriografii sovetskogo obshchestva*, (Moscow, 1967), pp. 104–34; *Za industrializatsiyu*, 23 September 1932, p. 3, deplored the fact that workers had to buy from 'speculators' stalls outside the factory gates'.
62. *Predpriyatie*, 1935, No.10, pp. 39–41.
63. *Voprosy profdvizheniya*, 1936, No.1, pp. 60–5.
64. *Voprosy profdvizheniya*, 1936, No.11, pp. 91–5.
65. *Voprosy profdvizheniya*, 1936, No.9, pp. 67–73.
66. Calculated on the basis of data given in *Voprosy profdvizheniya*, 1936, No.1, pp. 51–9, and 1934 No.11, p. 9.
67. *Predpriyatie*, 1935, No.10, pp. 39–41.
68. Gudov, I., *op.cit.*, p. 21.
69. *Trud*, 27 September 1936.
70. Rabkina, N.E. and Rimashevskaya, N.M., 'Raspredelitel'nye otnosheniya i sotsial'noe razvitie', *EKO*, 1978, No.5, p. 20. I am indebted for this reference to Ken Straus, at present a PhD student at the University of Pennsylvania.
71. Smith, A., *op.cit.*, p. 41; *Voprosy truda*, 1933, No.8–9, pp. 106–10; *Za industrializatsiyu*, 29 April 1937, p. 2.

72. *Voprosy profdvizheniya*, 1936, No.5, pp. 52–6; Kiselev, Ya.L. and Malin, S.E. (eds.), *Sbornik vazhneishikh postanovlenii po trudu* (Moscow, 1936), pp. 108–9.
73. Rabkina, and Rimashevskaya, *op.cit.*, p. 20.
74. *Trud*, 6 June 1936, named a Stakhanovite who earned 1429 roubles in one month.
75. *Za industrializatsiyu*, 29 April 1937, p. 2; also *Trud*, 16 September 1936.
76. *Trud*, 10 February 1933.
77. Chapman, J.G., *Real Wages in Soviet Russia since 1928* (Harvard University Press, Cambridge, Mass., 1963), pp. 138–40.
78. *Voprosy profdvizheniya*, 1933, No.3, p. 45; 1936, No.11, pp. 62–71.
79. *Voprosy profdvizheniya*, 1933, No.8, p. 2.
80. *Trud*, 5 May 1936.
81. *Voprosy profdvizheniya*, 1936, No.6, pp. 22–7.
82. *Trud*, 17 December 1933.
83. *Voprosy profdvizheniya*, 1936, No.9, pp. 28–37 (postscript from the editors); *Trud*, 17 November 1934; 9 December 1933.
84. *Trud*, 11 August 1935; 11 May 1936.
85. *Voprosy profdvizheniya*, 1936, No.1, pp. 60–5; 1936, No.2, pp. 71–6.
86. *Voprosy profdvizheniya*, 1936, No.1, pp. 60–5.
87. *Voprosy profdvizheniya*, No.8, pp. 69–75.
88. *Trud*, 10 January 1934; 17 November 1934; *Voprosy profdvizheniya*, 1936, No.10, pp. 75–9.
89. Hoover Archive, Zawodny Interviews, II/74 provides an autobiographical example where *blat* and bribery were used to obtain a place in a sanatorium in Crimea. Also see *Trud*, 10 September 1935, for allegations that singularly undeserving miners were finding their way to vacation resorts faster than deserving ones.
90. *Predpriyatie*, 1935, No.10, pp. 39–41.
91. *Za industrializatsiyu*, 29 April 1937, p. 2.
92. *Ibid.*; also *Voprosy truda*, 1933, No.8–9, pp. 106–10.
93. Hoover Archive, AER collection, e.g. Fisher to Burrell, 18 October 1933: Russian women tend to be 'as a rule, more efficient and dependable in their work than men'.
94. Kiselev and Malin (eds.), *op.cit.*, pp. 159–61.
95. *Predpriyatie*, 1935, No.8, pp. 7–10; Hoover Archive, Zawodny Interviews, II/17.
96. *Predpriyatie*, 1934, No.1–2, pp. 23–5.
97. There are, however reports from certain factory shopfloors where workers are said 'systematically' to work from 1 to 2 hours overtime, and from factories where workers do 'at least' 10 hours of overtime every month, see *Trud*, 11 October 1934. This does not seem a great amount by international standards. Scott, *op.cit.*, p. 49, mentioned 'up to 12-hour shifts' in Magnitogorsk; Smith, *op.cit.*, p. 41, found that shifts in the Leningrad *Elektrozavod* usually lasted 8–10 hours, because piece-rate quotas did not allow workers to earn enough within the normal seven hours.

98. *Trud*, 5 March 1934; 22 June 1935.
99. Gudov, *op.cit.*, p. 7.
100. *Predpriyatie*, 1928, No.5, pp. 7–9.
101. Some allotments were reported to be 10–12 km from the workers' homes. *Trud*, 1 March 1934.
102. *Predpriyatie*, 1930, No.15–16, p. 3.
103. *Za industrializatsiyu*, 29 April 1937, p. 2.
104. *Ibid.*
105. Scott, *op.cit.*, p. 45.
106. *Trud*, 12 January 1934, the story about *Rostsel'mash*.
107. *Za industrializatsiyu*, 29 April 1937, p. 2.
108. *Voprosy profdvizheniya*, 1935, No.4, pp. 74–8.
109. For example, one of the American engineers who had taken part in a *subbotnik*, i.e a stint of voluntary labour, in a collective farm, reported that some of his fellow workers did their best to work hard at weeding cabbages, 'but most of the young men and women turned the affair into a sort of picnic. There was little accomplished.' Hoover Archive, AER collection, Questionnaire W.C.A.
110. Hoover Archive, J.K. Zawodny Interviews, I/3.
111. *Ibid.*, I/2.
112. *Ibid.*, II/20, II/26.
113. Two-thirds of Zawodny's interviewees moved up from manual jobs in the factories to white-collar positions in the course of the 1930s.
114. Strøm, *op.cit.*, p. 25 and *passim*.
115. Hoover Archive, Zawodny Interviews, II/18.
116. *Ibid.*, II/21.
117. *Ibid.*, II/15.
118. *Trud*, 2 August 1935, story about Nizhnedneprovsk.
119. *Predpriyatie*, 1935, No.10, pp. 39–41.
120. *Sovetskoe gosudarstvo i pravo*, 1933, No.4, pp. 63–74.
121. *Ibid.*
122. In the Russian Federated Republic in 1934, only 16–17 per cent of the people sentenced under the 1932 decree on speculation were described as workers. *Sotsialisticheskaya zakonnost'*, 1935, No.11, pp. 9–12. Compare this with the 33 per cent of sentenced hooligans being workers, in the same territory three years earlier, when there were fewer workers relative to the overall population, cf. previous footnote.
123. As footnote 120.
124. *Trud*, 2 August 1935, story from Nizhnedneprovsk.
125. Gudov, *op.cit.*, pp. 78–79.
126. *Sovetskoe gosudarstvo i pravo*, 1933, No.4, pp. 63–74.
127. *Ibid.*
128. *Trud*, 4–6 January 1933.
129. According to an American engineer who was in Leningrad at the time, the banned persons were taken by the police 100 metres beyond the city boundaries and released there. Hoover Archive, AER collection, Questionnaire W.S.O.

130. In Leningrad alone, there were 50,000 fewer ration cards issued for January 1933 than for the previous month. *Trud*, 6 January 1933.
131. *Sovetskoe gosudarstvo i pravo*, 1933, No.4, pp. 63–74.
132. *Sotsialisticheskaya zakonnost'*, 1935, No.5, p. 30.
133. *Ibid.*
134. *Sovetskoe gosudarstvo i pravo*, 1933, No.4, pp. 63–74.
135. Of the rest, 78 per cent served their sentences in their own places of work, simply by incurring deductions from their salaries, and 11 per cent served their sentences in labour colonies. *Sotsialisticheskaya zakonnost'*, 1935, No.3, pp. 17–22.
136. *Voprosy profdvizheniya*, 1935, No.9, pp. 21–7.
137. *Voprosy profdvizheniya*, 1936, No.3, pp. 3–10.
138. Hoover Archive, Zawodny Interviews, I/12 and II/26.
139. Al'brecht, K.I., *Sud'by lyudskie v podvalakh GPU* (Berlin, 1941). Similar lack of correspondence between generalizations and examples in this respect is found in another memoir published in Nazi-occupied Europe after Germany had begun her military campaign against the USSR; see Klicka, J., *Zil jsem v SSSR* (Praha, 1942).
140. Hoover Archive, Zawodny Interviews, II/26. The presence of Poles presumably became dominant in the last stages of this interviewee's imprisonment, after the occupation of the eastern half of Poland by Soviet troops in accordance with the pact between Germany and USSR, in September 1939.
141. Hoover Archive, Zawodny Interviews, I/5, II/15, II/19, II/24, II/25. Not all of these stories of pressure on people end in *NKVD* arrests, and some of those that do are vague about the occupational identity of the arrested person. The following story (II/19), however, is from a large factory (10,000 employees) for the manufacture of tank engines.

One day [in 1939], the Party Committee called all workers to sign a voluntary gift to the State; we were supposed to work for a certain period of time without pay for the benefit of the State. You really couldn't refuse to sign this list. I tell you, everybody was there, all the bosses of the factory were sitting at this table. We were standing in line and everyone who entered this room, just signed it even without reading the paper. As I said, there was even a man who we knew worked for *NKVD* sitting at that table. When the time came for this girl, I am telling you, she was a real kozak and she belonged to the *komsomol*. She entered the room, and she asked, 'What am I supposed to sign now?' And they said, 'The Comrade Stalin and our great country . . . etc.', and they started to deliver this standardized speech to her, ending with the statement that she had to work for nothing for a while. Do you know what she did? She just turned around, bent down, put her skirt over her head, and she said, 'Comrade Stalin and you all can kiss me whenever it is most convenient for you', and she left. I am telling you, I saw that and I was numb with fear. All those men behind the table, they just sat silently. Finally, one of them said, 'Did you notice, she didn't have any pants on?', and everybody started to laugh. This was the shortest answer of this type that I have ever seen, and she got away with it. But this was unusual.'

142. Both interviewees were industrial managers at the time of their troubles with the authorities. One (II/26) was in prison from 1937 to 1939, on charges which probably included the fact that he had tried to hide his social origins by obtaining false documents, for which he was denounced by a rival for promotion in 1936, but remained unpunished until the arrest, in 1937, of the factory director who had protected him. Interestingly, he got a job in factory management again after his release.

The other (II/17) was sentenced by the courts to one year of deprivation of freedom, suspended for two years, after being denounced by a neighbour for anti-Semitism. This apparently happened after he told his neighbours who had scolded his child in the shared kitchen, 'Don't think that because you are Jews that you are the managers here.' The suspended sentence was annulled on appeal, after his friends, who were members of the party, testified that he was not anti-Semitic. Ironically, the interviewee concluded his story with, 'I have never had much love for Jews.'

143. The decree was signed by Kalinin and Enukidze, respectively the chairman and secretary of the central executive committee of the federal Soviet (*TsIK Soyuza SSR*), in 1933. The original decree granting special powers to *OGPU* in regard to alleged counter-revolutionary 'wrecking' (*vreditel'stvo*) had been issued in 1923. See *Za industrializatsiyu*, 15 March 1933.

144. Hoover Archive, Zawodny Interviews, II/15.

145. Scott, *op.cit.*, pp. 17, 22, 30, 194.

146. Hoover Archive, AER collection, Questionnaire M.K.

147. Scott, *op.cit.*, p. 194.

148. Gudov, *op.cit.*, p. 165.

CHAPTER 3

1. *Predpriyatie*, 1931, No.23–23, pp. 1–5.
2. *Za industrializatsiyu*, 24 November 1934, p. 1.
3. *Za industrializatsiyu*, 9 January 1934, p. 1; *Predpriyatie*, 1936, No.7, pp. 5–6; *Za industrializatsiyu*, 3 February 1937, p. 1.
4. Berliner, J.S., *Factory and Manager in the USSR* (Harvard University Press, Cambridge, Mass, 1957).
5. Scott, J., *Behind the Urals* (Cambridge, Mass., 1942), p. 22.
6. *Predpriyatie*, 1931, No.12, pp. 1–2.
7. Wheatcroft, S.G., *Changes in the pattern of employment in the USSR*, (Conference paper, University of Birmingham, 1982).
8. In 1934–36, more than one-quarter of factory directors had come to

their posts within the past 12 months, and about three-quarters within the past three years, judging by the estimates provided by David Granick in *Management and the Industrial Firm in the USSR* (Columbia University Press, 1954), pp. 47–56 and 290–6.

9. Hoover Archive, American Engineers in Russia Collection, M.K. to H.H.F.
10. Hoover Archive, AER collection, Questionnaire J.H.G.
11. Hoover Archive, AER collection, Qustionnaires, C.R.O., A.W.H., G.F.
12. *Sovetskoe gosudarstvo i pravo*, 1935, No.1–2, pp. 108–25.
13. *Za industrializatsiyu*, 3 February 1937, p. 1.
14. Scott, *op.cit.*, p. 159.
15. Hoover Archive, AER collection, L.D.A. to H.H.F.; Questionnaires W.S.O., L.D.A.
16. Hoover Archive, AER collection, Questionnaire A.W.H.
17. Hoover Archive, AER collection, Questionnaires L.D.A., J.H.G.
18. *Predpriyatie*, 1928, No.4, pp. 11–13.
19. Smolensk Archive, file WKP 189, contains the minutes of such a meeting, held by the inner circle of a district party committee (*byuro raikoma*) in February 1935, in response to an exposé about the management of a castings factory published in a local newspaper six days earlier. The 'signals' made by the newspaper were found in this case to be correct and the meeting recommended that the 'class alien' managers should be replaced by promotees from the shop floor (*vydvizhentsy*) and 'young specialists'. This sort of outcome was not inevitable; the national newspapers often complained that local party organs were inclined to protect some of the culprits named in newspaper revelations, but sometimes had to print retractions of earlier allegations after the local party organs made their enquiries.
20. Strøm, A., *Uncle Give us Bread* (Allen & Unwin, London, 1936), p. 113.
21. *Za industrializatsiyu*, 3 July 1932, p. 3.
22. *Za industrializatsiyu*, 2 July 1931, p. 2.
23. *Predpriyatie*, 1928, No.6, pp. 12–15.
24. *Predpriyatie*, 1929, No.11, pp. 1–2.
25. *Predpriyatie*, 1929, No.10, pp. 23–7.
26. *Ibid.*
27. *Predpriyatie*, 1930, No.1, pp. 36–7.
28. *The American Magazine*, April 1932; Hoover Archive, AER collection, correspondence between Fisher and J.J. Calder.
29. *Za industrializatsiyu*, 24 November 1930, p. 4.
30. Likhachev, M.A., *Direktor* (Moskva, 1971), p. 40.
31. Gudov, I., *Sud'ba rabochego* (Politizdat, Moskva, 1970) p. 62.
32. *Predpriyatie*, 1928, No.1, pp. 7–8; and *Predpriyatie*, 1934, No.8, pp. 1–3.
33. *Predpriyatie*, 1935, No.8, pp. 7–10.
34. Beynon, H., *Working for Ford* (Penguin, Harmondsworth, 1973).
35. *Predpriyatie*, 1931, No.9, pp. 5–8; also see *Predpriyatie*, 1928, No.1, pp. 7–8.

36. *Predpriyatie*, 1935, No.8, pp. 7–10.
37. Hoover Archive, AER collection, Questionnaire H.H.A. The respondent's experience of Soviet industry consisted of helping to set up new iron-ore mines in 1930–32.
38. Meyer, S., 'Adapting the immigrant to the line: Americanisation in the Ford factory, 1914–1921', *Journal of Social History*, vol.14, No.1 (1980), pp. 67–82.
39. Rose, M., *Industrial Behaviour* (Allen Lane, London, 1975); Bendix, R., *Work and Authority in Industry* (Harper & Row, New York, 1963); Littler, C.R., 'Understanding Taylorism', *British Journal of Sociology*, vol.29, No.2 (1978), pp. 185–202.
40. Burawoy, M., *Manufacturing Consent: changes in the labour process under capitalism* (University of Chicago Press, 1979), p. 126.
41. Littler, C.J., *The Development of the Labour Process in Capitalist Societies: a comparative analysis of work organisation in Britain, USA and Japan* (Heinemann, London, 1982).
42. *Predpriyatie*, 1935, No.5–6, pp. 2–8.
43. *Ibid.*
44. *Predpriyatie*, 1935, No.21–2, pp. 4–9.
45. *Predpriyatie*, 1930, No.5–6, pp. 27–32; *Predpriyatie*, 1930, No.19–20, pp. 35–40; *Predpriyatie*, 1930, No.8.
46. *Tekhnicheskoe normirovanie*. Also see *Predpriyatie*, 1931, No.15–16, pp. 25–32.
47. *Predpriyatie*, 1930, No.19–20, pp. 13–16, and.27.
48. *Predpriyatie*, 1930, No.11–12, pp. 17–18; *Predpriyatie*, 1935, No.8, pp. 43–4.
49. *Predpriyatie*, 1928, No.4, pp. 8–11.
50. *Voprosy truda*, 1929, No.8, pp. 7–15; *Predpriyatie*, 1931, No.12, pp. 40–1.
51. *Za industrializatsiyu*, 28 September 1932.
52. *Voprosy truda*, 1932, No.1, pp. 10–22.
53. Ermanskii, O.A., *Nauchnaya organizatsiya truda i sistema Teilora* (1922, subsequent editions in 1923, 1924 and 1925; German edition in Berlin, 1925); *Teoriya i praktika ratsionalizatsii* (Gos. izdatel'stvo, Moskva i Leningrad, 1928).
54. Ermanskii, O.A., *Teoriya i praktika, op.cit.*, pp. 123–72; also *Voprosy truda*, 1932, No.5–6, pp. 10–15.
55. Osip A. Ermanskii first developed this argument in *Nauchnaya organizatsiya truda i sistema Teilora, op.cit.*, where he counterposed 'scientific organization of work' to Taylor's own Taylorism which was contaminated, thought Ermanskii, by a desire to cheat workers into giving a higher intensity of effort. Ermanskii wrote this book in part as an explicit polemic against the tendencies within the early Soviet government to make the intensification of labour in industry a major policy goal, to the detriment of efficient organization of work. But the theme of identifying the deliberate cultivation of efficient work organization with socialist ideals is already evident in his first substantial publication, a revolutionary pamphlet, *Nashi blizhaishiya trebovaniya*

i konechnaya tsel' (Rabochaya biblioteka, Petrograd, 1904, 1906 and 1917), pp. 27–8 in the 1917 edition.

56. *Voprosy truda*, 1932, No.1, pp. 3–9. The charges of Menshevism were close to the bone in Ermanskii's case, as he had been a prominent leader of the non-Bolshevik majority in the Russian Social Democratic Workers' Party. A close associate of Martov, he contested Lenin's seat on the party's Presidium at the conference held in Stockholm in 1905–6, to lose by only one vote. The 1917 edition of *Nashi blizhaishiya trebovaniya i konechnaya tsel'*, published soon after the October *coup*, included a passage criticizing the Bolshevik government for basing itself on demagogic appeals to a backward (*temnye*) people and on authoritarian methods of rule, thus jeopardizing the liberation of the working class. He was the person who spoke on behalf of the Menshevik movement at the funeral of the prominent anarchist Peter Kropotkin in 1921, one of the last public gatherings at which the various branches of revolutionary Russia were able to make a public demonstration of their presence. Later in the same year, Ermanskii left the Social Democratic Party but refused the temptations to join the Bolsheviks; instead, he made public his withdrawal from active politics, and started a new career as a social scientist and a professor of rational management. He clearly commanded much respect amongst government circles, to the extent of being able to publish a political autobiography, *Iz prezhitogo, 1887–1921* (Gos. izdatel'stvo, Moskva, 1927), where he defended the revolutionary credentials and realism of the Menshevik movement. He survived the purges and resurfaced with the publication of a book about the Stakhanovite movement, *Stakhanovskoe dvizhenie i stahanovskoe metody* (Gos. sots.-ek. izd., Moskva, 1940), where he returned to his favourite theme of promoting organizational rationalization and denouncing drives to get workers to expend more than 'physiologically optimal' amounts of effort. He prefaced this book by apologizing to the reader for the damage that had been done to its contents by two years of making compromises with publishers. The publishers printed a note dissociating themselves from the views expressed in the book.

Ermanskii's earlier books also included one about Fordism, *Legenda o Forde* (Gosizdat, Moskva, 1926) and one about the organization of the distributive networks, *Ratsionalizatsiya torgovli* (Moskva, 1924).

57. *Predpriyatie*, 1936, No.6, pp. 28–31.
58. Cf., e.g., *Predpriyatie*, 1935, No.14, pp. 3–8.
59. *Predpriyatie*, 1935, No.19, pp. 37–42.
60. *Voprosy profdvizheniya*, 1933, No.11, p. 77; for earlier examples see *Predpriyatie*, 1928, No.4, pp. 11–13; *Predpriyatie*, 1929, No.1, pp. 23–25; *Predpriyatie*, 1929, No.7, p. 40.
61. *Voprosy profdvizheniya*, 1933, No.9, p. 48.
62. *Voprosy truda*, 1929, No.3–4, pp. 9–13, reported that these factors were found to constitute the main cause of high production costs, by a special government commission (*kommissiya VSNKh RSFSR*) set up in 1928.

63. *Za industrializatsiyu*, 19 February 1931, p. 2.
64. *Ibid.*
65. *Za industrializatsiyu*, 28 September 1932, p. 3.
66. *Voprosy truda*, 1929, No.7, pp. 95–9.
67. Stalin quoted in *Voprosy profdvizheniya*, 1933, No.5, p. 25.
68. *Za industrializatsiyu*, 14 August 1930. p. 3.
69. E.g. *Predpriyatie*, 1932, No.16, pp. 22–3; *Predpriyatie*, 1935, No.10, pp. 39–41.
70. *Za industrializatsiyu*, 19 February 1931, p. 2.
71. *Predpriyatie*, 1935, No.11–12, pp. 3–6; *Voprosy truda*, 1929, No.7, pp. 95–9.
72. *Za industrializatsiyu*, 5 January 1932, p. 3.
73. *Voprosy profdvizheniya*, 1934, No.8–9, pp. 48–56.
74. *Za industrializatsiyu*, 28 September 1932, p. 3; *Za industrializatsiyu*, 24 January 1930, p. 4.
75. *Predpriyatie*, 1929, No.8, pp. 64–5.
76. *Voprosy profdvizheniya*, 1934, No.5, pp. 81–7; *Voprosy profdvizheniya*, 1937, No.7–8, pp. 36–41.
77. *Za industrializatsiyu*, 24 November 1930, p. 3; *Predpriyatie*, 1929, No.12, pp. 20–2.
78. *Voprosy profdvizheniya*, 1936, No.6, pp. 22–7.
79. *Trud*, 5 May 1936.
80. *Za industrializatsiyu*, 14 August 1930, p. 2.
81. *Predpriyatie*, 1930, No.13–14, pp. 1–3; *Voprosy truda*, 1930, No.4, pp. 18–29.
82. *Voprosy truda*, 1932, No.1, pp. 3–9.
83. *Voprosy profdvizheniya*, 1933, No.1, p. 65; *Voprosy profdvizheniya*, 1934, No.5, pp. 81–7.
84. *Voprosy profdvizheniya*, 1934, No.5, pp. 81–7.
85. Gudov, I., *Sud'ba rabochego* (Politizdat, Moskva, 1970), pp. 18, 43, 51; *Trud*, 26 December 1933; *Voprosy profdvizheniya*, 1935, No.4, pp. 3–4; *Predpriyatie*, 1935, No.11–12, pp. 3–6.
86. Hoover Archive, AER collection, W.C.A. to H.H.F.
87. Hoover Archive, AER collection, Questionnaire W.N.P.
88. Hoover Archive, AER collection, Questionnaire T.R.H.
89. Hoover Archive, AER collection, Questionnaire G.D.J.
90. Hoover Archive, AER collection, Questionnaire C.B.
91. Hoover Archive, AER collection, Questionnaire E.P.E.
92. Hoover Archive, AER collection, Questionnaire T.H.O.
93. Hoover Archive, AER collection, Questionnaire J.K.J.
94. *Predpriyatie*, 1936, No.5, pp. 1–2.

CHAPTER 4

1. Hoover Archive, AER collection, Questionnaire EPE.
2. Meyer, S., 'Adapting the immigrant to the line: Americanisation in

the Ford factory, 1914–1921', *Journal of Social History* vol.14, No.1, (1980) pp. 67–82.

3. Hoover Archive, AER collection, Questionnaire THO.
4. Wells, F.A. and Warmington, W.A., *Studies in Industrialisation: Nigeria and the Cameroons* (London, 1962), p. 128.
5. Moore, W.E., *Industrialization and Labour: social aspects of economic development* (Russell & Russell, New York, 1965), p. 309.
6. Southall, A. (ed.), *Social Change in Modern Africa* (Oxford University Press, 1961), p. 19.
7. Burawoy, M., *Manufacturing Consent: changes in the labour process under capitalism* (The University of Chicago Press, 1979), pp. 212–13.
8. Meyer, *op.cit.*
9. For an excellent discussion of this hitherto neglected theme see Campbell, C.B., *The Romantic Ethic and the Spirit of Modern Consumerism* (Blackwell, Oxford, 1987), part I.
10. Baldamus, W.G., *Efficiency and Effort* (Tavistock Publications, London, 1961).
11. *Ibid.*, Chapters 5–7.
12. *Ibid.*, pp. 60–61.
13. Roy, D., 'Quota restriction and goldbricking in a machine shop', *American Journal of Sociology*, vol.57 (1952), pp. 427–42; 'Efficiency and "the fix": informal intergroup relations in a piecework machine shop', *American Journal of Sociology*, vol.60 (1955), pp. 255–66; 'Satisfaction and reward in quota achievement', *American Sociological Review*, vol.18 (1953).
14. *Ibid.*
15. Burawoy, *op.cit.*
16. *Ibid.*, p.63.
17. *Ibid.*, pp. 82–3.
18. Roy, 'Efficiency and "the fix" ', *op.cit.*
19. Burawoy, *op.cit.*, p. 176.
20. Gouldner, A., *Patterns of Industrial Bureaucracy* (Free Press, New York, 1964).
21. Baldamus, *op.cit.* Chapters 3–4.
22. Burawoy, *op.cit.*, p. 175.
23. Roy, 'Quota restriction and goldbricking', *op.cit.*
24. Burawoy, *op.cit.*, p. 51.
25. *Ibid.*, pp. 130–1.
26. *Ibid.*, pp. 141–57.
27. *Za industrializatsiyu*, 11 March 1933.
28. *Ibid.*
29. *Voprosy profdvizheniya*, 1933, No.1, p. 57.
30. *Voprosy truda*, 1929, No.1, pp. 21–5.
31. *Voprosy truda*, 1929, No.3–4, pp. 9–13.
32. *Voprosy truda*, 1929, No.1, pp. 21–5.
33. *Voprosy truda*, 1930, No.6, p.30; Drobizhev, V.Z. and Vdovin, A.I., *Rost rabochego klassa v SSSR* (Moskva, 1976), p. 224.
34. *Za industrializatsiyu*, 5 August 1930, p. 3.

35. *Za industrializatsiyu*, 3 July 1931, p. 3; *Za industrializatsiyu*, 5 May 1932, p. 3.
36. *Voprosy truda*, 1929, No.8, pp. 7–15; *Predpriyatie*, 1929, No.7, pp. 23–5; *Voprosy truda*, 1929, No.3–4, pp. 9–13. The reported decrees are *SNK SSSR*, 6 March 1929; *SNK RSFSR*, 2 June 1929; and a circular *NKT SSSR*, 9 March 1929.
37. Kiselev, Ya.L. and Malin, S.E. (eds.), *Sbornik vazhneiishikh post-anovlenii po trudu* (Moskva, 1936), p. 140. The original is in *Sbornik zakonov 1932g.*, No.78, p. 475.
38. Filtzer, D., *Soviet Workers and Stalinist Industrialisation: the formation of modern Soviet production relations, 1928–1941* (Pluto Press, London, 1986), Chapter 9.
39. *Za industrializatsiyu*, 23 August 1930, p. 3.
40. *Voprosy truda*, 1929, No.8, pp. 7–15.
41. *Za industrializatsiyu*, 19 July 1931, p. 1, interview with the Commissar for Labour, Tsikhon.
42. 'Postanovlenie TsIK i SNK SSSR, 15.11.1932g.' and 'Instruktsiya NKT SSSR, 26.11.1932g.', reprinted in Kiselev and Malin, *op.cit.*, p. 139.
43. *Voprosy profdvizheniya*, 1933, No.5, pp. 45–7.
44. *Sovetskoe gosudarstvo i pravo*, 1933, No.5, pp. 52–60.
45. *Ibid.*
46. *Ibid.*; *Voprosy profdvizheniya*, 1933, No.13, p. 20; *Trud*, 4 January 1933; *Trud*, 5 and 28 February 1933; *Trud*, 18 June 1935.
47. *Predpriyatie*, 1934, No.3, pp. 24–6.
48. *Voprosy profdvizheniya*, 1933, No.13, p. 15; *Trud*, 10 February 1933.
49. *Trud*, 5 February 1933.
50. *Trud*, 10 February 1933; *Voprosy truda*, 1933, No.4, pp. 61–4.
51. *Trud*, 10 February 1933; *Voprosy profdvizheniya*, 1933, No.5, pp. 45–7; *Voprosy truda*, 1933, No.4, pp. 61–4.
52. *Voprosy profdvizheniya*, 1933, No.13, p. 20.
53. *Trud*, 10 February 1933; *Voprosy profdvizheniya*, 1933, No.5, p. 22 and 45–7.
54. The text of the decree itself in fact is not unambiguous on this point: '(one day's absence "without a worthy reason") makes the employee subject to dismissal from the enterprise . . .'. In Kiselev and Malin (eds.), *op.cit.*, p. 140. The flood of commentaries that followed the decree, however, made its mandatory nature quite clear. See *Voprosy truda*, 1933, No.5 p. 23. Also, the Instruction of the Commissariat of Labour dated 26 November 1932, reprinted in Kiselev and Malin (eds.), *op.cit.*, p. 141, makes managers who are 'guilty of a failure to fulfil the duties set by the decree of 15 November 1932' liable to either administrative punishment or prosecution in courts.
55. *Voprosy profdvizheniya*, 1933, No.13, pp. 17–18; *Voprosy profdvizheniya*, 1935, No.2–3, pp. 64–72.
56. *Voprosy profdvizheniya*, 1933, No.5, p. 43; and *Voprosy profdvizheniya*, 1933, No.13, p. 17.
57. *Voprosy truda*, 1933, No.5, p. 23; *Voprosy profdvizheniya*, 1933, No.5, pp. 45–7 and 61.

58. *Voprosy profdvizheniya*, 1933, No.5, p. 61.
59. *Voprosy profdvizheniya*, 1933, No.13, pp. 16–17; Kiselev and Malin (eds.), *op.cit.*, p. 141. The re-hire of dismissed workers was not allowed for one year following the dismissal.
60. *Voprosy truda*, 1933, No.4, pp. 61–4.
61. *Ibid*.
62. *Trud*, 14 February 1933.
63. *Voprosy truda*, 1933, No.4, pp. 61–4.
64. *Ibid*.
65. *Trud*, 3 February 1933.
66. *Trud*, 18 June 1935.
67. *Voprosy truda*, 1933, No.4, pp. 61–4.
68. *Trud*, 27 February 1933.
69. *Voprosy profdvizheniya*, 1935, No.2–3, pp. 64–72.
70. *Voprosy profdvizheniya*, 1933, No.3, p. 4; *Voprosy profdvizheniya*, 1935, No.2–3, pp. 64–72; 'Postanovlenie NKT SSSR 18.1.1931g.', in Kiselev and Malin (eds.), *op.cit.*, p. 139.
71. *Voprosy profdvizheniya*, 1933, No.5, p. 62.
72. *Trud*, 14 February 1933.
73. Filtzer, *op.cit.*
74. *Trud*, 3 February 1933.
75. *Trud*, 18 June 1935, see the story about workplace victimization of a for(wo)man and member of *VTsIK* in the leading article.
76. *Voprosy truda*, 1929, No.3–4, pp. 9–13.
77. *Za industrializatsiyu*, 7 February 1930, p. 4.
78. *Za industrializatsiyu*, 1 June 1933.
79. *Za industrializatsiyu*, 16 August 1930, p. 3; *Za industrializatsiyu*, 15 May 1932, p. 3.
80. *Voprosy truda*, 1930, No.2, pp. 7–12.
81. *Voprosy profdvizheniya*, 1936, No.8, pp. 28–32.
82. Drobizhev, V.Z. and Drobin, A.I., *Rost rabochego klassa v SSSR* (Moskva 1976), p. 224.
83. *Voprosy profdvizheniya*, 1935, No.2–3, pp. 64–72.
84. *Voprosy profdvizheniya*, 1936, No.9, pp. 28–37.
85. *Voprosy profdvizheniya*, 1937, No.4, pp. 26–31.
86. In Leningrad industry, 84 per cent were members in April 1933 – *Voprosy profdvizheniya*, 1933, No.9, p. 47.
87. Wheatcroft, S.G., *Famine and Factors Affecting Mortality in the USSR; the demographic crises of 1914–1922 and 1930–1933*, CREES Discussion Papers (University of Birmingham, 1981).
88. *Voprosy profdvizheniya*, 1936, No.9, pp. 28–37.
89. *Voprosy profdvizheniya*, 1933, No.9, p. 39.
90. *Trud*, 9 and 17 December 1933.
91. *Voprosy profdvizheniya*, 1937, No.4, pp. 26–31. Also *Predpriyatie*, 1929, No.7, pp. 23–5; *Voprosy profdvizheniya*, 1936, No.9, pp. 28–37.
92. *Voprosy profdvizheniya*, 1936, No.6, pp. 90 and 36–41; *Voprosy profdvizheniya*, 1936, No.9, pp. 28–37; *Voprosy profdvizheniya*, 1936, No.11, pp. 62–71.

93. *Voprosy profdvizheniya*, 1933, No.7, pp. 66–71.
94. *Voprosy profdvizheniya*, 1933, No.10, p. 14.
95. *Trud*, 12 February 1933; *Trud*, 8 January 1934.
96. *Za industrializatsiyu*, 31 January 1930, p. 3.
97. Hoover Archive, AER collection, EPE to F; Scott, J., *Behind the Urals* (Cambridge, Mass., 1942), pp. 186–7.
98. Körber, L., *Life in a Soviet Factory* (London, 1933), p. 183.
99. *Voprosy truda*, 1929, No.7, pp. 95–7.
100. *Za industrializatsiyu*, 31 January 1930, p. 3.
101. *Sovetskoe gosudarstvo i pravo*, 1933, No.4, pp. 63–74.
102. Kiselev and Malin (eds.), *op.cit.*, pp. 148–9.
103. *Ibid.*
104. *Voprosy profdvizheniya*, 1933, No.5, p. 59.
105. *Voprosy profdvizheniya*, 1933, No.11, p. 74.
106. *Za industrializatsiyu*, 16 July 1934.
107. *Predpriyatie*, 1935, No.13, pp. 1–3.
108. *Voprosy profdvizheniya*, 1933, No.11, p. 74; *Predpriyatie*, 1935, No.13, pp. 1–3.
109. *Za industrializatsiyu*, 3 July 1932, p. 3.
110. *Trud*, 3 January 1933; *Trud*, 8 January 1934.
111. *Voprosy profdvizheniya*, 1933, No.5, p. 61.
112. *Voprosy profdvizheniya*, 1933, No.7, pp. 66–71.
113. *Voprosy profdvizheniya*, 1934, No.2, p. 45.
114. *Za industrializatsiyu*, 19 July 1931, p. 1.
115. *Voprosy truda*, 1929, No.1, pp. 21–5.
116. *Ibid.*
117. *Za industrializatsiyu*, 20 October 1931, p. 2; *Za industrializatsiyu*, 5, 14 and 20 August 1930, p. 3.
118. *Voprosy truda*, 1929, No.1, pp. 21–5.
119. *Za industrializatsiyu*, 6 September 1932, p.3.
120. *Za industrializatsiyu*, 20 October 1931, p. 2.
121. *Za industrializatsiyu*, 23 August 1930, p. 3.
122. *Predpriyatie*, 1929, No.8, pp. 64–5; *Za industrializatsiyu*, 14 August 1930, p. 3.
123. *Za industrializatsiyu*, 20 April 1930; *Za industrializatsiyu*, 22 January 1930, p. 3.
124. *Za industrializatsiyu*, 8 August 1930, p. 3.
125. 'Prikaz No.850', *Sbornik postanovlenii NKTP*.
126. *Ibid.*
127. *Voprosy profdvizheniya*, 1934, No.7, p. 41.
128. *Za industrializatsiyu*, 29 September 1933; *Voprosy profdvizheniya*, 1933, No.11, p. 74; *Voprosy profdvizheniya*, 1934, No.6, p. 95; *Voprosy profdvizheniya*, 1934, No.7, p. 41.
129. *Za industrializatsiyu*, 29 September 1933.
130. *Voprosy profdvizheniya*, 1933, No.5, p. 62; *Voprosy profdvizheniya*, 1934, No.7, p. 50.
131. *Voprosy profdvizheniya*, 1934, No.7, p. 50.
132. *Za industrializatsiyu*, 8 April 1931, p.2; 'Prikaz No.850', *Sbornik postanovlenii NKTP*.

133. *Za industrializatsiyu*, 6 June 1937, p. 1; *Za industrializatsiyu*, 24 and 29 April 1937.
134. *Predpriyatie*, 1928, No.12, pp. 43–7.
135. *Predpriyatie*, 1930, No.13–14, pp. 1–3.
136. Stalin, J.V., *Collected Works* (Moscow, 1955), vol.13, pp. 53–82.
137. *Voprosy profdvizheniya*, 1936, No.11, pp. 91–5.
138. Kuromiya, H., 'Between shovel and conveyor; Russian workers' *cartels* and Soviet industrialisation', unpublished paper presented at CREES, University of Birmingham, in March 1987.
139. *Sovetskoe gosudarstvo i pravo*, 1933, No.4, pp. 75–87.
140. *Voprosy profdvizheniya*, 1933, No.1, p. 78.
141. *Voprosy profdvizheniya*, 1933, No.1, pp. 65 and 78; *Voprosy profdvizheniya*, 1936, No.7, pp. 19–26.
142. *Trud*, 26 June 1935.
143. *Za industrializatsiyu*, 12 March 1933; *Voprosy profdvizheniya*, 1934, No.2, p. 44.
144. *Za industrializatsiyu*, 15 March 1933.
145. *Ibid*.
146. *Voprosy profdvizheniya*, 1933, No.11, p. 24; *Za industrializatsiyu*, 15 March 1933.
147. *Voprosy profdvizheniya*, 1933, No.8, p. 7; *Voprosy profdvizheniya*, 1935, No.4, pp. 74–8; *Voprosy profdvizheniya*, 1933, No.1 p. 32.
148. *Voprosy profdvizheniya*, 1936, No.5, pp. 52–6.
149. *Za industrializatsiyu*, 14 July 1932, p. 3; *Voprosy profdvizheniya*, 1934, No.2, p. 44.
150. *Voprosy profdvizheniya*, 1934, No. 2, p. 49.
151. *Voprosy profdvizheniya*, 1936, No.5, pp. 52–6.
152. *Voprosy profdvizheniya*, 1934, No.2, p. 49.
153. *Voprosy profdvizheniya*, 1933, No.6, p.7; *Voprosy profdvizheniya*, 1934, No.1, pp. 85–92.
154. *Voprosy profdvizheniya*, 1933, No.8, p. 8; *Voprosy profdvizheniya*, 1936, No.2, pp. 3–11.
155. Smolensk Archive, file WKP 189, circular dated 22 March 1935.
156. *Voprosy profdvizheniya*, 1935, No.2–3, pp. 14–21.
157. *Voprosy profdvizheniya*, 1934, No.11, p. 10.
158. *Trud*, 5 January 1934.
159. Smolensk Archive, file WKP 89, the minutes of a factory party committee meeting dated 15 November 1935.
160. *Trud*, 4 January 1934.
161. *Ibid.*, *Voprosy profdvizheniya*, 1933, No.1, p. 82.
162. Smolensk Archive, file WKP 189.
163. *Voprosy profdvizheniya*, 1936, No.7, pp. 19–26.
164. *Voprosy profdvizheniya*, 1933, No.13, p. 59; *Voprosy profdvizheniya*, 1934, No.11, p. 17; *Voprosy profdvizheniya*, 1935, No.2–3, pp. 14–21.
165. *Voprosy profdvizheniya*, 1933, No.1, p. 5; *Voprosy profdvizheniya*, 1935, No.2–3, pp. 3–13; *Voprosy profdvizheniya*, 1936, No.1, pp. 3–8; 'Prikaz No.1724, 21.10.1936g.', *Sbornik postanovlenii NKTP*.

166. Calculated from Strumilin's industrial output data presented in Davies, R.W., *Soviet Industrial Production 1928–1937: the rival estimates*, CREES Discussion Papers (University of Birmingham, 1978), p. 67.

167. Estimated on the basis of data found in *Voprosy profdvizheniya*, 1933, No.1; *Trud*, 20 December 1933; *Voprosy profdvizheniya*, 1934, No.11, p. 9; *Voprosy profdvizheniya*, 1936, No.1, pp. 51–9; *Voprosy profdvizheniya*, 1936, No.2, p. 50; *Voprosy profdvizheniya*, 1935, No.2–3, pp. 14–21; *Voprosy profdvizheniya*, 1936, No.9, pp. 67–73; *Trud*, 5 July 1936; *Trud*, 27 September 1936; *Voprosy profdvizheniya*, 1936, No.11, pp. 91–5.

168. *Voprosy profdvizheniya*, 1936, No.7, pp. 19–26; *Za industrializatsiyu*, 4 December 1933.

169. 'Prikaz No.715, 11.8.1933g' and 'Prikaz No.1143, 27.8.1934g.', *Sbornik postanovlenii NKTP; Trud*, 5 February 1933; *Trud*, 9 January 1934; *Trud*, 14 February 1935; *Voprosy profdvizheniya*, 1935, No.2–3, pp. 3–13.

170. *Voprosy profdvizheniya*, 1935, No.4, pp. 74–8.

171. Article 68 of the Labour Code, in *Kodeks zakonov o trude*, (Moskva, 1938), p. 23; *Voprosy profdvizheniya*, 1933, No.3, p. 9; *Trud*, 12 February 1933; *Voprosy profdvizheniya*, 1934, No.11; 'Prikaz No.11724, 21.10.1936g.', *Sbornik postanovlenii NKTP*.

172. *Voprosy profdvizheniya*, 1933, No.13, pp. 56–9; *Voprosy profdvizheniya*, 1934, No.6, p. 84; *Voprosy profdvizheniya*, 1935, No.4, pp. 74–8; *Za industrializatsiyu*, 15 March 1933.

173. 'Prikaz No.1724, 21.10.1936g', *Sbornik postanovlenii NKTP; Voprosy profdvizheniya*, 1933, No.8, pp. 5–6; *Voprosy profdvizheniya*, 1934, No.11, p. 9; *Za industrializatsiyu*, 8 January 1934.

174. *Voprosy profdvizheniya*, 1933, No.6, p. 6.

175. *Za industrializatsiyu*, 5 and 11 July 1933.

176. *Voprosy truda*, 1929, No.8, pp. 7–18.

177. Littler, C.J., *The Development of the Labour Process in Capitalist Societies: a comparative analysis of work organisation in Britain, USA and Japan* (Heinemann, London, 1982).

178. Davies, R.W., *Planning and the Soviet Factory, 1926–1934*, mimeo, West European Conference on Soviet Industry, University of Birmingham, June 1981; *Za industrializatsiyu*, 13 February 1931, p. 4.

179. *Ibid.*

180. *Predpriyatie*, 1928, No.12, pp. 11–14; *Predpriyatie*, 1929, No.8, pp. 64–5; *Predpriyatie*, 1929, No.9, pp. 19–21; *Voprosy truda*, 1929, No.8, pp. 7–15.

181. *Za industrializatsiyu*, 7 February 1930, p. 4.

182. *Za industrializatsiyu*, 3 February 1931, p. 1; *Za industrializatsiyu*, 15 July 1931, p. 2.

183. *Za industrializatsiyu*, 13 February 1931, p. 4.

184. *Za industrializatsiyu*, 7 May 1930.

185. *Predpriyatie*, 1935, No.8, pp. 7–10.

186. *Za industrializatsiyu*, 13 February 1931, p. 4.

187. The Commissariat for Labour was abolished in 1933.
188. *Za industrializatsiyu*, 18 September 1932, p. 3.
189. *Predpriyatie*, 1933, No.22, pp. 10–14.
190. *Za industrializatsiyu*, 23 September 1932, p. 3; *Predpriyatie*, 1936, No.4, pp. 36–7.
191. *Predpriyatie*, 1933, No.22, pp. 10–14; *Predpriyatie*, 1934, No. 23, M. Bogart.
192. *Predpriyatie*, 1933, No.22, pp. 10–14.
193. See esp. the references in notes 7 and 13 above.
194. *Predpriyatie*, 1935, No.11–12, pp. 3–6; *Predpriyatie*, 1935, No.13, pp. 1–3; *Predpriyatie*, 1935, No.16, p. 21.
195. *Predpriyatie*, 1935, No.1, pp. 41–3.
196. *Za industrializatsiyu*, 7 February 1930 p. 4.
197. *Predpriyatie*, 1935, No.11–12, pp. 3–6; *Predpriyatie*, 1932, No.4, pp. 16–20.
198. *Ibid.*
199. *Za industrializatsiyu*, 6 September 1932, p. 2; *Za industrializatsiyu*, 4 July 1932, p. 2; *Voprosy truda*, 1932, No.10, pp. 14–24.
200. E.g. Lupton, T., *On the Shop Floor; two studies of workshop organisation and output* (Pergamon Press, Oxford, 1963), p. 129.
201. *Predpriyatie*, 1935, No.11–12, pp. 3–6.
202. *Predpriyatie*, 1934, No.23, M. Bogart.
203. *Predpriyatie*, 1932, No.15, pp. 1–3.
204. *Predpriyatie*, 1933, No.22, pp. 10–14.
205. *Predpriyatie*, 1933, No.9–10, pp. 1–4.
206. For an example of implementation, see *Predpriyatie*, 1934, No.15, pp. 17–19.
207. *Predpriyatie*, 1934, No.4., pp. 7–9.
208. *Predpriyatie*, 1935, No.2, pp. 36–8; *Predpriyatie*, 1933, No.9–10, pp. 1–4.
209. *Predpriyatie*, 1935, No.2, pp. 36–8; *Predpriyatie*, 1935, No.15, p. 23.
210. *Predpriyatie*, 1935, No.8, pp. 4–5.
211. *Predpriyatie*, 1933, No.9–10, pp. 1–4.
212. *Za industrializatsiyu*, 9 May 1932, p. 4.
213. *Predpriyatie*, 1933, No 9–10, pp. 17–18.
214. *Predpriyatie*, 1935, No.21–22, pp. 4–9.
215. *Ibid.*
216. E.g. *Predpriyatie*, 1934, No.4, pp. 7–9; *Predpriyatie*, 1935, No.16, p. 21.
217. *Predpriyatie*, 1934, No.23, M. Bogart.
218. *Za industrializatsiyu*, 4 June 1937, p. 3.
219. E.g. *Predpriyatie*, 1936, No.7, pp. 5–6; *Voprosy profdvizheniya*, 1936, No.2, pp. 64–70.
220. *Voprosy truda*, 1929, No.7, pp. 95–9.
221. *Predpriyatie*, 1935, No.11–12, pp. 3–6.
222. Roy, D., 'Efficiency and "the fix": informal intergroup relations in a piecework machine shop', *American Journal of Sociology*, vol.60 (1955), pp. 255–66; *Predpriyatie*, 1935, No.1, pp. 41–3; *Za industriali-*

zatsiyu, 11 May 1932, p. 3; *Predpriyatie*, 1928, No.12, pp. 43–7.
223. *Predpriyatie*, No.1, pp. 41–3.
224. Cunnison, S., *Wages and Work Allocation* (Tavistock Publications, London, 1966), pp. 55–7.
225. *Predpriyatie*, 1935, No.11–12, pp. 3–6.
226. *Ibid.*
227. *Predpriyatie*, 1935, No.11–12, pp. 3–6.
228. *Za industrializatsiyu*, 4 September 1932, p. 3.
229. *Voprosy profdvizheniya*, 1935, No.4, pp. 74–8.
230. *Za industrializatsiyu*, 9 January 1932, p. 2; *Predpriyatie*, 1928, No.12, pp. 11–14; *Predpriyatie*, 1929, No.8, pp. 64–5; *Predpriyatie*, 1929, No.9, pp. 19–21; *Voprosy truda*, 1929, No.8, pp. 7–15.
231. Gudov, I., *Sud'ba rabochego* (Politizdat, Moskva, 1970), pp. 46–47.
232. *Predpriyatie*, 1930, No.13–14, pp. 1–3.
233. *Za industrializatsiyu*, 4 January 1932, p. 3.
234. *Voprosy truda*, 1930, No.4, pp. 18–29.
235. *Ibid.*
236. *Za industrializatsiyu*, 5 January 1930.
237. *Predpriyatie*, 1930, No.13–14, pp. 1–3.
238. *Predpriyatie*, 1929, No.12, pp. 23–24.
239. *Voprosy truda*, 1930, No.4, pp. 18–29.
240. *Predpriyatie*, 1929, No.12, pp. 23–4.
241. *Za industrializatsiyu*, 27 July 1930, p. 2.
242. *Voprosy truda*, 1930, No.4, pp. 18–29.
243. *Za industrializatsiyu*, 24 January 1930, p. 4.
244. *Predpriyatie*, 1929, No.8, pp. 64–5.
245. *Voprosy profdvizheniya*, 1934, No.5, p. 83.
246. *Trud*, 2 January 1934.
247. *Voprosy truda*, 1933, No.8–9, pp. 106–10.
248. *Voprosy truda*, 1932, No.5–6, pp. 10–15; *Voprosy profdvizheniya*, 1936, No.6, pp. 22–7.
249. See the *komsomol* central committee resolution publicized in *Za industrializatsiyu*, 14 August 1930, p. 2.
250. *Za industrializatsiyu*, 15 November 1930, p.3.
251. *Voprosy truda*, 1930, No.10–11, p. 41.
252. *Trud*, 2 January 1934, the cartoons.
253. *Voprosy profdvizheniya*, 1935, No.9, pp. 21–7.
254. *Voprosy profdvizheniya*, 1935, No.4, pp. 3–11.
255. *Voprosy profdvizheniya*, 1934, No.5, p. 83.
256. *Za industrializatsiyu*, 15 November 1930, p. 3; *Za industrializatsiyu*, 8 February 1930, p. 3.
257. Berliner, J.S., *Factory and Manager in the USSR* (Cambridge, Mass., 1957).

CHAPTER 5

1. Getty, J.A., *Origins of the Great Purges: The Soviet Communist Party reconsidered, 1933–1938* (Cambridge University Press, 1985), Chapters 3–4.
2. *Voprosy profdvizheniya*, 1935, No.7–8, pp. 88–96; Trud, 11 May 1936.
3. *Trud*, 14 August 1935.
4. *Voprosy profdvizheniya*, 1935, No.7–8, pp. 88–96.
5. *Voprosy profdvizheniya*, 1937, No.9–10, pp. 6–30.
6. *Voprosy profdvizheniya*, 1936, No.9, pp. 3–9; *Voprosy profdvizheniya*, 1937, No.12, pp. 7–13.
7. *Voprosy profdvizheniya*, 1936, No.4, p. 39.
8. *Voprosy profdvizheniya*, 1936, No.4, pp. 39, 50–1 and 65–70; *Voprosy profdvizheniya*, 1936, No.7, pp. 11–15 and 19–26; *Voprosy profdvizheniya*, 1936, No.5, pp. 52–6; *Voprosy profdvizheniya*, 1937, No.2, pp. 40–1; *Voprosy profdvizheniya*, 1937, No.11, pp. 51–2; *Voprosy profdvizheniya*, 1936, No.2, pp. 3–11; *Voprosy profdvizheniya*, 1936, No.7, pp. 56–8; *Za industrializatsiyu*, 24 and 29 April 1937; *Voprosy profdvizheniya*, 1937, No.7–8, pp. 46–7; *Trud*, 11 May 1936.
9. *Trud*, 16 July 1935; *Trud*, 2 August 1935.
10. *Trud*, 5 September 1935.
11. *Voprosy profdvizheniya*, 1935, No.5–6, pp. 3–6.
12. Gudov, I., *Sud'ba rabochego* (Politizdat, Moskva, 1970), pp. 25–6.
13. *Sotsialisticheskaya zakonnost'*, 1934, No.1.
14. *Op.cit.*, pp. 29 and 38.
15. *Ibid.*, pp. 12 and 30–4.
16. *Ibid.*, p. 41.
17. *Ibid.*, pp. 38–9.
18. *Ibid.*, pp. 51–5.
19. *Ibid.*
20. *Voprosy profdvizheniya*, 1936, No.5, pp. 86–9.
21. *Predpriyatie*, 1936, No.6, pp. 28–31.
22. *Za industrializatsiyu*, 29 April 1937, p. 2.
23. *Trud*, 5 July 1936.
24. *Voprosy profdvizheniya*, 1936, No.10, pp. 59–63.
25. Gudov, *op.cit.*, pp. 69–76.
26. *Za industrializatsiyu*, 28 April 1937, p. 3.
27. Gudov, *op.cit.*, p. 66.
28. *Trud*, 5 July 1936.
29. *Voprosy profdvizheniya*, 1936, No.2, pp. 39–45.
30. *Predpriyatie*, 1936, No.5, Zhilin.
31. *Voprosy profdvizheniya*, 1936, No.1, pp. 3–8.
32. *Sbornik postanovlenii NKTP*, March–April 1936.
33. *Za industrializatsiyu*, 9 April 1937.
34. *Za industrializatsiyu*, 12 April 1937.

35. *Voprosy profdvizheniya*, 1936, No.8, pp. 69–75.
36. Bailes, K.E., 'Alexei Gastev and the Soviet controversy over Taylorism, 1918–1924', *Soviet Studies*, vol.29, No.3 (July 1977), pp. 373–94.
37. *Predpriyatie*, 1936, No.7, pp. 5–6.
38. *Predpriyatie*, 1936, No.3, pp. 1–2.
39. *Predpriyatie*, 1936, No.7, pp. 3–4.
40. *Predpriyatie*, 1936, No.1 and 8.
41. *Za industrializatsiyu*, 4 June 1937, p. 3.
42. *Za industrializatsiyu*, 5 June 1937, p. 2.
43. *Trud*, 14 July 1936; *Voprosy profdvizheniya*, 1936, No.7, pp. 19–26.
44. *Trud*, 9 July 1936.
45. *Predpriyatie*, No.7, pp. 3–4.
46. *Trud*, 1 June 1936.
47. *Voprosy profdvizheniya*, 1936, No.7, pp. 19–26.
48. *Predpriyatie*, 1936, No.4, pp. 22–4.
49. *Predpriyatie*, 1935, No.20, pp. 32–5.
50. *Za industrializatsiyu*, 2 February 1937, interview with Sushkov.
51. *Predpriyatie*, 1936, No.6, pp. 19–22.
52. See Chapter 4, pp. 155–76 above.
53. *Predpriyatie*, 1936, No.6, pp. 19–22.
54. *Za industrializatsiyu*, 15 February 1937, p. 2.
55. *Predpriyatie*, 1936, No. 3, pp. 1–2.
56. *Voprosy profdvizheniya*, 1936, No. 2, pp. 64–70.
57. *Trud*, 16 September 1935.
58. *Voprosy profdvizheniya*, 1936, No.2, pp. 64–70.
59. *Voprosy profdvizheniya*, 1936, No.2, pp. 64–70; Smolensk Archive, file WKP 89, reports from party cell meetings.
60. *Trud*, 10 July 1936.
61. *Predpriyatie*, 1936, No.4, pp. 22–4.
62. *Predpriyatie*, 1936, No.2, pp. 64–70; *Predpriyatie*, 1936, No.3, pp. 11–19.
63. *Voprosy profdvizheniya*, 1936, No.1, pp. 51–9.
64. *Voprosy profdvizheniya*, 1936, No.1, pp. 60–5; Smolensk Archive, WKP 89.
65. *Voprosy profdvizheniya*, 1936, No.1, pp. 3–8.
66. *Trud*, 8 May 1936; *Voprosy profdvizheniya*, 1936, No.1, pp. 3–8.
67. *Trud*, 16 September 1935.
68. Smolensk Archive, WKP 89; *Voprosy profdvizheniya*, 1936, No.1, pp. 60–5; *Trud*, 10 September 1935.
69. *Voprosy profdvizheniya*, 1936, No.1, pp. 3–8.
70. *Voprosy profdvizheniya*, 1936, No.8, pp. 69–75; *Za industrializatsiyu*, 29 April 1937, p. 2.
71. *Trud*, 12 July 1936.
72. *Za industrializatsiyu*, 28 April 1937, p. 3.
73. *Trud*, 17 September 1936; *Predpriyatie*, 1936, No.7, pp. 5–6.
74. *Predpriyatie*, 1936, No.7, pp. 5–6.
75. *Trud*, 16 September 1936.
76. *Za industrializatsiyu*, 29 April 1937, p. 2.

77. *Trud*, 10 July 1936.
78. *Trud*, 16 September 1936.
79. *Za industrializatsiyu*, 28 April 1937, p. 3.
80. *Trud*, 6 May 1936.
81. *Predpriyatie*, 1936, No.7, pp. 5–6.
82. *Voprosy profdvizheniya*, 1936, No.2, pp. 39–45.
83. *Trud*, 5 June 1936; *Voprosy profdvizheniya*, 1936, No.7, pp. 19–26; *Predpriyatie*, 1936, No.4, pp. 22–4.
84. *Za industrializatsiyu*, 9 April 1937, p. 2.
85. *Predpriyatie*, 1936, No.7, pp. 5–6.
86. 'Prikaz No.1724', *Sbornik postanovlenii NKTP*.
87. *Za industrializatsiyu*, 12 April 1937, p. 1.
88. *Za industrializatsiyu*, 9 June 1937, p. 2.
89. *Predpriyatie*, 1936, No.8, pp. 1–5.
90. *Za industrializatsiyu*, 1 March 1937.
91. *Za industrializatsiyu*, 16 February 1937, p. 1.
92. *Za industrializatsiyu*, 11 February 1937, p. 3; *Za industrializatsiyu*, 12 February 1937, p. 1.
93. *Za industrializatsiyu*, 29 April 1937, p. 2.
94. *Za industrializatsiyu*, 1 and 9 June 1937.
95. *Za industrializatsiyu*, 11 February 1937, p. 3.
96. Filtzer, D., *Soviet Workers and Stalinist Industrialisation: the formation of modern Soviet production relations, 1928–1941* (Pluto Press, London, 1986), pp. 233 and 310–11.
97. *Ibid.*, Chapters 5 and 9.
98. This argument is pursued by Getty, *op.cit.*
99. See Chapter 1.
100. McAuley, M., 'Political change since Stalin', *Critique*, No.2; that the Soviet working class was thoroughly atomized in the 1930s is argued by Filtzer, *op.cit.* For a general discussion of totalitarianism and the destruction of social bonds see Arendt, H. *The Origins of Totalitarianism* (Allen and Unwin, London, 1969), Chapter 10.
101. Rittersporn, G.T., 'L'état en lutte contre lui-même: Tensions sociales et conflits politiques en U.R.S.S. 1936–1938', *Libre*, (1978), pp. 3–37.

Bibliography

Al'brekht, K.I., *Sud'by lyudskie v podvalakh GPU* (Berlin, 1941).

Bailes, K.E., 'Alexei Gastev and the Soviet controversy over Taylorism, 1918–1924', *Soviet Studies*, vol.29, No.3 (1977), pp. 373–94.

Baldamus, W.G., *Efficiency and Effort* (Tavistock Publications, London, 1961).

Bendix, R., *Work and Authority in Industry* (Harper & Row, New York, 1963).

Benvenuti, F., 'La "lotta per la redditivita" nell'industria sovietica (1935–1936)', *Studi Storici*, no.2 (1984).

Berliner, J.S., *Factory and Manager in the USSR* (Harvard University Press, Cambridge, Mass., 1957).

Beynon, H., *Working for Ford* (Penguin, Harmondsworth, 1973).

Burawoy, M., *Manufacturing Consent: changes in the labour process under capitalism* (University of Chicago Press, 1979).

Campbell, C.B., *The Romantic Ethic and the Spirit of Modern Consumerism* (Blackwell, Oxford, 1987).

Carr, E.H. and Davies, R.W., *The Foundations of a Planned Economy 1926–1929* (Macmillan, London, 1969), vol.1.

Chapman, J.G., *Real Wages in Soviet Russia since 1928* (Harvard University Press Cambridge, Mass., 1963).

Conquest, R., *The Great Terror* (Macmillan, London, 1968).

Cunnison, S., *Wages and Work Allocation* (Tavistock Publications, London, 1966).

Dale, P., 'The instability of the infant vanguard: worker party members of 1928–1932', *Soviet Studies*, vol.35, No.4, pp. 504–24.

Davies, R.W., *The Socialist Offensive: the collectivisation of Soviet agriculture, 1929–1930* (Macmillan, London, 1980).

Davies, R.W., 'The socialist market: a debate in Soviet industry, 1932–1933', *Slavic Review*, vol.42 (1984).

233

Davies, R.W., 'Soviet industrial production, 1928–1937: the rival estimates', *CREES Discussion Papers*, SIPS No.18 (CREES, University of Birmingham, 1979).

Drobizhev, V. and Lel'chuk, V., *in Ocherki po istoriografii sovetskogo obshechestva* (Moscow, 1967).

Drobizhev, V. and Vdovin, A., *Rost rabochego klassa v SSSR* (Moscow, 1976).

Ermanskii, O.A., *Teoriya i praktika ratsionalizatsii* (Moscow, 1928).

Ermanskii, O.A., *Stakhanovskoe dvizhenie i stakhanovskie metody* (Moscow, 1940).

Filtzer, D.A., *Soviet Workers and Stalinist Industrialisation: the formation of modern Soviet production relations, 1928–1941* (Pluto Press, London, 1986).

Fitzpatrick, S. (ed.), *Cultural Revolution in Russia, 1928–1931* (Indiana University Press, Bloomington and London, 1978).

Getty, J.A., *Origins of the Great Purges: the Soviet Communist Party reconsidered, 1933–1938* (Cambridge University Press, 1985).

Gouldner, A., *Patterns of Industrial Bureaucracy* (Free Press, New York, 1964).

Granick, D., *Management and the Industrial Firm in the USSR* (Columbia University Press, New York, 1954).

Gudov, I., *Sud'ba rabochego* (Politizdat, Moscow, 1970).

Khrushchev, N.S., *Khrushchev Remembers* (Penguin, Harmondsworth, 1977).

Kiselev, Ya. and Malin, S. (eds.), *Sbornik vazhneishikh postanovlenii po trudu* (Moscow, 1936).

Klicka, J., *Zil jsem v SSSR* (Prague, 1942).

Körber, L., *Life in a Soviet factory* (London, 1933).

Kravchenko, V., *I Chose Freedom: the personal and political life of a Soviet official* (Readers Union and R. Hale Ltd, London, 1949).

Kuromiya, H., 'The crisis of proletarian identity in the Soviet factory, 1928–1929', *Slavic Review* (Summer 1985).

Kuromiya, H., 'Edinonachalie and the Soviet industrial manager, 1928–1937', *Soviet Studies*, vol.36, No.2, pp. 185–204.

Lampert, N., *The Technical Intelligentsia and the Soviet State: a study of Soviet managers and technicians 1928–1935* (Macmillan, London, 1979).

Lewin, M., *The Making of the Soviet System: essays in the social history of interwar Russia* (Methuen, London, 1985).

Lewin, M., *Political Undercurrents in Soviet Economic Debates* (Princeton University Press, New York, 1974).

Likhachev, M., *Direktor* (Moscow, 1971).

Littler, C.J., 'Understanding Taylorism', *British Journal of Sociology*, vol.29, No.2 (1978), pp. 185–202.

Littler, C.J., *The Development of the Labour Process in Capitalist Societies: a comparative analysis of work organisation in Britain, USA and Japan* (Heinemann, London, 1982).

McAuley, M., 'Political change since Stalin', *Critique*, No.2.

Meyer, S., 'Adapting the immigrant to the line: Americanisation in the Ford factory 1914–1921', *Journal of Social History*, vol.14, No.1 (1980).

Moore, W.E., *Industrialisation and Labour: social aspects of economic development* (Russell & Russell, New York, 1955).

Nove, A., *An Economic History of the USSR* (Allen & Unwin, London, 1972).

Pisarev, M.I., *Naselenie i trud v SSSR* (Moscow, 1966).

Rittersporn, G., 'L'état en lutte contre lui-même: Tensions socialies et conflits politiques en U.R.S.S. 1936–1938', *Libre* (1978), pp. 3–37.

Rose, M., *Industrial Behaviour* (Allen Lane, London, 1975).

Rosefielde, S., 'An assessment of the sources and uses of forced labour, 1929–1956', *Soviet Studies*, vol.33, No.1.

Rosefielde, S., 'Excess mortality in the Soviet Union: a reconsideration of the demographic consequences of forced industrialisation, 1929–1949', *Soviet Studies*, vol.35, No.3, pp. 385–409.

Rosefielde, S., 'Incriminating evidence: excess deaths and forced labour under Stalin: a final reply to critics', *Soviet Studies*, vol.39, No.2, pp. 292–313.

Roy, D., 'Quota restriction and goldbricking in a machine shop', *American Journal of Sociology*, vol.57 (1952), pp. 427–42.

Roy, D., 'Efficiency and the "fix": informal intergroup relations in a piecework machine shop', *American Journal of Sociology*, vol.60 (1955), pp. 255–66.

Roy, D., 'Satisfaction and reward in quota achievement', *American Sociological Review*, vol.18 (1953).

Scott, J., *Behind the Urals* (Cambridge, Mass., 1942).

Shiokawa, N., 'Labor turnover in the USSR, 1929–1933: a sectoral analysis', *Annals of the Institute of Social Science*, No.23 (University of Tokyo, 1982).

Siegelbaum, H., 'Soviet norm determination in theory and practice, 1917–1941', *Soviet Studies*, vol.36, No.1, pp. 45–68.

Smith, A., *I was a Soviet Worker* (London, 1937).

Smith, S.A., *Red Petrograd: revolution in the factories, 1917–1918* (Cambridge University Press, 1985).

Stalin, J.V., *Collected Works* (Moscow, 1955), vol.13.

Strøm, A., *Uncle Give us Bread* (Allen & Unwin, London, 1985).

Thompson, E.P., 'Time, work discipline and industrial capitalism', *Past and Present*, vol.38 (December 1967), pp. 56–97.

Thurston, W.R., 'Fear and belief in the USSR's "Great Terror": response to arrest, 1935–1939', *Slavic Review*, vol.45, No.2, pp. 213–44.

Ward, C.E., *Russian Cotton Workers and the NEP* (PhD thesis, University of Essex, 1985).

Wells, F.A. and Warmington, W.A., *Studies in Industrialisation: Nigeria and the Cameroons* (London, 1962).

Wheatcroft, S.G., 'A re-evaluation of Soviet agricultural production', in Stuart, R.C. (ed.), *The Soviet rural economy* (Rowman & Allenheld, Totowa NJ, 1983).

Wheatcroft, S.G., Davies and Cooper, 'Soviet industrialisation reconsidered: some preliminary conclusions about economic developments between 1926 and 1941', *Economic History Review* (May 1986).

Wheatcroft, S.G., 'On assessing the size of forced concentration camp labour in the Soviet Union, 1929–1956', *Soviet Studies*, vol.33, No.2, pp. 265–95.

Wheatcroft, S.G., 'Towards a thorough analysis of Soviet forced labour statistics', *Soviet Studies*, vol.35, No.2, pp. 223–37.

Wheatcroft, S.G., 'A note on Steven Rosefielde's calculation of excess mortality in the USSR, 1929–1949', *Soviet Studies*, vol.36, No.2, pp. 277–81.

Wheatcroft, S.G., 'Famine and factors affecting mortality in the USSR: the demographic crises of 1914–1922 and 1930–1933', *CREES Discussion Papers*, SIPS No.20 (University of Birmingham).

Zaleski, E., *Planning for Economic Growth in the Soviet Union, 1918–1932* (Chapel Hill, 1971).

Index

237